LAW AND LA

Completed in 1964, Harold J. Berman's long-lost tract shows how properly negotiated, translated, and formalized legal language is essential to fostering peace and understanding within local and international communities. Exemplifying interdisciplinary and comparative legal scholarship long before they were fashionable, it is a fascinating prequel to Berman's monumental *Law and Revolution* series. It also anticipates many of the main themes of the modern movements of law, language, and ethics.

In his Introduction, John Witte, Jr., a student and colleague of Berman, contextualizes the text within the development of Berman's legal thought and in the evolution of interdisciplinary legal studies. He also pieces together some of the missing sections from Berman's other early writings and provides notes and critical apparatus throughout. An Afterword by Tibor Várady, another student and colleague of Berman's, illustrates via modern cases the wisdom and utility of Berman's theories of law, language, and community.

HAROLD J. BERMAN (1918–2007) was the Robert W. Woodruff Professor of Law and Senior Fellow at the Center for the Study of Law and Religion, Emory University. He was also James Barr Ames Professor of Law, *Emeritus*, at Harvard Law School. A scholarly giant in the fields of Soviet law, international trade, legal history, legal philosophy, and law and religion, he published 25 books and 450 articles.

JOHN WITTE, JR., is Jonas Robitscher Professor of Law, Alonzo McDonald Distinguished Professor, and Director of the Center for the Study of Law and Religion at Emory University.

LAW AND LANGUAGE

Effective Symbols of Community

By

HAROLD J. BERMAN
Emory University

Edited by

JOHN WITTE, JR.
Emory University

CAMBRIDGE
UNIVERSITY PRESS

University Printing House, Cambridge CB2 8BS, United Kingdom

Cambridge University Press is part of the University of Cambridge.

It furthers the University's mission by disseminating knowledge in the pursuit of education, learning and research at the highest international levels of excellence.

www.cambridge.org
Information on this title: www.cambridge.org/9781316619339

© John Witte, Jr. and the estate of Harold J. Berman 2013

First published 2013
Reprinted 2014
First paperback edition 2016

A catalogue record for this publication is available from the British Library

Library of Congress Cataloguing in Publication data
Berman, Harold J. (Harold Joseph), 1918–2007
Law and language : effective symbols of community / by Harold J. Berman,
Emory University, edited by John Witte, Jr., Emory University.
pages cm
Includes bibliographical references and index.
ISBN 978-1-107-03342-9 (hardback)
1. Law–Language. I. Witte, John, 1959– editor. II. Title.
K213.B475 2013
340'.14–dc23
2013012176

ISBN 978-1-107-03342-9 Hardback
ISBN 978-1-316-61933-9 Paperback

For my children,
Stephen, Jean, Susanna, and John

CONTENTS

PREFACE

"I need to get back to that book. It's just sitting there gathering dust. I just can't find the time." That was Harold J. Berman in September, 1982. We were sitting in his office at Harvard Law School, where I was getting my next assignment as his research assistant. The book in question was the *Law and Language* text that you are now holding. "Hal" (as Professor Berman was affectionately known) had completed a first draft of the book in 1964, but he just could not finish it. He had been writing and lecturing feverishly in the interim on Soviet law, international trade, legal philosophy, and legal history, and was always fighting deadlines. I asked him if he wanted me to take a crack at the "Law and Language" manuscript. "No, no, we have other things to do," he replied memorably. "We have the Reformation to conquer!" Then he handed me the first of many research assignments on the influence of the Protestant "revolutions" on the Western legal tradition – a topic that absorbed both of us for the next quarter century.

Hal never did find the time to get back to the "Law and Language" manuscript, and I never got the chance to work on it either – until recently. After we moved from Harvard Law School to Emory Law School in 1985, the manuscript disappeared, somehow lost in transit. Hal and I looked for it a few times after we both were at Emory, but he eventually gave up. He had many more books and articles to write, many more deadlines to fight, and of course "the Reformation to conquer."

When he died in 2007, I became Hal's literary executor, and spent many pleasant months digging through the veritable mountains of papers he left. Only near the end of that literary excavation did I come upon his old manuscript on "Law and Language." It was sitting in a rusty old filing cabinet in his unheated garage, buried under some old rags and newspapers. Mold, mildew, and mice had all done their best to be sure the manuscript would never be found. But there it was, still readable, and still unfinished.

It has been a special privilege to be able to finish my late great mentor's old book and to publish it in modern critical edition. The book is a creature of its time and place – America in the 1960s. It reflects concerns over the Cold War, the violent student protests and union strikes, the rise of Marxism in the academy and McCarthyism in Congress. It talks easily of the gradual senescence of legal realism and legal positivism, and prophesizes grandly about the rise of world law and a new interdisciplinary legal studies movement. But the book is also a timeless statement about the intricacies of legal translation, transmission, and transplantation over time and the essential role and power of law and legal language in building culture and community both locally and globally. It's written in a buoyant and accessible style, which typifies a lot of Berman's writing, especially in this period of his career. Its main themes and recommendations about law and language are as relevant in our day as they were half a century ago when Hal wrote them – even if we now have fancier tools and terms of comparative hermeneutics, literary theory, legal philology, and semiotics to describe them.

I have tried to preserve and present what Hal wrote, with minimal editorial intrusion. The manuscript had only partial footnotes and only for Chapter 1. I have provided citations to his undocumented quotes throughout, using his own library as much as possible to find the original sources. I have added further footnotes to direct readers to writings where Hal and other scholars he influenced elaborated certain key themes. In a few places where the text or argument breaks off, I have tipped in a passage from his other writings that elaborate the point, adding footnotes to explain what I have done and why. And I have added a Conclusion drawn from his other contemporaneous writings. But this book is, so much as possible, vintage Berman, 1964.

I owe a special debt of gratitude to Professor Tibor Várady, an LLM and SJD student of Berman at Harvard Law School from 1967 to 1970. After his studies, Tibor became a distinguished scholar of international and comparative law at Central European University in Budapest, where he was dean, as well as Cornell Law School and Emory Law School, where he taught regularly over the past two decades. Tibor was a generous friend and genial colleague to both Hal and me at Emory. He gave me invaluable advice on the preparation, production, and publication of this book. He also wrote the lovely Afterword that appears herein attesting to Berman's enduring insights into delicate issues of legal translation, especially in international tribunals. I thank him deeply for his generous cooperation and contribution.

I owe special thanks as well to Christopher Manzer and Andrew Stevens, two fine students in our Center for the Study of Law and Religion at Emory University, for their excellent work in helping to edit this book and in tracking down so many of the relevant sources and cross-references. My associate, Amy Wheeler, again did her magic in the production of the final manuscript and working with the Press. Our Center public relations director, April Bogle, did fine work with sundry Emory librarians to prepare a digital library of all Professor Berman's writings, which aided greatly the work of cross-referencing. And, Anita Mann, our Center business manager, did a superb job managing the Harold J. Berman Fund to support the work on the Berman digital library, this publication, and related publications and public lectures.

It has been a privilege to work with Finola O'Sullivan and Richard Woodham and their colleagues at Cambridge University Press. I appreciate their work in masterminding the production and marketing of this book and their earlier efforts to secure the valuable reviews of the preliminary incomplete manuscript.

I think Hal would have agreed with my decision to dedicate this book to his and Ruth's four children – Stephen, Jean, Susanna, and John.

~

Introduction

JOHN WITTE, JR. AND CHRISTOPHER J. MANZER

I should like to revive and revitalize historical jurisprudence, and I think the way to do it is with linguistic jurisprudence. History is group memory. Language is the record of history. Speech is the recording of the remembered past, and the envisioned future. I shall no doubt be scorned or ignored for the identification of history, speech, and law ... But not in all quarters. More and more people are now ready for this message.

Harold J. Berman (1966)[1]

Harold Berman is a giant, whose work defies the banalities of the age and allows us to take their measure. In a scholarly world drifting toward the particularistic exploration of "unique" contexts, Berman points in a different direction – toward holistic descriptions of entire systems of legal thought ... Berman's work, and especially his *Law and Revolution*, will endure when almost everything is forgotten. He is the only American who might be paired with Max Weber in the depth of his historical and comparative understanding of the remarkable character of legal modernity.

Guido Calabresi, Dean, Yale Law School (1996)[2]

1

Harold J. Berman was one of the great polymaths of American legal education, and taught for sixty years before his death in 2007. After completing his LLB and MA in History at Yale – interrupted by military service in World War II from 1942 to 1945 – he began his teaching career at Stanford Law School in 1947. From 1948 to 1985, he taught at Harvard Law School – for twelve years as the Joseph Story Professor of Law and Legal History, for sixteen more as the James Barr Ames Professor of

---

[1] Excerpts from Letter to his Dartmouth College mentor, Eugen Rosenstock-Huessy (May 28, 1966) (on file in the Emory Law Library Archives), see below, note 15.

[2] Jacket endorsement for Howard O. Hunter, ed., *The Integrative Jurisprudence of Harold J. Berman* (Boulder, CO: Westview Press, 1996). Dean Calabresi by this point had been appointed to the United States Court of Appeals for the Second Circuit.

Law. He also served as Founder and Director of Harvard Law School's Liberal Arts Fellowship Program in Law, Fellow of the Russian Research Center of Harvard University, and Member of the Legal Committee of the US–USSR Trade and Economic Council.

From 1985 to 2007, Berman taught at Emory Law School, serving as the first Robert W. Woodruff Professor of Law, a university professorship. He was also a Fellow in The Carter Center at Emory University, Founding Director of the American Law Center in Moscow, Founding Director of the World Law Institute at Emory Law School, and Senior Fellow of the Center for the Study of Law and Religion at Emory University. He was also co-founder of the *Journal of Law and Religion* and a member of its sponsoring organization, the Council on Religion and Law.

In the first three decades of his career, Berman's scholarly energies were focused on the Soviet legal system and the law of international trade. He developed several new courses, testified frequently before courts, commissions, and Congressional committees, and traveled regularly to Europe and the Soviet Union – fifty-five times to Russia alone. He spent the 1961–62 academic year at the Moscow Institute of State and Law, where he encountered, among others, a rising young star named Mikhail Gorbachev.[3] In the spring of 1982, he served as Fulbright Professor at Moscow State University. He produced a massive body of new writing in this early period. Of these writings, his *Justice in the USSR* (1950; rev. edn. 1963)[4] will long endure as a classic, as will several of his lengthy law review articles on the *lex mercatoria*.[5] Also important publications in this period,

---

[3] True story: it was the winter of 1982, with Brezhnev still in power in the USSR. Hal and Ruth had me over for dinner. After a few rounds of drinks, he stood up and announced grandly: "I have a prophecy to make. I predict that, in a decade, the Soviet Union will be revolutionized, and the leader of the revolution will be a young man I have been watching for a long time – Mikhail Gorbachev." Within a decade, *glasnost, perestroika,* and *demokratizatsiia* had become the watchwords of a new Russian revolution. See later Harold J. Berman, "Book Review of Mikhail Gorbachev, *PERESTROIKA: New Thinking for Our Country and the World* (1987)," *The Atlanta Constitution* (December 13, 1987): 12J; "Gorbachev's Law Reforms in Historical Perspective," *Emory Journal of International Affairs* 5 (Spring, 1988): 1–10; "The Challenge of Christianity and Democracy in the Soviet Union," in *Christianity and Democracy in Global Context*, ed. John Witte, Jr. (Boulder, CO: Westview Press, 1993), 287–96.

[4] Cambridge, MA: Harvard University Press, 1950, 1963 and New York: Random House, 1963.

[5] Harold J. Berman, "The Legal Framework of Trade Between Planned and Market Economies: The Soviet–American Example," *Law and Contemporary Problems* 24 (Summer 1959): 482–528; Harold J. Berman and George L. Bustin, "The Soviet System of Foreign Trade," in *Business Transactions with the USSR, The Legal Issues,*

for purposes of this book, were his exquisite translations of sundry Soviet laws – nearly 2,800 printed pages in English translation.[6]

In the first three decades of his career, Berman also developed a keen interest in bringing legal education into the undergraduate college – a different exercise in translation, now of professional legal language, concepts, and methods into something accessible to young students of the social, humane, and exact sciences. These pedagogical interests he distilled in two other signature titles, *On the Teaching of Law in the Liberal Arts Curriculum* (1956)[7] and *The Nature and Functions of Law* (1958; 6th edn., 2004),[8] the latter a standard text in American college courses on law. He extended this interest further in arranging a multilingual series of *Talks on American Law*, which started as Voice of America broadcasts. Here was yet another early example of legal translation and transmission – making the intricacies of American public, private, penal, and procedural law accessible to radio audiences throughout the Americas, Europe, Africa, Asia, Australia, the Middle East, and even the Soviet Union.[9]

In the last three decades of his career – with *Law and Language* coming right at the transition point – Berman expanded his legal scholarship to include legal philosophy, legal history, and law and religion. He produced a series of path-breaking volumes, most notably *The Interaction of Law and Religion* (1974),[10] *Faith and Order: The Reconciliation of Law and Religion* (1993),[11] and his massive *Law and Revolution: The Formation*

---

ed. Robert Starr (Chicago: ABA Press, 1975), 25–75; Harold J. Berman, "The Law of International Commercial Transactions (*Lex Mercatoria*)," *Emory Journal of International Dispute Resolution* 2 (Spring 1988): 235–310.

[6] Harold J. Berman and James W. Spindler, eds. and trans., *Soviet Criminal Law and Procedure: The RSFSR Codes* (Cambridge University Press, 1966); Harold J. Berman and Peter B. Maggs, eds. and trans., *Disarmament Inspection Under Soviet Law* (Dobbs Ferry, NY: Oceana Publications, 1967); Harold J. Berman and John B. Quigley, eds. and trans., *Basic Laws on the Structure of the Soviet State* (Cambridge, MA: Harvard University Press, 1969); Harold J. Berman, ed. and trans., *Soviet Statutes and Decisions, A Journal of Translations I–V* (Fall, Spring 1964 – Summer 1969).

[7] Brooklyn, NY: Foundation Press, 1956.

[8] Brooklyn, NY: Foundation Press, 1958; with William R. Greiner and Samir N. Saliba, 6th rev. edn. (New York: Foundation Press, 2004).

[9] Harold J. Berman, ed., *Talks on American Law* (New York: Random House, 1961); Portuguese translation published in Rio de Janeiro, 1963; Arabic translation published in Cairo, 1964; French translation published in Paris, 1965; Spanish translation published in Chile and Mexico, 1965; Vietnamese translation published in Saigon, 1968; Japanese translation published in Tokyo, 1963 and 1969.

[10] Nashville, TN: Abingdon Press, 1974.

[11] Atlanta, GA: Scholars Press, 1993; repr. edn., Grand Rapids, MI: Wm. B. Eerdmans, 1996.

of the Western Legal Tradition (1983)[12] and *Law and Revolution II: The Impact of the Protestant Reformations on the Western Legal Tradition* (2003).[13] The final volume of this series – on the American, French, and Russian revolutions – was on his writing desk when he died, along with a dozen articles in progress.

Berman left a scholarly legacy of 25 books and 458 articles, book chapters, and book reviews. These writings were collectively published in twenty-one languages; a few of his books are still being translated, and this new book will deserve translation, too. A comprehensive collection of his writings and some of his correspondence from 1948 to 1985 are included in the "Red Set" of faculty publications in the Harvard Law Library.[14] Digital and hard copies of all his (published and unpublished) non-book writings from 1938 to 2007 are available through the Emory University Libraries.[15] His work continues to be mined and cited with alacrity in the main fields that he worked. This new book on *Law and Language* will provide a further window, if not gateway, into his writings and the development of his legal thought.

Berman taught some 8,000 law students at Harvard and Emory, more than 300 of whom have become professors, in at least 33 countries. His students and colleagues honored him with three *Festschriften*,[16] and three law journal symposia are dedicated to his work.[17] He was a member of both the American Academy of Arts and Sciences and the Russian Academy of Sciences. He received more than a hundred prizes and awards for his scholarly achievements, including the prestigious Scribes Award from the American Bar Association, and honorary doctorates from the Catholic

---

[12] Cambridge, MA: Harvard University Press, 1983.

[13] Cambridge, MA: Harvard University Press, 2003.

[14] Harvard Law School Library, Collections, The Red Set, (accessed January 1, 2013), www.law.harvard.edu/library/special/collections/red_set/index.html

[15] Emory Libraries, EmoryFindingAids, Harold J. Berman Papers,1938–2007, (accessed January 1, 2013), http://findingaids.library.emory.edu/documents/L-027/; Zotero, Harold J. Berman Collection, (accessed January 1, 2013), https://www.zotero.org/harold_j_berman/items.

[16] John Witte, Jr. and Frank S. Alexander, eds., *The Weightier Matters of the Law: Essays on Law and Religion in Tribute to Harold J. Berman* (Atlanta, GA: Scholars Press, 1988); William E. Butler, Peter B. Maggs, and John B. Quigley, Jr., eds., *Law after Revolution: Essays on Socialist Law in Honor of Harold J. Berman* (Dobbs Ferry, NY: Oceana Press, 1988); and Hunter, *Integrative Jurisprudence*.

[17] "A Conference on the Work of Harold J. Berman," *Emory Law Journal* 42 (1993): 419–589; "The Foundations of Law," *Emory Law Journal* 54 (2005): 1–376; "In Praise of a Legal Polymath: A Special Issue Dedicated to the Memory of Harold J. Berman (1918–2007)," *Emory Law Journal* 57 (2008): 1393–469.

University of America, the Virginia Theological Seminary, the University of Ghent, and the Russian Academy of Sciences. The newly dedicated Harold J. Berman Library in the Center for the Study of Law and Religion at Emory University houses some of his personal books and effects. The Harold J. Berman Lecture Series at Emory Law School offers regular lectures on the many legal topics that Berman long championed.

2

Throughout his long career, Berman had the remarkable ability to think above, beyond, and against his times. In the 1950s and 1960s, the dominant Cold War logic taught that the Soviet Union was a lawless autocracy. Berman argued to the contrary that the Russians would always honor contracts and treaties that were fairly negotiated.[18] His views prevailed and came to inform various nuclear treaties, trade agreements, and East–West accords. In the 1970s and 1980s, the conventional belief persisted that the Middle Ages were the dark ages as the West waited impatiently for Enlightenment and modernization. Berman argued the contrary, that the medieval era was the first modern age of the West and the founding era of our Western legal tradition.[19] This view is now standard lore. In the 1980s and 1990s, jurists fought fiercely over whether legal positivism or natural law or some other perspective was the better legal philosophy. Berman called for an integrative jurisprudence that reconciled these views with each other and with other perspectives on law.[20] This view now prevails in

[18] See sources above, note 5. See further Harold J. Berman, "The Challenge of Soviet Law," *Harvard Law Review* 62 (December 1948 and January 1949): 220–65, 449–66; "The Law of the Soviet State," *Soviet Studies* 6 (January 1955): 225–37; "Suggestions for Future US Policy on Communist Trade," *Export Trade and Shipper* 35 (July 16, 1956): 11–12; "Negotiating Commercial Transactions with Soviet Customers," *Aspects of East-West Trade, American Management Association Report No. 45* (1960), 68–75; "The Dilemma of Soviet Law Reform," *Harvard Law Review* 76 (March 1963): 929–51; "Law in American Democracy and Under Soviet Communism," *New Hampshire Bar Journal* 5(3) (April 1963): 105–13; "Soviet Law Reform and Its Significance for Soviet International Relations," in *Law, Foreign Policy and the East-West Detente*, ed. Edward McWhinney (Toronto: University of Toronto Press, 1964), 3–17; "Law as an Instrument of Peace in US–Soviet Relations," *Stanford Law Review* 22 (1970): 943–62.
[19] This is the central thesis of his *Law and Revolution* series.
[20] See esp. Harold J. Berman, "Toward an Integrative Jurisprudence: Politics, Morality, History," *California Law Review* 76 (1988): 779–801; and elaboration in *Faith and Order*, 239–310. See analysis in Peter Teachout, "'Complete Achievement': Integrity of Vision and Performance in Berman's Jurisprudence," in Hunter, *Integrative Jurisprudence*, 75–98. Already in his 1958 edition of *The Nature and Functions of Law*, 25ff., Berman had

a world dedicated to interdisciplinary legal study. And, in the 2000s, with the world hell-bent on waging "a clash of civilizations,"[21] Berman called for a world law, grounded in global structures and processes, and universal customs and principles of peace, cooperation, and reconciliation.[22] This view holds so much more promise than the jingoism and jihadism of the past decade and more.

"First it was Russian law, then it was Western law, now it is world law. What's next, cosmic law?" This is how Professor Berman's beloved wife, Ruth, once summarized (with a blend of exasperation and astonishment) the stages of Berman's storied and storied legal career. There is keen insight in this statement. For Berman, every legal system – even the budding legal system of the world – must ultimately be founded upon cosmic commandments and contemplation, divine examples and exemplars. Berman has long prophesied that those legal systems that build on immanent and material foundations alone will fail. The spectacular failure of the Soviet legal system in the later twentieth century was ample vindication of his insight into the essential religious foundations of law.

Berman repeated this message in China, too, when in 2006, as a still energetic 88-year old, he gave a series of lectures on law to packed houses in a dozen universities. One of his Chinese respondents asked whether one needed to believe in God in order to have a just legal order. "It would certainly help!" Berman quipped immediately. "But no," he went on diplomatically:

> You don't necessarily have to believe in God, but you have to believe in *something.* You have to believe in law at least. If you can't accept God, then just focus on the law that God has written on all of our hearts.

formed his basic, three-part analytical framework for jurisprudence, combining natural law, legal positivism, and historical jurisprudence.

[21] Samuel P. Huntington, *The Clash of Civilizations and the Remaking of World Order* (New York: Simon & Schuster, 1996).

[22] Harold J. Berman, "Law and Religion in the Development of a World Order," *Sociological Analysis: A Journal in the Sociology of Religion* 52 (Spring 1991): 27–36; "Law and Logos," *DePaul Law Review* 44 (Fall 1994): 143–65; "The Tri-Une God of History," *The Living Pulpit* (April 1999): 18–19; "World Law in the New Millennium," *Twenty-First Century* 52 (April 1999): 4–11 (in Chinese); "The God of History," *The Living Pulpit* (July–September 2001): 27; "Integrative Jurisprudence and World Law," in Manuel Atienza et al., *Rechtstheorie: Theorie des Rechts und der Gesellschaft: Festschrift für Werner Krawietz zum 70. Geburtstag* (Berlin: Duncker & Humblot, 2003), 3–16; "The Holy Spirit: The God of History," *The Living Pulpit* (April–June 2004): 32–33; "Faith and Law in a Multicultural World," in Mark Juergensmeyer, ed., *Religion in Global Civil Society* (Oxford University Press, 2005), 69–89; "World Law: An Ecumenical Jurisprudence of the Holy Spirit," *Theology Today* 63 (October 2006): 365–74.

Even children intuitively sense this law within us. Every child in the world will say, "That's *my* toy." That's property law. Every child will say, "But you *promised* me." That's contract law. Every child will say, "It's not my fault. He hit me first." That's tort law. Every child will say, too, "Daddy said I could." That's constitutional law. Law ultimately comes from our human nature, and our human nature is ultimately an image of God.[23]

Such views reflect, in part, Berman's life-long effort to integrate his religious faith with his legal learning. In his chapel talks delivered in the Harvard Memorial Church over the years, Berman contrasted "the wisdom of the world" with "the wisdom of God." The wisdom of the world, he declared, "assumes that God's existence is irrelevant to knowledge, and that truth is discoverable by the human mind unaided by the Spirit." Jewish and Christian wisdom, by contrast, "seeks God's guidance ... in order to discover the relationship between what we know and what God intends for us." Knowledge and intellect are "intimately connected with faith, with hope, and with love." "God does not call us to be merely observers of life; rather he calls all of us – even the scholars in all that we do – to participate with him in the process of spiritual death and rebirth which is fundamental religious experience."[24]

Early on, Berman made clear that dialogue was essential to our relationships with God, neighbor, and self, and that language was an essential sinew of all our relationships. God is a God of words, Berman believed, drawing on the Bible. "In the beginning was the Word, and the Word was with God, and the *Word was God*," reads John 1. "In the beginning God created the heavens and the earth," Genesis 1 reads. And He did so by speech: "And God *said*, 'Let there be ...'" is how each day of creation starts. When it came to the creation of men and women, it was by dialogue, by conversation, first among the members of the Trinity, then between God and humanity: "Let *us* make man in our image, after our likeness," the Trinitarian God says to its members. And thereafter, God walked and talked with the man and the woman whom he created, though he talked with no other creature. For Berman, humans, created in the image of God,

---

[23] This is based in part on my memory of a conversation with Professor Berman after his return from China. These same sentiments are conveyed in a newspaper article about this trip. See Meredith Hobbs, "Translating Western Law into Chinese: Emory Professor Harold J. Berman toured China, speaking to halls packed with Chinese students," *The Daily Report* 117 (Fulton County, GA) (June 1, 2006): 1.

[24] Berman, *Faith and Order*, 319–22.

are given the capacity for language and dialogue with each other and with God.[25] In a 1969 sermon in Harvard's Memorial Church he proclaimed:

> If we see Christianity as a dialogue which God has initiated with man, I think we can see that Christians are called to transform this dialogue into a dialogue also among men, in which we are brought into relationships with each other, so that we share common convictions, undertake common tasks, and recognize a common authority … All life is a great conversation, a discourse, a speaking together, which goes back to the very beginning, to God Himself.[26]

Dialogue was key, in Berman's view, to teaching and reaching reconciliation, and for building community both locally and globally. Both Jewish and Christian theology, he reminded his church listeners, teach that persons must reconcile themselves to God, neighbor, and self. For Berman, building on St. Paul, this meant that there can be "no real division between Jew and Gentile, slave and free, male and female"[27] – or, for that matter, black and white, straight and gay, old and young, rich and poor, citizen and sojourner. For every sin that destroys our relationships, there must be grace that reconciles them. For every Tower of Babel that divides our voices, there must be a Pentecost that unites them and makes them understandable to all.[28]

Such spiritual sentiments could shackle the narrow-minded. They liberated Berman from conventional habits of mind and traditional divisions of knowledge. He challenged Max Weber, Karl Marx, and Jeremy Bentham for their separation of fact and value, is and ought.[29] He criticized Alexander Solzhenitsyn for his contradistinction of law and morals, law and love.[30] He fought against the divisions of the very world itself into East and West, old and new, developed and undeveloped. His favorite

---

[25] Berman and I sometimes did devotions together, and I remember spending weeks discussing the meaning of these quoted statements, which in his view said a lot about the dialogical nature of God.

[26] See Conclusion herein, p. 161.

[27] Galatians 3:28, Ephesians 2:14–15, Colossians 3:10–11. See also John Witte, Jr., "A New Concordance of Discordant Canons: Harold J. Berman on Law and Religion," *Emory Law Journal* 42 (1993): 523–60, at 531.

[28] See sources in note 22, and Tibor Várady's Afterword herein.

[29] See Berman, *Justice in the USSR*, 15–24; *Faith and Order*, 239, 280; *Law and Revolution*, 538, 546. For criticisms of Bentham, see his unpublished (but available in Emory Law School Library archives), "World Law and the Crisis of the Western Legal Tradition," *The William Timbers Lecture, Dartmouth College, Hanover, NH*, April 21, 2005.

[30] See Berman, *Faith and Order*, 314, 381. For similar criticisms of Emil Brunner, see Berman, *Interaction*, 81–91.

jurists were Gratian, Matthew Hale, and Joseph Story, who wrote con-cordances of discordant canons.[31] His favorite philosophers were Peter Abelard, Philip Melanchthon, and Michael Polanyi, who developed inte-grative holistic philosophies.[32]

"The era of dualism is waning," Berman wrote in 1974. "We are entering into a new age of integration and reconciliation. Everywhere synthesis," the overcoming of false opposites, is "the key to this new kind of think-ing and living." Either–or must give way to both–and. Not subject versus object, not fact versus value, not is versus ought, not soul versus body, not faith versus reason, not church versus state, not one versus many, "but the whole person and whole community thinking and feeling, learning and living together" – that is the common calling of humankind, Berman wrote.[33]

Berman applied this gospel of reconciliation and integration most vig-orously to his legal studies. He called for the reintegration of the classic schools of legal positivism, natural-law theory, and historical jurispru-dence – which, in his view, had been separated since God was cast out of the legal academy. He called for the integration of public law and private law, of common law and civil law, of Western law and Eastern law into a global legal system. He urged that law be given a place among the human-ities and enrich itself with the ideas and methods of sundry humane dis-ciplines. He urged that legal language be cast in terms understandable to all, and be enriched by the power of poetry, liturgy, literature, and art. And he urged most strongly that the subjects and sciences of law and reli-gion be reconciled to each other. Their separation was, for him, a theo-logical "heresy" and a jurisprudential "fallacy" that cannot survive in the new era of synthesis and integration. "[L]aw and religion stand or fall together," he wrote. "[I]f we wish law to stand, we shall have to give new life to the essentially religious commitments that give it its ritual, its trad-ition, and its authority – just as we shall have to give new life to the social, and hence the legal, dimensions of religious faith."[34]

Berman's talk of the death of dualism and the birth of an age of syn-thesis points to his further belief in a teleological, if not, providential view of history. Both Jewish and Christian theology, he reminded his readers,

[31] See Berman, *Law and Revolution*, 144–48; *Law and Revolution II*, 100–30; *Faith and Order*, 170ff.
[32] See Berman, *Law and Revolution*, 132; *Law and Revolution II*, 77–80; and Chapter 1 herein.
[33] Berman, *Interaction*, 113; "Law and Religion in the Development of World Order," 35.
[34] Berman, *Faith and Order*, 13.

teaches that time is continuous, not cyclical, that time moves forward from a sin-trampled garden to a golden city, from a fallen world to a perfect end-time. Berman was convinced that slowly but surely all the peoples of the world would come into contact with each other, and ultimately, after revolutionary struggle and even apocalyptic explosion, would seek finally to be reconciled with each other forever.[35]

Berman's grand account of evolution and revolution in Western history, set out in his *Law and Revolution* series, is rooted in this basic belief about the nature and pattern of time. There is a distinctive Western legal tradition, he argued, a continuity of legal ideas and institutions, which grow by accretion and adaptation. The exact shape of these ideas and institutions is determined, in part, by the underlying religious belief systems of the people ruling and being ruled. Six great revolutions, however, have punctuated this organic gradual development: the Papal Revolution of 1075, the German Lutheran Reformation of 1517, the English Puritan Revolution of 1640, the American Revolution of 1776, the French Revolution of 1789, and the Russian Revolution of 1917. These revolutions were, in part, rebellions against a legal and political order that had become outmoded and ossified, arbitrary and abusive. But, more fundamentally, these revolutions were the products of radical shifts in the religious belief systems of the people – shifts from Catholicism to Protestantism to Deism to the secular religion of Marxist-Leninism. Each of these new belief systems offered a new eschatology, a new apocalyptic vision of the perfect end-time, whether that be the second coming of Christ, the arrival of the heavenly city of the Enlightenment philosophers, or the withering away of the state. Each of these revolutions, in its first radical phase, sought the death of an old legal order to bring forth a new order that would survive the Last Judgment. Eventually, each of these revolutions settled down and introduced fundamental legal changes that were ultimately subsumed in and accommodated to the Western legal tradition.[36]

In this new millennium, Berman believed, the Western legal tradition is undergoing a profound integrity crisis, graver and greater than any faced in the past millennium. The old legal order of the West is under attack both from within and from without. From within, Western law is suffering from the critical and cynical attacks relentlessly issued by jurists and judges – a "form of lawyerly self-loathing," he once called it. These legal skeptics have dismissed legal doctrine as malleable, self-contradictory

---

[35] See section 6 of "Conclusion" herein. See also Berman, *Interaction*, 119–20; *Law and Revolution*, 166–72.

[36] See a good summary in the "Introduction," to Berman, *Law and Revolution II*, 1–28.

rhetoric. They have depicted the law as an instrument of oppression and
exploitation of women, of minorities, of the poor, of the different. They
have derided the legal system for its promotion of the political purposes
of the powerful and the propertied. This assault from within the law, from
within the legal academies and within the courts – devoid as it is of a positive agenda of reconstruction – reflects a cynical contempt for law and
government, a deep loss of confidence in its integrity and efficacy. The
"secular priests of the law," its officials and its educators, no longer seem to
believe in what they are doing.[37]

From without, the radical transformation of economic life and the
rapid acceptance of new social forms and customs, many born of Eastern,
Southern, and new-age thinking, have stretched traditional Western legal
doctrines to the breaking point. Each of the major branches of Western
law – contract, property, tort, family, criminal, commercial, and constitutional law – have transformed several times over in the past two generations. Many of these changes may well be necessary to modernize the
law, to conform it to contemporary social needs and ideals, to purge it of
its obsolete ideas and institutions. But as a consequence, Western law –
always something of a patchwork quilt – has become more of a collection
of disjointed pieces, with no single thread, no single spirit holding it in
place and giving it integrity and direction. This also has led to profound
disillusionment with and distrust of the law.[38]

For Berman, these are signs of end-times. We are reaching the end of
an age and the end of the Western legal tradition, as we have known it.
Western law is dying, he wrote, a new common law of all humanity is
struggling to be born out of the counter-forces of violent balkanization,
radical fundamentalism, and belligerent nationalism that now beset us
all. Western law, rooted in the soils and souls of Christianity, Judaism,
and their secular successors, will have a place in this new common law of
humanity. But so will the laws of the East and the South, of the tribe and
the jungle, of the country and the city, each with its own belief system.
What needs to be forged in this new millennium, Berman challenged his

[37] This is Hugo Grotius's phrase, which Berman has often used in personal conversations.
See Hugo Grotius, "[The Poem] Het Bcrocp van Advocaat [The Calling of the Advocate]
(February 18, 1602)," reprinted in Hugo Grotius, *Anthologia Grotiana* (The Hague:
Martinus Nijhoff, 1955), 33. See Berman, *Faith and Order*, 351; "The Prophetic, Pastoral,
and Priestly Vocation of the Lawyer," *The NICM Journal* 2 (1977): 5–9.
[38] See Harold J. Berman, "The Crisis of the Western Legal Tradition," *Creighton Law Review*
9 (1975): 252–65; "The Moral Crisis of the Western Legal Tradition and the Weightier
Matters of the Law," *Criterion* 19(2) (1980): 15–23; "The Crisis of Legal Education in
America," *Boston College Law Review* 26 (1985): 347–52.

readers, is a comprehensive new religious belief system, a new pattern of language and ritual, a new eschaton, that will give this common law of humanity its cohesion and direction. We need a new common law and a new common faith on a world scale, a new *ius gentium* and *fides populorum* for the whole world. We need global structures and symbols, global processes and principles. These cannot be found only in worldwide science and commerce, or in global literature and language. They must also be sought in a new "world law" and a new "world religion." For law and religion are the only two universal solvents of human living that can ultimately bring true peace, order, and justice to the world.

A streak of mystical millenarianism colors Berman's historical method – much of it already conceived while he was a young man witnessing the carnage of World War II and still brimming with the heady instruction of his Dartmouth mentor, Eugen Rosenstock-Huessy.[39] Description and prescription run rather closely together in his account, occasionally stumbling over each other. Historical periods and patterns are rather readily equated with providential plans and purposes. But here we have one of the deepest sources of many of Berman's insights and ambitions as a legal scholar. He was, as he put in an April 17, 1966 letter to Rosenstock, on a scholarly "pilgrimage."

> It is a very long, slow, hard journey. It goes through law and language, history, comparison of legal systems and cultures, the Great Revolutions, the communification of the nations, trade between planned and market economies, the hard struggle for peace, the reconciliation of man to his destiny and to God … I have hope that I can make meaningful and important what you have taught me – and can possibly rescue a good deal of scholarship and make a contribution to peace – by showing, first, that American law is a human, creative response to the continued danger of disintegration and alienation, and that law altogether is a great hope for uniting mankind. But law, to fulfill this hope, must be felt to be Speech, and a response to God's Word.[40]

---

[39] See, e.g., Eugen Rosenstock-Huessy, *Speech and Reality* (Norwich, VT: Argo Books, 1970); *The Christian Future, or The Modern Mind Outrun* (New York: Charles Scribner's Sons, 1946); *Out of Revolution: Autobiography of Western Man*, introduction by Harold J. Berman, (Providence, RI: Berg, 1993). For Berman's assessment of his mentor, see, e.g., Harold J. Berman, "Renewal and Continuity: The Great Revolutions and the Western Tradition," in *Eugen Rosenstock-Huessy: Studies in His Life and Thought*, eds., M. Darrol Bryant and Hans R. Huessy (Lewiston, NY: Edward Mellen Press, 1986): 19–29; "Recollections of Eugen [Rosenstock-Huessy], 1936–1940," March 29, 1999, unpublished (available at Emory Law School Library archives).

[40] Harold J. Berman, Letter to Eugen Rosenstock-Huessy (April 17, 1966) (on file in the Emory Law School Library archives).

3

All of these cardinal themes of Berman's life work can already be seen in this little book on *Law and Language*, written right in the middle of his legal career. The book distills some of the keen insights he had developed in his earlier international and comparative law work. It anticipates crisply some of the key themes that he went on to explore at great length in his *Law and Revolution* series and other writings in legal history, law and religion, and legal philosophy. And the book has a typical Berman-like interdisciplinary edge, with the methods and insights of jurisprudence, history, sociology, psychology, anthropology, theology, philosophy, and more all adeptly and seamlessly integrated into his analysis.

What makes the book all the more interesting is that Berman wrote this manuscript in the early 1960s when interdisciplinary approaches to legal study – including the study of law and language[41] – were only in their infancy. The regnant legal philosophy at the time was still the legal positivism that had dominated American, and broader Western, legal education for the first half of the twentieth century. Law, according to legal positivists, was simply the sovereign's rules. Legal study was simply the analysis of the rules that were posited, and their application in particular cases. Why these rules were posited, whether their positing was for good or ill, how these rules affected society, politics, or morality were not relevant questions for legal study. It was rather common to read in legal textbooks of the day that law is an autonomous science, that its doctrines, language, and methods are self-sufficient, that its study is self-contained. It was rather common to think that law has the engines of change within itself; that, through its own design and dynamic, law marches teleologically through time "from trespass to case to negligence, from contract to quasi-contract to implied warranty."[42]

To be sure, American legal positivism was not without its detractors. Already in the 1920s and 1930s, sociologists of law argued that the nature and purpose of law and politics cannot be understood without reference

---

[41] The first prominent discussion of law and literature in legal scholarship came with Judge Cardozo's essay, "Law and Literature," in his 1931 collection, *Law and Literature, and Other Essays and Addresses* (New York: Harcourt, Brace & Co, 1931), 3–40. See collection of later materials in William R. Bishin and Christopher D. Stone, *Law, Language, and Ethics: An Introduction to Law and Legal Method* (Mineola, NY: Foundation Press, 1972) and James Boyd White, *The Legal Imagination* (Boston, MA: Little, Brown, 1973 [rev. edn., University of Chicago Press, 1985])), discussed further below.

[42] Barbara Shapiro, "Law and Science in Seventeenth-Century England," *Stanford Law Review* 21 (1969): 727–766, at 728.

to the spirit of a people and their times – of a *Volksgeist und Zeitgeist* as their German counterparts put it.[43] The legal realist movement of the 1930s and 1940s used the new insights of psychology and anthropology to cast doubt on the immutability and ineluctability of judicial reasoning.[44] The revived natural-law movement of the 1940s and 1950s saw in the horrors of Hitler's Holocaust and Stalin's gulags the perils of constructing a legal system without transcendent checks and balances.[45] The international human rights movement of the 1950s and 1960s pressed the law to address more directly the sources and sanctions of civil, political, social, cultural, and economic rights.[46]

By the 1960s, the confluence of these and other movements had exposed the limitations of a positivist definition of law standing alone. Berman was in the vanguard of leading jurists – which included his colleagues Roscoe Pound and Lon Fuller as well as Jerome Hall, Karl Llewellyn, and others – who were pressing for a broader interdisciplinary philosophy of law. Of course, they said in concurrence with legal positivists, law consists of rules – the black letter rules of contracts, torts, property, corporations, and sundry other familiar subjects. Of course, law draws to itself a distinct legal science, an "artificial reason," as Sir Edward Coke once put it.[47] But law is much more than the rules of the state and how we apply and analyze them. Law is also the social activity by which certain norms are formulated by legitimate authorities and actualized by persons subject to those authorities. The process of legal formulation involves legislating, adjudicating, administering, and other conduct by legitimate officials. The process of legal actualization involves obeying, negotiating, litigating, and other conduct by legal subjects. Law is rules, plus the social and political processes of formulating, enforcing, and responding to those rules.[48]

[43] See, e.g., Julius Stone, *The Province and Function of Law: Law as Logic, Justice, and Social Control* (London: Stevens, 1947); Gustav Radbruch, *Der Geist des englischen Recht* (Heidelberg: A. Rausch, 1946).
[44] William W. Fisher, Morton Horowitz, and Thomas Reed, eds., *American Legal Realism* (New York: Oxford University Press, 1993); Wilfred E. Rumble, *American Legal Realism: Skepticism, Reform, and the Judicial Process* (Ithaca, NY: Cornell University Press, 1968).
[45] Charles Grove Haines, *The Revival of Natural Law Concepts* (New York: Russell & Russell, 1965); Roscoe Pound, *The Revival of Natural Law* (Notre Dame, IN: University of Notre Dame Press, 1942).
[46] John Witte, Jr. and Johan D. Van der Vyver, eds., *Religious Human Rights in Global Perspective*, 2 vols. (The Hague: Martinus Nijhoff, 1996).
[47] John Underwood Lewis, "Sir Edward Coke (1552–1633): His Theory of 'Artificial Reason' as a Context for Modern Basic Legal Theory," *Law Quarterly Review* 84 (1968): 330–42, at 330.
[48] Berman, *Law and Revolution*, 44ff.; Jerome Hall, *Comparative Law and Social Theory* (Baton Rouge: Louisiana State University Press, 1963), 78ff. See Chapter 2.

Numerous other institutions, besides the state, are involved in this legal functionality. The rules, customs, and processes of churches, colleges, corporations, clubs, charities, and other non-state associations are just as much a part of a society's legal system as those of the state. Numerous other norms, besides legal rules, are involved in the legal process. Rule and obedience, authority and liberty are exercised out of a complex blend of concerns, conditions, and character traits – class, gender, persuasion, piety, charisma, clemency, courage, moderation, temperance, force, faith, and more.[49]

Legal positivism could not, by itself, come to terms with law understood in this broader sense. In the 1960s, American jurists thus began to turn with increasing alacrity to the methods and insights of other disciplines to enhance their legal formulations. This was the birthing process of the modern movement of interdisciplinary legal study. The movement was born to enhance the province and purview of legal study, to refigure the roots and routes of legal analysis, to render more holistic and realistic our appreciation of law in community, in context, in concert with politics, social sciences, and other disciplines.[50]

Berman's pithy little volume on *Law and Language*, like his equally pithy little volume on *The Interaction of Law and Religion* published ten years later, is a valuable artifact from these early days of interdisciplinary legal study in America. N. E. H. Hull calls this kind of early work "*bricolage* jurisprudence," given its "marvelously far-ranging and free-thinking eclecticism."[51] Hull got this term from French anthropologist, Claude Lévi-Strauss, who used it to describe primitive handymen, who worked with "whatever [was] at hand," tools that were not designed for the present task.[52] Berman and other early interdisciplinary legal scholars, like Pound and Llewellyn, similarly "collect[ed] ideas from their vast reading of their predecessors in jurisprudence, as well as of economists, social psychologists, sociologists, and historians."[53] Eclecticism was the spirit of

---

[49] See further, John Witte, Jr., "Introduction," to John Witte, Jr. and Frank S. Alexander, eds., *The Teachings of Modern Christianity on Law, Politics, and Human Nature*, 2 vols. (New York: Columbia University Press, 2006), xx–xxxvii.

[50] See, e.g., Richard A. Posner, "The Present Situation in Legal Scholarship," *Yale Law Journal* 90 (1981): 1113–30; Robert C. Clark, "The Interdisciplinary Study of Legal Evolution," *Yale Law Journal* 90 (1981): 1238–74; Symposium, "American Legal Scholarship: Directions and Dilemmas," *Journal of Legal Education* 33 (1983): 403–11.

[51] N. E. H. Hull, *Roscoe Pound & Karl Llewellyn: Search for an American Jurisprudence* (University of Chicago Press, 1997), 8–10.

[52] Ibid., 9.   [53] Ibid., 10–11.

the times, and Berman was exuberantly broad in his use of sources from all manner of disciplines to aid his study of law.

Not only was intellectual eclecticism the new fashion of legal education in the early 1960s, but political danger was the perennial worry. The world was gripped by deep fear born of the Cold War and the Cuban Missile Crisis, while still reeling from the devastation of World Wars I and II. For Berman, the academy was no ivory tower refuge. "Two world wars, and the threat of a third," he wrote, with the Cuban Missile Crisis just averted, "have joined all mankind in a common destiny. We are all in contact with each other. Paradoxically, the human race is becoming unified by its capacity for self-destruction."[54]

The Cold War between the United States and the USSR, in particular, shaped Berman's efforts in *Law and Language* to work out a theory of "communification": to form sympathetic bonds of community through better mutual understanding of each other's cultures, languages, and laws, and more conversation to overcome the "tragic disunity which now threatens to destroy us."[55] In the 1950s and 1960s, he wrote a series of popular articles in the American press, designed to bring greater understanding of Russian families, farms, and workers, of Russian religion, morality, and values, of Russian science, education, and sports.[56] He also wrote popular articles and longer law reviews recommending concrete legal measures to open up commerce, trade, and travel between the USSR and the United States – a theme to which he returned many times.[57] He saw more

[54] See Conclusion herein.   [55] See Chapter 1, p. 48, herein.
[56] Harold J. Berman, "Divorce and Domestic Relations in Soviet Law," *Virginia Law Weekly* 2(2) (April 1950): 28–33; "Soviet Planning," *Atlantic Monthly* (December 1951): 11–12, 14; "The Soviet Family," *Atlantic Monthly* (February 1952): 18–20; Harold J. Berman and Miroslav Kerner, "Soviet Military Discipline," *Military Review* 32(3) (June 1952): 19–29; "Soviet Military Discipline," *Military Review* 32(4) (July 1952): 3–15; Harold J. Berman, "The Soviet Worker," *Atlantic Monthly* (July 1952): 8–10; "The Soviet Soldier," *Atlantic Monthly* (September 1952): 4, 6, 8; "The Soviet Peasant," *Atlantic Monthly* (March 1953): 15–18; "Soviet Education," *Atlantic Monthly* (April 1953): 16–19; "Soviet Trade," *Atlantic Monthly* (August 1954): 14–17; "Real Property Actions in Soviet Law," *Tulane Law Review* 29 (June 1955): 687–96; "Impressions of Moscow," *Harvard Law School Bulletin* 7(3) (December 1955): 7–8; "The Current Movement for Law Reform in the Soviet Union," *American Slavic and East European Review* 15 (April 1956): 179–89; "Soviet Legal Reforms," *The Nation* 182 (June 30, 1956): 546–48; "Soviet Law and Government," *Modern Law Review* 21 (January 1958): 19–26; "Limited Rule of Law," *Christian Science Monitor* (April 29, 1958): 9; "The Devil and Soviet Russia," *The American Scholar* 27 (Spring 1958): 147–52.
[57] Harold J. Berman, "The Problems That Unite Us," *The Nation* 192 (February 18, 1961): 132; see also, interview by Michael J. Ryan, "Berman: Losing Enemies by Making Friends," *Harvard Law Record* (February 25, 1965): 5–6.

international trade and travel to be essential initial steps of communication and intercourse that would lead to deeper and more stable understanding and peace.[58] He also arranged to have broadcast into the Soviet Union, his series of *Talks on American Law*, to give Russian listeners a better and a clearer understanding of what American law was all about.

These were first steps in Berman's gradual development of the field of comparative legal studies – especially comparisons of the Soviet and American legal systems, analyses of particular Soviet legal institutions, and linguistic analysis and translation of Soviet codes, statutes, and other legal materials.[59] Mastering the legal language and legal concepts of another people would prove to be a lasting feature of Berman's scholarly work, not only on Russia in these early days, but also eventually on other big foreign legal systems like China and Japan.[60] He pressed his students relentlessly to learn foreign languages and to translate their work to and from foreign languages. He also urged his readers to learn to parse closely the letter and spirit, the anatomy and physiology of foreign legal materials. He demonstrated that hermeneutic brilliantly in his many translations of Russian private, public, and military laws, and in his careful linguistic analysis of the recent Soviet Criminal Code, where he showed the many layers of ancient Christian morality and socialist innovation in the palimpsest of Soviet criminal law.[61]

[58] Harold J. Berman, "Thinking Ahead: East–West Trade," *Harvard Business Review* 32(5) (1954): 147–58; "The Legal Framework of Trade Between Planned and Market Economies"; "Negotiating Commercial Transactions with Soviet Customers."

[59] Harold J. Berman, "The Comparison of Soviet and American Law," *Indiana Law Journal* 34 (1959): 559–70, at 559; "Law in American Democracy and Under Soviet Communism"; Harold J. Berman and James W. Spindler, "Soviet Comrades' Courts," *Washington Law Review* 38 (1963): 842–910.

[60] Harold J. Berman, "Soviet Perspectives on Chinese Law," in Jerome A. Cohen, ed., *Contemporary Chinese Law* (Cambridge, MA: Harvard University Press, 1970), 313–28; Harold J. Berman, Susan Cohen, and Malcolm Russell, "A Comparison of the Chinese and Soviet Codes of Criminal Law and Procedure," *The Journal of Criminal Law and Criminology* 73 (Spring 1982): 238–58; Harold J. Berman, *The Role of Law in Trade Relations Between the United States and Japan*, a talk given to the Industrial Association in Osaka May 23, 1981, and to the Industrial Law Center in Tokyo May 27, 1981, unpublished (available at Emory Law School Library archives); Harold J. Berman and Van R. Whiting, Jr., "Impressions of Cuban Law," *The American Journal of Comparative Law* 28 (Summer 1980): 475–86.

[61] See Harold J. Berman, "A Linguistic Approach to the Soviet Codification of Criminal Law and Procedure," in Donald D. Barry, F. J. M. Feldbrugge, and Dominic Lasok, eds., *Codification in the Communist World* (Leiden: A. W. Sijthoff, 1975), 39–52. See his earlier work *Soviet Criminal Law and Procedure*; "Principles of Soviet Criminal Law," *Yale Law Journal* 56 (May 1947): 803–36; and with Donald H. Hunt, "Criminal Law and Psychiatry: The Soviet Solution," *Stanford Law Review* 2 (1950): 635–63.

For Berman, a comparative legal scholar had to understand not only the law on the books, but also the law in action. And that required him to be on site in the nations he studied – to interview judges and lawyers, to observe the legislature and courts in session, to have open talks with fellow scholars, ambassadors, and state officials about their legal systems and the American legal system. Russia was again his most critical laboratory in the years that he wrote *Law and Language*. In the late 1950s and 1960s he pressed relentlessly to get visas to travel to Russia. When state bureaucrats on both sides blocked him, he began writing directly to Soviet Chairman Nikita Khrushchev. On February 13, 1955, he sent this cable:

> NIKITA KHRUSHCHVEV THE KREMLIN MOSCOW USSR NEW YORK TIMES REPORTS TODAY YOU DESIRE MORE NORMAL TRADE RELATIONS BETWEEN UNITED STATES AND SOVIET UNON PERIOD ... I APPLIED ONE YEAR AGO FOR SOVIET VISA TO DISCUSS WITH EXPORT AND IMPORT OFFICIALS CONCRETE COMMERCIAL AND LEGAL PROBLEMS OF TRADING IN VARIOUS COMMODITIES PERIOD. I HAVE RECEIVED NO REPLY ... PERIOD.[62]

Within a month, Berman had his visa, and took the first of his many trips to the USSR. A few years later, he applied for a visiting law professorship in Moscow, and again got caught up in miles of red tape. He again wrote to Chairman Khrushchev, revealing his belief in comparative legal study as a source of better mutual understanding between nations:

> I am taking the liberty of writing to you about a matter which deeply concerns me as an American jurist who is working for better relations between the United States of America and the Soviet Union – namely, the matter of exchanges of visits between Soviet and American jurists ...
> I am convinced that Soviet officials charged with responsibility for cultural exchanges with the United States have failed to grasp a very simple point: that the very best Soviet propaganda in the United States is to send us your jurists. The United States is governed by jurists more than by any other professional group. [But] the view is very widespread in the United States (even among our jurists, who should know better), that law and legality play a very minor role in the Soviet Union. Many Americans are surprised to learn that jurists even exist in the Soviet Union ...
> Perhaps what I have written so far might give the impression that I am thinking only in terms of the benefit to the Soviet Union which can result from visits by Soviet jurists to the United States. But I am thinking primarily of the benefit to both of our countries, and to the cause of peace.

[62] Quoted by Robert C. Clark, "Preface to A Conference on the Work of Harold J. Berman," *Emory Law Journal* 42 (1993): 427–32, at 428.

> Frankly, I believe that the Soviet Union has at least as much to learn about the United States, and especially about our legal system, as the United States has to learn about Soviet law. Even more important is what we can learn from each other about the necessary conditions for establishing better legal relations between our countries, and among all countries.[63]

Berman followed this up with a direct appeal to Chairman Khrushchev at a reception in New York, following Khrushchev's famous shoe-banging speech at the United Nations. When he met the Chairman in the receiving line, he explained in Russian why he wanted to come to the Soviet Union to teach. Khrushchev listened intently, nodded, then instructed an aide to "take care of him." Berman soon got his visa to teach in Moscow for a year.[64] There he finished the new edition of his classic monograph, *Justice in the USSR.*

4

It was in that same year of 1963, flush with interdisciplinary and international ambition, that Berman began work in earnest on *Law and Language.*[65] His basic aim in this book is to provide an understanding of law that reveals its ability to build community and foster peaceful relationships among individuals and nations. Berman was convinced that the Western legal tradition, and the world community altogether, had the resources in its linguistic heritages to overcome its most dangerous tensions and divisions. Candid, learned, empathetic, and peaceful conversation across religions, cultures, and nations was the key.

"Communification" was Berman's new term for the process by which humans make and sustain communities, from the local to the global.[66] Language plays a critical role in this process, since language is ultimately a social phenomenon. Though words mean particular things, language as a practice is as much about meaning-making as it is about the "reciprocal transfer of meanings."[67] We need a new verb, says Berman, to capture this reciprocal dynamic in language: "speak-listen."[68] This heritage of

[63] April 16, 1960, quoted in Clark, "Preface," 430–31.
[64] See Erwin N. Griswold, "Preface to A Conference on the Work of Harold J. Berman," *Emory Law Journal* 42 (1993): 424–26.
[65] In a letter to his mentor, Eugen Rosenstock-Huessy, September 3, 1963, Berman wrote: "I am particularly anxious to have your opinions on the first chapter 'Law and Language'." (On file in Emory Law School Library archives.)
[66] See Chapter 1, p. 47, herein.   [67] Ibid., p. 38, herein.   [68] Ibid., p. 38, herein.

language, its socializing function, defends society from dissolution and disintegration:

> [L]anguage is a social event, not only in the sense that it brings together the participants in a conversation or dialogue ... but also in the sense that it brings together all the members of the language-community – those who have created the expressions we use, those who have taught them to us, our ancestors, our nation, our family, our teachers, our colleagues.[69]

Language is also the historical deposit of a community's social life, Berman continued. Each community has, in a sense, its own language, and we all inhabit many communities with distinctive languages. The loss of these linguistic communities, or their inability to speak to each other, is a grave threat. This was particularly true during the Cold War, whose propaganda machines and censorship campaigns on both sides violated the vital community-building power of language. The Cold War divisions were exacerbated by the inability of both sides to understand the other's language, culture, and law, which stymied meaningful negotiation. But since all humans speak language and all language bears similar marks and performs similar functions in each community, broader communities, even between bitter enemies, can be formed through the common experience and judicious translation of their most essential texts, not least their legal texts. Translation and conversation, Berman argued, are the beginning of making peace and the basis for lasting peace. The words we share, the common language we build, become symbols of our budding new community. Though there are no easy solutions to deep conflicts, especially those as vast as the Cold War, understanding the other in our own language, and having a common language to understand the tensions that exist on both sides, is an essential beginning point.

"Conviviality" – from "con" and "vivere," meaning "living together" – is another term that captures part of Berman's efforts in these pages. While words are important, Berman always moves outward, towards the whole. Words are part of language, which is the substance of a community's social life. This social life takes shape in rituals and rites that are marked by "conviviality."[70] Language and tradition are the stable ground of a community's life together, giving those people with common cause the common means to talk together, to work together, and to live peaceably together. "Even faculty meetings serve a necessary function in this respect," Berman writes, "and academicians are wrong to disparage them."[71] (Academics: please lower your eyebrows, and read on.)

---

[69] Ibid., p. 44, herein.   [70] Ibid., p. 61, herein.   [71] Ibid., p. 62, herein.

This also serves as a reminder to traditionalists that traditions serve the purpose of allowing individuals to share life together – amidst conflict – rather than to obfuscate and exclude. Berman is quite aware of the dangers of specialization in modern, industrialized society: "all are threatened by a polyglot culture, in which the only words that everybody hears or reads are the slogans of commercial advertisements and of political propaganda. Our common speech is threatened with debasement."[72] The tension between expertise and generality, between cultures and legal traditions, is the same: "the health of any society depends upon its ability to maintain and develop its common language without destroying the identity of the separate languages into which the common language is continually being broken."[73] Law is especially susceptible to this problem, since legal language is almost continually maligned as an alien tongue.

When it functions properly, however, legal language creates venues for speaking of and hearing about conflict and how to resolve it. Legal language also creates channels of negotiating, cooperating, and planning our lives together. In this way, law serves an important communifying function, since it works to prevent disintegration and injustice in a community, "creating order and giving orders," convincing and exhorting. Instead of just "referring" to things, Berman writes, legal terms create relationships and rights among persons. For these purposes, legal language needs formality and ceremony – words which show the legal relationships overlaying the parties, and a setting like a courtroom to show that justice is being done with impartiality and authority:

> Especially in primitive societies, and in primitive situations in modern societies, that is, when passions run high, the law-speaking authority needs words which characterize the grievance (or the economic or social problem demanding solution) to the satisfaction of both sides and which at the same time command the respect of the community as a whole.[74]

Given the essential relationship between language, experience, community, and law, Berman argues further for a historical approach to law. Such an approach gives proper place to tradition in the process of creating law and maintaining legal meaning:

> [T]he ability of a society to maintain traditions is absolutely essential to progress, for it alone makes it possible to introduce changes that will themselves, in turn, have stability. The capacity to change is a negation

---

[72] Ibid., p. 63, herein.   [73] Ibid., 63, herein.
[74] Ibid., p. 92, herein.

of progress when it is not linked with the capacity to preserve. For, without the capacity to preserve, there is no change in the sense of taking a new direction but only a perpetual series of changes, each canceling the other.[75]

This historical view of language is important for the American legal tradition, Berman writes, a vital part of the distinctive American understanding of the "rule of law." "America inherited the idea of the historicity of law from England, and ultimately from the Western concept of historical development. But America embodied that idea [both in its vital doctrine of precedent, as well as] in a written document, thereby fixing permanently the language of American Constitutional law."[76] The Constitution itself is an example of the developmental power of tradition and stabilizing force of tradition.

5

Berman's argument in *Law and Language* was grounded in the best philosophical and social science literature of the day. While the text is rife with references, Bronistaw Malinowski, Edward Sapir and Benjamin Lee Whorf, and Kenneth Burke deserve special mention. Each of these theorists prized cultural particularity, the bounded-ness of language to thought, the subjectivity of the individual, and the dramatic, dialogical character of human existence. Each of them also challenged the naïve objectivism and false universalism of some earlier social scientists – criticisms that Berman took to heart in *Law and Language*.

Prior to Bronistaw Malinowski's work, it was commonly thought that "savage" societies were developmentally inferior, having few social or cultural conventions. According to anthropologists Jane Hill and Bruce Mannheim, the intellectual life of the late nineteenth and early twentieth centuries was marked by "a naïve ... universalism in grammar, and an equally vulgar evolutionism in anthropology and history."[77] Malinowski's field work with the Trobriand islanders showed that "primitive" culture was as complex and refined in its cultural objects and systems of meaning as that of modern European nations. Through his fine-grained studies of Trobriand life, Malinowski became the "father" of ethnography in

---

[75] Ibid., p. 129, herein.   [76] Ibid., p. 143, herein.
[77] Jane H. Hill and Bruce Mannheim, "Language and World View," *Annual Review of Anthropology* 21 (1992): 381–404, at 384.

anthropology.[78] His fieldwork manifested the anthropological necessity of first-hand, fact-based, empirical analysis obtained through living together with the communities being studied. At the same time, Malinowski challenged anthropologists and ethnographers to understand the challenges of the ethnographer, who is both "chronicler and historian." There is an interpretive distance between the ethnographer, his anthropological facts, and his final presentation, Malinowski insisted, which required critical exercises of subjective judgment and interpretive discretion.[79]

The problem of subjectivity in scientific work was addressed in detail by anthropologist Edward Sapir and his student Benjamin Lee Whorf. On several occasions in *Law and Language*, Berman acknowledges his debt to both men. While allowing that there is some objective and universal "fact" at the heart of understanding, Whorf and Sapir argued that these facts are construed through the idiomatic and habitual patterns of language which shape the thought and method of anthropology. Even this binary fact–language picture is problematic, since language is more than just a cultural "label" for objective facts, but is constitutive of the entire process and object of research. The "real world," the world of "facts," is as mediated by cultural and linguistic habits and particularities as the most idiomatic English expression.[80] Sapir and Whorf's emphasis on the fundamental, constitutive importance of language is a critical reference point for Berman's argument in *Law and Language*. It shapes his response to Jeremy Bentham's attempt to reduce language to its "neutral, objective" meaning, and it leads him to endorse Friedrich Carl von Savigny's emphasis on history and cultural particularity in law reform.[81]

The final important social science touchstone for Berman is rhetorician and philosopher Kenneth Burke. His major work, *A Rhetoric of Motives*, translates this view of language into a holistic account of human interaction with other humans and with the world. For Burke, the material world is already cast through the "filter" of language when humans come to understand it. These syntheses of material reality and linguistic symbol are called motives. Rhetorical devices, scientific viewpoints, and moral systems are all interpretive lenses for material reality, which can

[78] Dominik Bartmanski, "How to Become an Iconic Social Thinker," *European Journal of Social Theory* 15 (2012): 433–36.
[79] Lodewijk Brunt, "Thinking About Ethnography," *Journal of Contemporary Ethnography* 28 (October 1999): 500–9, at 502.
[80] Hill and Mannheim, "Language and World View," 383–85.
[81] See Chapters 2 and 3 herein.

lead to different ideas of what is important about material reality or even what material reality is. The sharing and identification of these motives among groups of people leads to "consubstantiality," that is, a shared identity though shared interpretations of a common symbol. Burke uses the United States Constitution as an example, which may have inspired Berman's appropriation of Burke in the legal context. Since we are speaking beings, our common nature is produced through the dramatic and rhetorical sharing of common symbols and motives; law is especially relevant as an example of shared identity through communication.[82]

These debates in linguistics and anthropology were accompanied by analogous disputes and developments in mid-twentieth-century philosophy. These Berman also followed, albeit at a greater distance; technical philosophy was never his thing. By the early 1950s, Ludwig Wittgenstein's *Philosophical Investigations* had decisively put to rest the efforts of Anglo-American philosophers to render a pure and perfectly rational language. Wittgenstein's *Investigations* explored the roots of linguistic meaning in social forms of life. Words are not primarily or only arrows that point to things; words are used in different ways as parts of social practices.[83] Similarly, Hans-Georg Gadamer, a student of Martin Heidegger, had just finished his magisterial *Truth and Method*, where he declared that hermeneutics was ontology – that is, language and interpretation preceded and undergirded our most basic philosophical understanding of the *being* of anything at all. Things, in a certain sense, have "existence" through language.[84] Almost every discipline in the university experienced a "turn to language" in the middle of the twentieth century. This was the intellectual climate of Berman's foray into the most linguistic of disciplines – that of law.

Two other critical figures for Berman in *Law and Language* are the later eighteenth-century English political philosopher, Edmund Burke, and

[82] Jeffrey W. Murray, "Kenneth Burke: A Dialogue of Motives," *Philosophy & Rhetoric* 35(1) (2002): 31–34.

[83] Ludwig Wittgenstein, *Philosophical Investigations*, trans. G. E. M. Anscombe (Oxford: B. Blackwell, 1953); see *Tractatus Logico-Philosophicus*, trans. Frank P. Ramsey and C. K. Ogden, (New York: Harcourt, Brace & Co., 1922) for Wittgenstein's earlier, partly repudiated reference theory of meaning. See A. J. Ayer, *Language, Truth, and Logic* (London: Victor Gollancz, 1936) for a traditional Anglo-American account of language as simple reference between word and thing.

[84] Hans-Georg Gadamer, *Truth and Method*, trans. Joel Weinsheimer and Donald G. Marshall, 2nd rev. edn. (New York: Continuum, 2000); originally published as *Warheit und Methode* (Tubingen: J.C.B. Mohr, 1960).

the nineteenth-century German jurist, Friedrich Carl von Savigny. Both of these scholarly giants anticipated many of the developments in linguistics and anthropology that Berman found attractive.[85] Savigny and Burke were alike in viewing law as the unique achievement of a culture. As the law responds to its particular problems, they argued, it develops common solutions that have wide consensus and moral weight. These insights led both men to oppose needless or hasty law reform or legal codification by whoever happened to be in power. Law, they said, is a fragile, interdependent historical heritage of the entire people, rather than a series of neutral and transient commands of a sovereign. Each nation has its own character and its own legal needs, and their law has moral force because it builds on the customs of a people responding to their common needs. Berman took to heart this historical, communitarian view of law, and adapted it to address the international tensions that so shaped the 1960s. If law is a product of communities, citizens of all communities need to form an international community, and each of their legal systems needs to be discussed, understood, and sifted for their convergences, common elements, and creative tensions.

Law and Language is not without its sympathetic villains. The English utilitarian philosopher and law reformer, Jeremy Bentham, stands in for an entire perspective on law, scholarship, and language that Berman rejects. This is not only the legal positivism for which Bentham was famous, but also the reference theory of word meaning and a legal reformism insensitive to the historical framework and cultural context of law. Berman does not begrudge Bentham his accomplishments as a reformer and theorist of legal language. Nor does he begrudge the keen insights of Bentham's modern disciple, the preeminent Oxford jurist, H. L. A. Hart. While admiring Bentham for his energetic attack on self-deception in the law, Berman also criticizes Bentham for his single-minded attempt to neuter legal language.[86] As Berman explains in the text, Bentham attempted to root out the emotional and rhetorical characteristics of legal language. If legal language is neutered, however, Berman argues, the critical "communifying" function of law is impaired. By the same token, if legal scholars choose to separate the moral (and emotional and rhetorical) characteristics of law from its positive "legal" content, they lose their perception of

---

[85] See Peter Stein, *Legal Evolution: The Story of an Idea* (Cambridge University Press, 1980) and Symposium, "Savigny in Modern Comparative Perspective," *American Journal of Comparative Law* (Winter 1989): 1–169.

[86] See Chapter 2, part 1 herein.

the critical role law plays in shaping a group's moral life and uniting individuals into enduring bonds of community. Here we see, in the ripples of Kenneth Burke's *A Rhetoric of Motives*, a tacit interdisciplinary response to the new legal positivism.

Bentham's linguistic reformism was taken up by practicing lawyer and UCLA professor David Mellinkoff, in his classic text *The Language of Law*. Legal scholars at the time viewed this book as a novel and important achievement. "Here is a book unlike any other," said reviewer Saul Cohen in 1964.[87] Early reviewers seemed to agree that Mellinkoff's book was an important *cri de coeur* against the problems of antiquated linguistic habits that prized ambiguity and esotericism, and they praised his efforts to bring about a critical program of legal and linguistic reform.[88] The book was popular enough to end up in the hands of distinguished poet and "ex-lawyer" Archibald Macleish, who carved out a space in public letters for him: "Mr. Mellinkoff is wittier than Mencken as well as being considerably more civilized."[89] Berman's copy of this text is well marked, and his comments on the history and poetics of legal language in Chapter 3 herein may be his (tacit) response to Mellinkoff's path-breaking text.

In a late-life reflection, Mellinkoff recalled the early days of his corporate law practice. As a young associate, he wrote, "I did as I was told. I followed the office pattern: Sentences long enough to choke a horse. I looked at the opinions: Words repeated endlessly in different forms: *by and with, each and every, null and void, made and provided, keep and maintain.* On and on. English grammar became a matter of twists and turns."[90] His magnum opus, *The Language of the Law*, recounts the history of Anglo-American linguistic habits, from the argot of Law French, twinned in the synthesis of English and French legal traditions, to the constant criticism of legalese through the colonial period to today.[91] What has resulted is a legal language and a legal profession that is "wordy," "unclear," "pompous," and "dull."[92] Though Berman was most interested in Mellinkoff's presentation of the history, Mellinkoff himself hoped to provoke the development of a

---

[87] Saul Cohen, "Book Reviews," *UCLA Law Review* 11 (1964): 461–64, at 461.
[88] Brainerd Currie, "Book Reviews," *Journal of Legal Education* 17 (1964): 227–30; Susan Westerberg Prager, "David Mellinkoff: An Affectionate Tribute," *UCLA Law Review* 33 (June 1985): 1247–49.
[89] Archibald Macleish, "Book Reviews," *Harvard Law Review* 78 (1964): 490–91, at 490.
[90] David Mellinkoff, "Plain English: Why I Wrote *The Language of the Law*," *Michigan Bar Journal* 79 (January 2000): 28.
[91] David Mellinkoff, *The Language of the Law* (Boston, MA: Little, Brown, 1963), 136–79, 230–31, 265.
[92] Ibid., 24.

durable, intelligible, precise, and concise language for practitioners which would redound to the benefit of clients, judges, and juries who live by and interpret this work-product.[93] Deferring to Mellinkoff, Berman himself recognizes these problems in legal language: "if the roots of law in the whole body of living language of the community are neglected, the power of law to hold it together is weakened."[94]

Altogether, Berman is to be admired for his open-minded and fair appropriation of the leading social scientists and historical jurists in his interdisciplinary approach to the study of law and language. While many of the scholars he used may now only be remembered in dusty books and on fading tombstones, their work did set the stage for our post-modern academy. The problems of language relativity, subjectivity, and objectivity in observation and method continue to haunt social science, post-colonial scholarship, and every shade of critical and cultural studies. The roles of history and tradition in shaping morality and legality are now hot topics of American constitutional theory, and in modern American cases dealing with fundamental rights and the appropriate constitutional relationships between citizens, states, and the federal government. And these matters are taken up in earnest by the law and language movements in the legal academy today.

6

The modern study of law and language can be divided, roughly, into two groups: a "rhetorical-humanistic" group and a "linguistic" group. While there are many treatments of language and law that fall outside or in between these groups, these are the mainstays in modern scholarship. Berman's *Law and Language* book anticipated a number of important themes at work in both these schools.[95]

The rhetorical-humanistic school of the "law and language" movement had an important early start in the 1984 conference on hermeneutics and law at the University of Southern California. The hefty symposium issue of the *Southern California Law Review* that resulted was marked by an

---

[93] Ibid., 285. [94] See Chapter 3, p. 103, herein.

[95] See, e.g., the papers collected in Anne Wagner, et al., *Interpretation, Law and the Construction of Meaning: Collected Papers on Legal Interpretation in Theory, Adjudication and Political Practice* (Dordrecht: Springer, 2007) and Janet Cotterill, ed., *Language in the Legal Process* (New York: Palgrave Macmillan, 2002) for important contributions that are not be addressed in this sample here.

exuberant diversity of methods and styles without a common approach, methodology, or theme.[96] A more systematic approach came the next year with the publication of University of Michigan law professor James Boyd White's *The Legal Imagination*. This was an elegant and judiciously assembled collection of literary excerpts, legal texts, and exercises in the style of a casebook, designed to help students understand the rhetorical aspects of legal practice and the moral and humane motives that should inform a humanistic practice of the law.[97]

James Boyd White's work in this and subsequent books has two principal themes that are congruent with the insights that Berman had proffered a generation earlier. First, White's theory of law and language emphasizes the role of language and dialogue in making community. Second, White brilliantly analyzes the rhetorical and moral content of American law and American community – the relationships between speaker and listener and the moral and communal values implicit in judicial and legal language. Unlike Berman, whose focus was legal history and comparative law, White focuses on American law today. In his *Living Speech*, for example, White observes that the inhumanity and dehumanization of persons in war, in advertising, and in electioneering are based on speech and its capacity to frame the world. Learning how to speak in a humanizing way is the first step to understanding the empire of force and learning "how not to respect it". Sentimentalities, trivialities, slogans, falsities, and denials, White argues, are all forms of dead speech that dehumanize persons and corrode the community.[98]

Also like Berman, White claims that the law *translates* ordinary life into legal argument, and vice versa. The incidental character of Supreme Court opinions calls the public and the court into a continual practice of making meaning, making sense, and making justice in life. The language of justice is critical for White, as it was for Berman: so is naming injustice, rather than reducing our discourse to "gratification," "power," or "instrumentalism." Practicing meaningful language, free from sentiment and cliché, is a necessary foundation for the difficult process of just judicial decision-making which is a *sine qua non* of the rule of law.[99]

[96] Collected in volume 58, nos. 1 & 2 of the *Southern California Law Review* (1985).
[97] White, *Legal Imagination*.
[98] James Boyd White, *Living Speech: Resisting the Empire of Force* (Princeton University Press, 2006), 1–13.
[99] Ibid., 196–206. White also submits American constitutional case law to critical, rhetorical analysis in his *Justice as Translation: An Essay in Cultural and Legal Criticism* (University of Chicago Press, 1990), "Part Two: The Judicial Opinion as Form of Life."

Advertising and sloganeering, White continues, reduce our world into commodities more than communities, and reduce individuals into consumers more than citizens or communal actors. A common theme of White's work is that living speech respects each individual as a source and site of narrative and meaning. Meaning-making is the essence of speech, and speech is the cornerstone of community. Courts must take account of the value of speech, with this in mind – not only in interpreting the First Amendment Free Speech Clause, but in crafting the language of their opinions in all cases. Speech as mere information for consumption is not valuable in the same way. "[The court] would see the world as a world of people talking, not making deals or transactions."[100]

Like Berman, White further notes that the danger of legal translation is abstraction, loss of context and cultural nuance. In his *Justice as Translation*, White argues that language makes a culture, with its own assumptions, values, and pictures of the world. "Conceptual" language is anti-linguistic, because it assumes that language is just pointing, rather than constitutive of thought and knowledge. This view of the world is imperialistic, says White, because one language is assumed to express a concept completely or sufficiently; the differences between languages and cultures are elided as mere differences in clarity. This view of language is also antagonistic, ruling out contradictions and conflicts in experience and other languages. This view reduces writing and speech to rationalistic outline.[101]

White's alternative view is this: language does not express concepts, but makes meaning; indeed, language is the very act of meaning and of being. Words get their meaning through their cultural, textual, and practical contexts. How they are used – in sentences, in books, in poems, in literature, or in judicial opinions alike – gives these words meaning, form, practicality, identity-marking functions. This means that language is individualized by context and by the speaker, who gains meaning, identity, understanding, and direction through the experience of language. The meaning we express isn't in an idea, concept, or sense datum, but in language as it is expressed in its entire context.

White would agree with Berman that good translation – across space, time, culture, discipline, and social place – is a preeminent example of the "communifying" characteristics of language. The effort of translating words, speeches, and texts reflects an ethic of respect for the other person,

---

[100] White, *Living Speech*, 206–11.
[101] White, *Justice as Translation*, 27–33.

the other language, the other culture. If done well, translation reflects an ethic of fidelity to the other, rather than dominance or replacement of a critical marker of identity and meaning. The practice of law, White argues, reflects this view of translation, too. Lawyers must speak lay language as well as legal language, respecting and taking up the client's story into the language of law, and using legal language to draw out meanings from the client's story that may not be as significant in the client's language. That, for White, is a fundamental ingredient of legal professionalism.[102]

All of life, in fact, White continues, involves this kind of translation, because each person is a unique source of meaning; the object is, in life as in law, to be individuals who respect the other without losing their sense of self. Out of this reciprocal engagement with others, we create ourselves and together we create community. The question for lawyers and the law is: will the law be a place for this reciprocal exchange and engagement, a place for "multivocality," or will it be the blunt object of "bureaucratic and theoretical power"? Human community and language lives through this process of reciprocal interaction, response, and translation.[103]

The problem of translation into legal argument, especially within the courtroom, is taken up in earnest by Milner S. Ball in *The Promise of American Law*. Ball, a longstanding friend and admirer of Berman, moves from the translation of legal languages to the translation of law into dramatic enactment. Ball conceives the entire legal process along the lines of theater, where justice must be done, but, just as importantly, justice must be seen to be done. The trial itself, for Ball, is an event of community ratification and belonging. Just as Malinowski would describe the rites of initiation, marriage, or reconciliation in primitive societies as absolutely necessary to community solidarity and social order, Ball describes the modern American courtroom as a place that reaffirms the commitment of every participant to the covenant of law in American society – whether litigants or advocates, judges or court officials, witnesses or audience members.[104] Ball provides a helpful analogue and extension to Berman's insights in *Law and Language*; he fills out the challenges and possibilities of translation, drama, and community.

Berman's basic picture of law is consonant with the "metaphor" of law as a "medium of social relationships" recommended in Milner Ball's signature title, *Lying Down Together*. According to Ball, the prevailing

---

[102] Ibid., 34ff.   [103] Ibid., 267.
[104] Milner Ball, *The Promise of American Law: A Theological, Humanistic View of Legal Process* (Athens, GA: University of Georgia Press, 1981), ch. 4.

metaphor for law today is "law as bulwark of freedom." Though this meta-phor has inspired protection of minority rights, it also underwrites laws that are firm, hard, unmoving, brutal – guaranteeing justice and equality only when law has been established with total authority. Seeing law as the medium of social relationships is better, Ball argues; law is a time-bound management of and coping with ineradicable features of human life.[105]

While Berman anticipates many of the themes in what we have called the "rhetorical-humanistic" school of law and language, represented by White and Ball, many scholars in this field today rely on literary analysis and critical theory which goes far beyond anything Berman found inter-esting.[106] What is lacking is the foundation in linguistics that Berman was careful to lay. This has led many critics, including federal judges Richard Posner and Harry Edwards to question the merit of this school of the law and language movement.[107] The ability of Berman to integrate the mean-ingful goals of the rhetorical-humanist movement with the scientific basis of contemporary linguistics suggests that there may still be common ground to be found between the economists, linguists, and literary theo-rists. As Posner himself has suggested, the legal academy cannot do with-out "the methods of scientific and humanistic inquiry" which "enlarge our knowledge of the legal system" as a whole.[108]

The second contemporary school of law and language that has emerged since Berman's seminal tract of 1964 can be termed the "linguist school." Lawyer-linguists Peter Tiersma and Lawrence Solan are exemplary; they have done much to show the contemporary relevance of linguistics to legal scholarship, especially in a time when textualism is a dominant method of statutory interpretation. Their co-edited *Oxford Handbook of Law and Language* is notable for its breadth of coverage in terms of theory and con-temporary concrete issues.[109] Solan's two monographs, *The Language of*

---

[105] Milner Ball, *Lying Down Together: Law, Metaphor, and Theology* (Madison, WI: University of Wisconsin Press, 1985), chs. 2 & 4.

[106] See, e.g., the diverse and provocative essays in Guyora Binder and Richard Weisberg, *Literary Criticisms of Law* (Princeton University Press, 2000).

[107] Richard A. Posner, *Law and Literature*, 3rd edn. (Harvard University Press, 2009), 382–85. See also Harry T. Edwards, "The Growing Disjunction Between Legal Education and the Legal Profession," *Michigan Law Review* 91 (1992): 34–78 and "The Growing Disjunction Between Legal Education and the Legal Profession: A Postscript," *Michigan Law Review* 91 (1993): 2191–219.

[108] Richard A. Posner, "The Decline of Law as an Autonomous Discipline: 1962–1987," *Harvard Law Review* 100 (1987): 761–80, at 778–79.

[109] Peter M. Tiersma and Lawrence M. Solan, eds., *The Oxford Handbook of Language and Law* (Oxford University Press, 2012).

Judges and *The Language of Statutes* offer expert linguistic analyses of the grammatical canons applied in judicial and statutory reasoning.[110] Solan ultimately concludes that, while linguistic analysis is helpful in some circumstances of legal ambiguity, ultimately, judges and politicians have to make political judgments. Candor about the ultimate ambiguities at the heart of language would be better for the legal system than strained linguistic analysis. Vagueness, indeterminacy, and ambiguity are critical issues for many philosophers of law as well.

Much contemporary work on law and language within the "linguistic school" is done to improve the conduct of trials before juries. The "plain language" movement has been an American echo of Bentham's original cry for clarity in legal vocabulary, later echoed by Mellinkoff. The basic goal of the movement is to form legal language that quickly and easily allows readers to understand and act based on the text; the text should be as simple as the complexity of the ideas permits.[111] According to Mark Adler, plain language is: (1) more precise, (2) less erroneous, (3) less expensive and more efficient, because lawyers do not have to translate legalese for their clients, (4) more persuasive by virtue of being easily understood, (5) more democratic and accessible, and (6) less tedious, more elegant, and more pleasant to use.[112]

This plain language movement goes beyond what Berman called for in *Law and Language*. Yes, Berman did argue that, especially in contexts where laypeople must understand the laws that apply to them, legal language should be clear, and lawyers and judges must work to translate the law into terms that laymen, even children, understand.[113] But Berman, like Milner Ball later on, focused further on the critical role of courtroom liturgy, pageantry, and ornate formal language to underscore the majesty, the justice-making power of the law.[114] Modern legal linguists may disagree with the latter accent. As Gail Stygall notes, courtroom discourse, though highly predictable if understood, is at a distance from ordinary language. This makes the trial itself, as well as the law writ large, incomprehensible to most laypeople. Given the importance of language in legal proceedings, Stygall argues, the trial should be positioned closer to ordinary language, or better explanations of the process should be given to

---

[110] Lawrence M. Solan, *The Language of Judges* (University of Chicago Press, 1993); *The Language of Statutes* (University of Chicago Press, 2010).
[111] Mark Adler, "The Plain Language Movement," in Tiersma and Solan, eds., *Oxford Handbook*, 67–68.
[112] Ibid., 71–72.   [113] See below, Chapter 3.
[114] See esp. Berman, *Interaction*, 31–39.

citizens, at the risk of delegitimizing the court.[115] These problems in the courtroom can present problems for Berman's communicative account of law and legal language, if legal language actually ends up alienating most of the community, rather than gathering it together and representing its basic norms and mores.

Translation is a critical issue in Berman's text, though he does not include detailed analyses of concrete problems of translation. The Afterword herein by his former prize student, Tibor Várady, draws out the implications of Berman's theory of law and language for modern legal problems and cases. Nevertheless, Berman's view of law and language, as a communifying practice oriented towards shared experience, has a concrete example in European Union legislators and courts. As these institutional bodies struggle to adopt common legal standards amidst a plurality of languages, modern linguists have wondered whether a common legal language is possible. Shared experience may indeed be a basis for a unified law of the European Union.[116] "Strong" language theorists reject this possibility, but "weak" language theorists, who emphasize the flexibility of language, suggest that language meaning can be shared across tongues and stabilized through common experience and dialogue.[117] The practice of EU legislators – writing without a source language, in a collaborative process of translation across each of the primary languages – is seeking the balance between a hegemony of a single legal language, and an incoherent mess of every European tongue having equal currency.[118]

The EU faces another problem in the development of a new "Court French" among the clerks of the European Court of Justice (ECJ). As Karen McAuliffe warns, the use of French by the court, coupled with the judicial clerks and law clerks who are not native French speakers, has led to a highly formalized version of "Court French," which obstructs simplicity and creativity, but allows for easy translation of opinions into the twenty-three official languages of the EU. The lawyer-linguists responsible for translating ECJ law must master two disciplines, since their work is comparative law as much as translation.[119]

---

[115] Gail Stygall, "Discourse in the US Courtroom," in *Oxford Handbook*, 369–70.
[116] Jan Engberg, "Word Meaning and the Problem of a Globalized Legal Order," in *Oxford Handbook*, 176–81.
[117] Michel Bastarache, "Bilingual Interpretation Rules as a Component of Language Rights in Canada," in *Oxford Handbook*, 170ff.
[118] Ibid., 182–85.
[119] Karen McAuliffe, "Language and Law in the European Union: The Multilingual Jurisprudence of the ECJ," in *Oxford Handbook*, 204–12.

Nevertheless, facing this situation, Lawrence Solan is optimistic. Using a theological analogy that may have pleased Berman, Solan suggests that the proliferation of languages in the European Union may end up helping the ECJ discover the meaning of a common legal text by helping the justices "triangulate" the meaning when there is no "original" text. This is an "Augustinian" approach to legal interpretation, as Saint Augustine compared translations of the Bible to ascertain its "true" meaning. If there is a common "original" meaning amidst the various versions, multiple legal texts will help the ECJ ascertain the shades of legal meaning in a text. Solan is hopeful that as citizens in the EU have more common experiences, the divergence in shades of meaning can be overcome.[120]

7

Berman understood that he was up to something very new and very controversial in this little volume. He was calling for a new understanding of law, language, and history that he thought would bring community and peace to a world torn asunder – by World Wars, the Korean War, the Cold War, and the Vietnam War, by the violent student riots and union strikes at home, by the savage Marxist and critical scholarly attacks on churches, states, and economies, on traditions, canons, and cultures alike. Many at the time would have viewed this argument as a fool's errand. Perhaps that reality, as much as his incessant busyness, was what kept Berman from finishing and publishing this book. "I shall no doubt be scorned or ignored," he confessed to his mentor Rosenstock-Huessy two years after completing the preliminary manuscript of this book.[121] He had the same trepidation ten years later in publishing his equally novel and equally controversial little book, *The Interaction of Law and Religion*. To his last days, he was smarting that his Harvard Law School colleagues just ignored his law and religion book.[122]

The Interaction of Law and Religion, however, helped to launch the modern law and religion movement, now embracing several hundred law professors in North America and Europe alone, with dozens of centers,

[120] Lawrence M. Solan, "The Interpretation of Multilingual Statutes by the European Court of Justice," *Brooklyn Journal of International Law* 34 (2009): 286–94.
[121] See above, note 1. Berman loved to quote the old adage of the scholar: "Though my sins be like scarlet, let my works be read."
[122] See Harold J. Berman, "Foreword," to Michael W. McConnell, Robert F. Cochran, Jr., and Angela C. Carmella, eds., *Christian Perspectives on Legal Thought* (New Haven, CT: Yale University Press, 2001), xii.

programs, journals, and associations around the world.[123] While Berman's *Law and Language* manuscript, unpublished and largely unknown, obviously did not have the same catalytic and generative effect, the field of law and language studies, and related fields of legal translation and legal interpretation (hermeneutics, semiotics, and philology), have certainly blossomed in the half century since Berman wrote this early work. At minimum, Berman's little book can be viewed as an interesting artifact, even a missing link, in the evolution of the field of law and language studies. But even more, it can be viewed as a profound prophetic example and call for deep legal scholarship that is at once rigorously interdisciplinary, international, and intercultural in reach and ambition, and that is resolutely directed toward greater understanding of the "weightier matters of the law: justice and mercy and faith."[124]

---

[123] See John Witte, Jr., "The Study of Law and Religion in the United States: An Interim Report," *Ecclesiastical Law Journal* 14 (2012): 327–54.

[124] Matthew 23:23. Berman often used this biblical trope. See, e.g., Harold J. Berman, "The Weightier Matters of the Law," *Address to the Opening of Vermont Law School, 1974*, repr. in *Royalton Review* 9(1 & 2) (1975): 32; "The Weightier Matters of the Law," in Ronald Berman, ed., *Solzhenitsyn at Harvard* (Washington, DC: Ethics and Public Policy Center, 1980), 99–113; "The Moral Crisis of the Western Legal Tradition and the Weightier Matters of the Law."

1

Language as an effective symbol of community

1

Speech is risky. The speaker must commit himself; and he must incur the risks of being misunderstood, disbelieved, resented, ignored. The listener, too, exposes himself to hazards. He may be deceived, offended, frightened, subverted, or, worst of all, bored.

Yet the risks of not speaking and not listening are greater. They are the risks of isolation, loneliness, and ultimately hatred, violence, and death. Melville's Billy Budd, unable to stammer out a protest of his innocence, struck a death-blow with his fist. "Could I have used my tongue, I would not have struck him," Billy Budd says to Captain Vere. "But he foully lied to my face and in the presence of my captain and I had to say something, and I could only say it with a blow."[1] This indeed is a parable of man's frustration when he loses the power to speak. We treasure that voluntary silence which is the aftermath of speech, or its precursor; but enforced silence is painful, and even voluntary silence, when prolonged, is likely to be uncomfortable and rude.[2] "To a natural man," wrote the anthropologist Bronisław Malinowski, referring to primitive societies, "another man's silence is not a reassuring factor, but, on the contrary, something alarming and dangerous."[3] In literate societies as well, silence – unless it contains the seeds of speech – is generally the mark of indifference or

---

[1] Herman Melville, "Billy Budd, Foretopman," in *Shorter Novels of Herman Melville* (New York: Horace Liverwright, 1928), 299.

[2] [Like Berman, James Boyd White has recognized the potent power of silence for authentic and capable speech, as well as the dehumanizing constrictions placed on "living speech" by the inundation of propaganda and advertising in public spaces. See James Boyd White, *Living Speech: Resisting the Empire of Force* (Princeton University Press, 2008), 14–16, 26.]

[3] Bronisław Malinowski, "The Problem of Meaning in Primitive Languages," appended to C. K. Ogden and I. A. Richards, *The Meaning of Meaning: A Study of the Influence of Language Upon Thought and of the Science of Symbolism* (New York: Harcourt, Brace & World, 1946), 309.

hostility, a denial of the "fundamental tendency of all human beings … to congregate, to be together, to enjoy each other's company."[4]

It is language, or speech – the two are inseparable[5] – which in the first instance brings us together. Language is, above all, a social activity; more than that, it is a socializing activity, a process of creating social relations.[6]

Many professional students of language have been content to treat it more narrowly, as a set of sounds or letter combinations (phonetics), or as the arrangement of such sounds or letter combinations according to the rules regulating their mutual relations (syntax), or as a body of words, phrases, and sentences, each having various meanings (semantics). To use a biological analogy, phonetics may be thought of as the anatomy of language, the study of its "barebones"; syntax may be thought of as the physiology of language, the study of its external functioning; and semantics may be thought of as the psychology of language, the study of its internal

---

[4] Ibid. Malinowski calls speech "the intimate correlate" of this tendency.

[5] Under the influence especially of Ferdinand de Saussure, linguists have thought it important to make a sharp distinction between the language (words) uttered by an individual speaker (*parole*), the particular language system of which that is a part (*langue*), and human language in general (*langage*). This breakdown is bolstered by a further distinction, also initiated by Saussure, between historical and descriptive linguistics. By taking these distinctions too seriously, many linguists have been led to analyze the structure of a language (*langue*) apart from the meaning of its various expressions, leaving the study of meanings to a special branch of linguistics and linguistic philosophy, generally called semantics. Indeed, the predominant trend of American linguistics in the 1930s and the 1940s was to exclude from consideration both the content of communication ("what is being talked about") and the normative aspects of communication ("why the individual wants to talk at all"), and to concentrate on making "a logical calculus … of the basic units of a language and their formal arrangements." John B. Carroll, *The Study of Language: A Survey of Linguistics and Other Related Disciplines in America* (Harvard University Press, 1953), 1–3, 8. Roman Jakobson, one of America's most distinguished authorities on linguistics, has deplored this tendency toward specialization within linguistics and toward the divorce of linguistics from other sciences. "Linguistics," Jakobson writes, "is concerned with language in all its aspects – language in operation, language in drift, language in the nascent state, and language in dissolution." See Roman Jakobson and Morris Halle, *Fundamentals of Language* (The Hague: Mouton & Co., 1956), 55. See also Jakobson's concluding statement in "Results of the Conference of Anthropologists and Linguists," in *Indiana University Publications in Anthropology and Linguistics: Memoir, Issue 8* (Baltimore, MD: Waverly Press, 1953). Jakobson's work may help to revive among American linguists the influence of Edward Sapir, whose path-breaking book, *Language: An Introduction to the Study of Speech* (New York: Harcourt, Brace & Co., 1921), seems to have had more impact upon anthropology than upon linguistics.

[6] In viewing language in these terms, I draw especially upon the works of Eugen Rosenstock-Huessy, Edward Sapir, G. H. Mead, Kenneth Burke, Georg Simmel, and others.

("mental") characteristics.[7] In this book I shall attempt to go beyond semantics, focusing attention not merely on the meanings of sentences (for it is sentences that we speak and write, not words) but also on the process of reciprocal transfer of meanings between speakers and listeners (or writers and readers); this, indeed, is the metabolism of language, its very life-process.

It should be stressed that language presupposes a transfer of meanings not only *from* speaker to listener (or writer to reader) but *between* them; for some response from the listener (or reader) is presupposed in every utterance. Such reciprocal interaction is not only a purpose of language but also what language *is* operationally: speech does inevitably effectuate an exchange, what the sociologist Georg Simmel calls a *Wechselwirkung*, an "interaction," between the parties engaged in the linguistic enterprise.[8] Even soliloquy is a kind of conversation, and presupposes an addressee; as John Dewey put it, soliloquy, or "inner dialogue" is "the product and reflex of converse with others ... [I]f we had not talked with others, and they with us, we should never talk with ourselves."[9] Thus monologue is only an imitation of dialogue, in which two or more persons engage in a mutual interchange thereby creating relationships between (or among) each other. We need a new verb, "speak-listen," to express the reciprocal character of language in action.

If language is thus understood in the first instance as a process of creating relationships among those who jointly engage in it, some of the most widespread fallacies of modern scholarship can be dispelled; more than

---

[7] [Berman drew this metaphor of anatomy and physiology from his colleague, Lon Fuller, who was working on this topic at the same time. See Lon L. Fuller, *The Anatomy of the Law* (New York: Praeger, 1968).]

[8] [Georg Simmel, *The Sociology of Georg Simmel*, trans. and ed. Kurt H. Wolff (Glencoe, IL: Free Press, 1950), 124.]

[9] John Dewey, *Experience and Nature* (London: George Allen & Unwin, 1929), 170. See also Michael Girdansky, *The Adventure of Language* (London: Allen & Unwin, 1963), 10: "[It] takes two to make a message – a sender and recipient ... Even in the act of talking to ourselves we play two roles, one after the other. This can be seen in our habit of frequently speaking so in the second person: 'You really made a fool of yourself that time, John my boy!' says John to himself. Additional proof that we always conceive of some listener to our statements lies in the fact that when we *do* use the 'I' in self-conversation – as in 'Oh, why did I do that?' – the remark is aimed at an imaginary audience around us, or at 'our better self'." [Berman included a note to himself: add "Jakubinski" [*sic*] on monologue. He was most likely referring to Lev Petrovich Iakubinskii, an early twentieth-century linguist from Russia. In 1922, Iakubinskii published an essay, in Russian, "On Dialogue Speech." See Lev Petrovich Iakubinskii, "*O dialogicheskoi rechi*," in A. A. Leont'ev, ed., *Izbrannye raboty: Iazyk i ego funktsionirovanie* (Moscow: Nauka, 1986), 15–56.]

that, by starting from this point we may be able to help restore the power of speech – a power that has been declining rapidly in recent generations, largely because of excessively individualistic and rationalistic conceptions of what speech is. For language is not the private property of individual minds; on the contrary, it is a social heritage, and our common defense against the forces of disintegration that threaten every community and every relationship within a community.

2

Language is most often defined as a set of symbols for expressing thoughts, or as a mechanism for transmitting information. Yet there is a growing recognition that this definition is entirely inadequate.[10] In the first place, the thoughts, the data or information, are themselves verbal in character. Thoughts without words – disembodied presences, as it were – do not have some prior Platonic existence in the mind; we can only think in representations, symbols – in short, words. In John Dewey's phrase, thinking is itself "preliminary discourse."[11] We may keep the words to ourselves, but they are in our minds or else we are not thinking. The reader may test this for himself by trying to think of something while excluding from his mind any words that symbolize that "something."

Moreover, even if it were possible to "think things, not words," as Justice Holmes supposed,[12] a thing identified by a word is vastly different from the thing not so identified – or from the thing identified by a different word. Words ("symbols") are sometimes said to refer to objects ("referents"), but what is in the mind, and what is transmitted to another, is not the referent but the symbol. Thus language is a set of symbols which transmit – themselves.

Even if the familiar definition of language is improved by adding to "thoughts" the words "or emotions," the basic difficulty remains:

---

[10] See Max Black, ed., *The Importance of Language* (Englewood Cliffs, NJ: Prentice Hall, 1962), Foreword; G. M. A. de Laguna, *Speech: Its Function and Development* (New Haven, CT: Yale University Press, 1927), 10ff.

[11] Dewey, *Experience and Nature*, 166.

[12] Oliver Wendell Holmes, Jr., "Science in Law – Law in Science," in *Collected Legal Papers* (New York: Harcourt, Brace & Co., 1920), 238. Holmes' view of language is also reflected in his famous aphorism that a word is but "the skin of a living thought." *Towne* v. *Eisner*, 245 US 418, 425 (1918). However, a word is not only the skin but the body of the thought and also its spirit; indeed, the very thought expressed by Holmes would vanish if it were "skinned" of the metaphor.

for although one may indeed experience sensations and primitive emotions – a feeling of horror, for example – without words, the symbolization of them in language is by no means a mere expression or transmission of emotion. As in the case of thoughts, the word creates something. The shout "Help!" transforms the preexisting feeling of fear which gives rise to it. "Even the dumb pang of an ache," to quote Dewey again, "achieves a significant existence when it can be designated and descanted upon; it ceases to be merely oppressive and becomes important; it gains importance because it becomes representative; it has the dignity of an office."[13] Thus words do not simply "have" meanings: they *give* meanings.

One recalls, in this connection, Helen Keller's moving account of how as a deaf mute she discovered the world of objects through language. At first, she writes, she experienced only "wordless sensations." Then she learned from her teacher, through pressures of her teacher's fingers upon her, the word "water." "Suddenly I felt a misty consciousness as of something forgotten – a thrill of returning thought; and somehow the mystery of language was revealed to me. I knew then that water means the wonderful cool something that was flowing over my hand. That living word awakened my soul, gave it light, hope, joy, set it free ... I left the well eager to learn. *Everything had a name and each name gave birth to a new thought.* As we returned to the house every object which I touched seemed to quiver with life."[14] Helen Keller learned what every poet knows: that words, names, themselves create thoughts and do not simply transmit preexisting thoughts.

The definition of language as a mechanism for transmitting thoughts and emotions is defective not only because the thoughts and emotions inhere in the language and are inseparable from it, but also because there is no language "mechanism" independent of the persons who are communicating. As polygraphs ("lie detectors") have demonstrated, one's blood pressure itself is involved in speech. The entire person speaks. The speaker himself is the "means" which he "uses" to speak: the words are generated within himself, his own mind and body, his own personality. Man, as the great German linguist Wilhelm von Humboldt put it, "spins language out of his own being" – language is "part of his constitution." Thus the language a man speaks is not an external device, a "tool," but a part of him.

---

[13] Dewey, *Experience and Nature*, 167.
[14] Helen Keller, *The Story of My Life* (New York: Doubleday, Page & Co., 1921), 23–24 (emphasis added by Berman).

It is himself that he uses and himself that he transmits.[15] No mechanical model can ever adequately represent these paradoxes, upon which much of traditional linguistics and philosophy has shattered.

Finally, the conception of language as a mechanism for transmitting thoughts, or thoughts and emotions, focuses attention on the speaker and neglects the listener. It suggests that we speak "at" each other instead of "with" each other. It is, of course, true that a speaker may treat a listener as an object rather than as a participant in a joint linguistic enterprise; yet this is clearly a distortion of language, a pretense that is rendered ineffective when it is discovered. "The most eager speaking at one another does not make a conversation," wrote Martin Buber, adding that "this is most clearly shown in that curious sport, aptly termed discussion, that is, 'breaking apart,' which is indulged in by men who are to some extent gifted with ability to think."[16] As soon as language is seen to be a joint enterprise, in which the participants do not merely speak but "speak-listen," it becomes apparent that no method for the analysis of language will suffice which treats words merely as tools and ignores their power over the very minds that utter them.[17]

It may well be that in linguistics the mechanistic theory of language is at last being rejected, as it has been for several decades by leading psychologists and anthropologists. The theory still exercises a pernicious influence, however, in all branches of learning, and especially in philosophy, sociology, and law; and it is still the "common sense" theory of most people, for it is what has been taught since the eighteenth century. As Ernst Cassirer pointed out, the age of Enlightenment "derived language from conscious reflection and considered it as something 'invented'."[18]

---

[15] [See later, Harold J. Berman, *The Interaction of Law and Religion* (Nashville, TN: Abington Press, 1974), 114: "Not intellect versus emotion or reason versus passion but the whole man thinking and feeling."]

[16] Martin Buber, "Dialogue," in *Between Man and Man* (New York: Macmillan, 1947), 3.

[17] [Berman anticipates James Boyd White's criticisms of "conceptual" language. See James Boyd White, *Justice as Translation: An Essay in Cultural and Legal Criticism* (University of Chicago Press, 1990), 29–36; *When Language Meets the Mind: Three Questions* (Nijmegen: Wolf Legal Publishers, 2007), 34. Conceptual language, according to White, is problematic because it denies the linguistic element in language; language is not just "pointing" to a thing. Rather, language taken as a whole is constitutive of all experience. Words *mean* in an active sense, through the cultural, linguistic, and practical associations they have.]

[18] Ernst Cassirer, *Language and Myth*, trans. Susanne K. Langer (New York: Dover Publications, 1946), 30; see also *The Philosophy of the Enlightenment*, trans. Fritz C.A. Koelln and James P. Pettegrove (Princeton University Press, 1951). Mario Pei, writing in 1962, states that "the predominant slant of linguistics in the past four decades has

Once language is conceived to be a conscious invention, the temptation is strong to deplore its "emotive" aspects and to extol its "utilitarian" and "scientific" aspects. The "proper" use of language is thus seen as the scientific representation of facts (or things). This naïve scientism has been carried by some writers on language to the point of attempting to apply mathematical laws to language, divorcing its form and structure from its meaning and ignoring its social and historical dimensions. The attempt to make language "scientific" fails to recognize that science itself is a linguistic phenomenon, and that scientific language – no less than other kinds of language – is a process of creating social relations, a process of exchange and interaction.

Unfortunately, the notion that science is emotionally and socially neutral is still prevalent, despite many convincing proofs to the contrary. Yet one does not have to live in a university community to know that the repressed emotions of the scientist (or academician generally) are nonetheless emotions, and that they usually flare up quite quickly when he is seriously challenged. But beyond that, the scientist is and should be at least as concerned as the politician or artist to influence, persuade, advance his cause, affirm his convictions and loyalties, be just in his judgments, denounce error, and seek truth. The language of science is not, to be sure, the language of the marketplace or of the campaign trail. However, the science of language must discover what these different

leaned heavily in the direction of the descriptive as against the historical – of phonology and, to a lesser degree, morphology and syntax as against etymology and semantics ... of the mechanical as against the spiritual manifestations of languages." Mario Pei, *Voices of Man: The Meaning and Function of Languages* (New York: Harper & Row, 1962), 13. The division between "mechanical" and "spiritual" manifestations of language leads, in semantics, to a false dichotomy between informative and emotive use of words, the former associated with statements of fact and the latter with expression and excitation of feelings. See also Ogden and Richards, *Meaning of Meaning*, 149. One writer who, following Ogden and Richards, makes this dichotomy central to his analysis is forced to conclude at the end of his book: "It is hard, certainly to separate the informative from the dynamic, expressive, emotional uses of language; they are seldom met with in pure forms." Emotive meanings, he concedes, "permeate every sort of language except that of academic and technical information and 'business'." Karl Britton, *Communication: A Philosophical Study of Language* (London: K. Paul, Trench, Trubner & Co., 1939), 279–80. It is apparent, however, that the language of "academic and technical information and 'business'" is also permeated with the emotive (just as emotive language is permeated with factual implications). This is amply demonstrated by Michael Polanyi in *Personal Knowledge* (University of Chicago Press, 1958). Polanyi, a distinguished physicist and chemistt as well as a philosopher, shows that scientific knowledge is "personal" knowledge, in the sense that it combines not only intellectual and emotional elements but also social and historical elements.

types of language have in common, and not only what separates them. One thing they have in common is what philosopher of science, Michael Polanyi, calls their "personal" character, but what might better be called their "inter-personal," or social character.[19]

3

In correcting the excesses of naïve scientism and rationalism in linguistics, it is not necessary to fall into the opposite error of mysticism or irrationalism. Language is not "invented" in the sense that electronic devices are invented; yet language is not simply "revealed" to the mind of the individual seeker either. We can avoid both a mechanical and a mystical interpretation by stressing, on the one hand, the social character, the interactive character, of language – and therefore of the thoughts and feelings which are realized in language; and on the other hand, its historical character – the fact that linguistic interaction takes place within limits imposed by the language community's linguistic tradition, that is, by the history of the language that is being spoken, and not only the desires of the immediate participants. Language is a dramatic expression of social confrontation, whereby men affirm, sustain, renew, and create social relationships.[20] It is at the same time the collective memory of such confrontations experienced in the past, the deposit left by history in our social consciousness, and hence a basis for a common future.

To stress these constructive aspects of language is not to deny its destructive uses. Language can, indeed, be a most dangerous – *the* most dangerous – weapon. It can be used to enslave an individual or, indeed, a whole nation. It can be used to whip men into fury against each other. It can be used to break a person down. Yet these destructive uses of language are only possible because of its constructive power – that is, the power of men through speech to reach out to each other, to share each other's experience, to achieve some sort of meeting of minds and hearts, some sort of agreement. These constructive uses of language are the basis upon which its power to confuse and divide is built. The scoundrel or demagogue or iconoclast counts on his hearers' faith in language in order to persuade them. Thus the most cynical speech presupposes that the

---

[19] Ibid.

[20] Kenneth Burke has stressed the dramatic quality of all language. See Kenneth Burke, *A Rhetoric of Motives* (New York: Prentice-Hall, 1950); see also H. D. Duncan, *Communication and Social Order* (New York: Bedminster Press, 1962), who, following Burke, has sought to create a model of socialization based on language.

listener can understand the meaning of the words spoken in the way in which the speaker intends him to understand them. Similarly, the skeptic who assures us that no statement can mean to the listener what it means to the speaker assumes that *that* statement, at least, can mean to us what it means to him. You do expect me to interpret what you say, to understand, and possibly to agree, when you tell me that we really do not speak a common language. Even one who tells lies usually wishes to be believed.

Of course, this is not to say that even with the best intentions we can ever achieve a perfect understanding. That is why we must go on speaking with each other. Most often, indeed, we only partly understand. No interpretation of your statements by me, or of my statements by you, will ever wholly satisfy. Yet it is only by speech that we can make common sense and common cause. And even the simplest statements tell a great deal. If we only exchange words about the weather, we display a common acceptance of nature – or at least of the requirement of civility that such acceptance be acknowledged.[21] If you are my teacher, your words transmit our common heritage. If we sit opposite each other at an international conference table and exchange verbal thrusts, even then our words symbolize our common allegiance to the techniques of international diplomacy.

Thus language is a social event, not only in the sense that it brings together the participants in a conversation or dialogue (however numerous they may be, as, for example, at a televised political convention or in the publication of the morning newspaper), but also in the sense that it brings together all the members of the language community – those who have created the expressions we use, those who have taught them to us, our ancestors, our nation, our family, our teachers, our colleagues. As Edward Sapir has put it, each of us is a member of different language communities which may be thought of as overlapping circles of varying radii, some concentric, and some non-concentric.[22] The different groups to which we belong may speak their own languages, and yet the language of each group is related to that of every other, if only through us. By speaking we affirm our membership in the various communities – the various traditions – which have given us our language, including the community of language-speaking mankind. By speaking ("speak-listening") we sustain, reinforce, and renew such communities. Indeed, it is through such

[21] Mikel Dufrenne, *Language and Philosophy*, trans. Henry B. Veatch (Bloomington: Indiana University Press, 1963), 99.
[22] See Sapir, *Language*, 158–59.

speaking and listening that we achieve our identity. *Colloquimur ergo summus*: we speak with each other, therefore we are.

At the same time, it is the existence of language that enables us to speak. This, indeed, is the central paradox of language: we create it, by speaking, and yet it creates us, for without it we could not speak. Clearly, language is not instinctive: no person can speak unless he is taught to speak; but he can only be taught to speak by the speech of others, and those others – society – can only teach him what is already inherent in their language.

4

Many writers have emphasized that just as language and thought are inseparable in each individual, so the language of each community conveys its conception of life. Implicit in our various national languages are various attitudes toward time and space, toward people, and toward nature.[23] As Benjamin Lee Whorf wrote, "users of markedly different grammars are pointed by their grammars toward different types of observations and different evaluations of externally similar acts of observation, and hence are not equivalent as observers but must arrive at somewhat different views of the world."[24] Whorf showed that the language of Hopi Indians, which treats time solely as a psychological phenomenon and cannot give to it a number greater than one (they cannot say, for example, "five days"), inevitably creates in Hopi children, as they grow up, a different attitude toward time from that learned by children in our tradition, who are taught early that hours, days, weeks, months, and years have an objective reality independent of their personal consciousness. Further, "A language whose verb has clear precise tense distinctions," Whorf wrote, "will induce in its speakers a keen consciousness of time values and punctuality."[25] In a similar vein, Friedrich Waismann points out that classical Greek and Latin have no equivalent for "to become" (*devenire*, in medieval Latin), expressing continuous change, and that as a result the Greeks "were mightily impeded in coming to grips with the problem of change," and never mastered the problem of motion or evolved a science of

---

[23] [See later, Berman, *Interaction*, 34, 148–51.]

[24] Benjamin Lee Whorf, "Linguistics as an Exact Science," in John B. Carroll, ed., *Language, Thought and Reality: Selected Writings of Benjamin Lee Whorf* (Cambridge, MA: Harvard University Press, 1964), 221.

[25] Ibid., 216ff.

dynamics.[26] As we shall see in a later chapter, Soviet citizens today, partly because of the absence of any word in contemporary Russian corresponding to our word "privacy," or any word which adequately expresses our concept of "the market," will not easily develop thoughts similar to those which are provoked in us by those words.[27]

Even words which are roughly equivalent in two languages may have quite different ranges of meanings and hence lead to quite different ranges of thought. Our word "science," for example, derived from the Latin word *scire*, "to know," has come to refer primarily to the natural sciences and mathematics, despite alternative dictionary meanings, whereas the German equivalent *Wissenschaft*, like the French *science*, has kept the connotation of a more general body of knowledge. The German word *Rechtswissenschaft*, "the science of law," is what we refer to as "jurisprudence," meaning legal philosophy or, literally, legal wisdom. The equivalent in Russian, *nauka*, derived from *nauchit'*, meaning literally "to teach," carries the additional connotation of a learned discipline. As a result, it is more difficult for Americans than for French or Germans or Russians (or other Continental Europeans) to think of law as a systematic body of knowledge based on general principles that can be taught, in some way akin to other practical sciences such as medicine or engineering.

The word "law," as well, has different connotations in different language communities. In all European languages except English, there are two words for law, corresponding to the distinction in Latin between *ius* and *lex*. The French *droit*, the German *Recht*, the Italian *diritto*, and the Russian *pravo* all refer to law as a whole, the system of "right," which encompasses the particular "laws" (*lois, Gesetze, leggi, zakony*) that comprise a legal system. In later chapters we shall have occasion to discuss the significance of this distinction, and of its absence in England and America. For present purposes it is enough to suggest that the words "law" and "*loi*" may conjure up quite different responses in the minds of an American and a Frenchman, respectively, and further, that legal scholarship in the two countries may diverge precisely because of the necessity of explaining the distinction between *loi* and *droit* in France and the absence of a corresponding necessity in the United States.

---

[26] Friedrich Waismann, "The Resources of Language," in Black, ed., *The Importance of Language*, 107–11.

[27] [See elaboration in Harold J. Berman, *Faith and Order: The Reconciliation of Law and Religion*, repr. edn. (Grand Rapids, MI: Wm. B. Eerdmans, 1998), 388, where Berman tied the Russian conception of law as cold and impersonal to the fact that the Russian language only has one word for "legalism," "legality," "legalistic," and "legal"].

Likewise, the word "language" itself has different connotations in different "languages." It is harder, for example, to show the identity of language and speech in English, where there are two separate words for what *can* mean the same thing, than in German, where there is only one word (*Sprache*) for both. Similarly it is easier in German than in English to relate both "language" and "speech" to "conversation" since the German word for conversation (*Gespräch*) is derived from the same root. By the same token, it is harder in German than in English to show the different connotations of language, speech, and conversation.

Thus the language of the community, the way we have been taught to speak, preconditions – indeed, as Helen Keller said, *generates* – not only the perceptions, attitudes, ideas, feelings, relationships, and actions, of the public generally, but also the theories held by scholars concerning society, law, nature, man, and language itself.[28] Through language, then, the community makes us what we are, just as through language we make the community what it is. Language is the dramatic process by which community is made and remade, a process of what might be called "communification."[29]

---

[28] It has often been pointed out that the existence in classical Greek of the grammatical form of the unmodified noun was an indispensable condition for the development of Platonic idealism. Fritz [Mauthner] wrote: "If Aristotle had spoken Chinese or Dacotan, he would have had to adopt an entirely different theory of Categories." [Fritz Mauthner, *Beiträge zu einer Kritik der Sprache*, 3 vol., repr. edn. (Frankfurt: Ullstein, 1982 [1901]), 3:4. Translated and] quoted in Ogden and Richards, *Meaning of Meaning*, 35. It would be hard for Greenlanders, for example, to develop the concept of the "eye" since they have no generic name for eye but only names for blue eye, brown eye, green eye, etc. It would be interesting to explore the significance of the fact that the Russian cannot say "brother-in-law" but only "sister's husband" (*ziaf*'), "wife's brother" (*shurin*), "husband-and-wife's sister" (*svoiak*) and "husband's brother" (*dever*'); of the fact that the Romans had no word for gray or brown and no generic term for blue; and many other similar examples of linguistic differences that affect social relations, perceptions of nature, and the like. Some anthropologists have done significant work in this direction. See Clyde Kluckhohn and Dorothea Leighton, *The Navaho* (Cambridge, MA: Harvard University Press 1946); A. L. Kroeber, "Some Relations of Linguistics and Ethnology," *Language* 17 (1941): 287–91; B. L. Whorf, "An American Indian Model of the Universe (circa 1936)" and "A Linguistic Consideration of Thinking in Primitive Communities," in Carroll, *Language, Thought and Reality*, 57, 67–72.

[29] [See later, Harold J. Berman, "Religious Freedom and the Rights of Foreign Missionaries Under Russian Law," *The Parker School Journal of East European Law* 2 (1995): 446, where Berman wrote that the word "*sobornost*" in the Russian Orthodox Tradition stood for the resolution of conflict at the level of dialogue. Though he described this word as "almost untranslatable," he translated it as "communification." See also Berman, *Interaction*, 122.]

5

If this is so, then clearly language has a profound relevance to the tragic disunity which now threatens to destroy us.[30] Such disunity is manifested not only in international conflicts – the Cold War, colonial revolutions, and the like – which put in issue the physical survival of the human race, but also, within nations, in racial and religious conflicts, as well as in those less easily defined but nonetheless real conflicts between the generations, between the sexes, between man and the machine civilization that he has created, and within each man himself – conflicts which give rise to family disorganization, juvenile delinquency, crime, and psychopathic frustrations and fears. Of course, each of these types of conflict has its own causes; but behind them all stands a deeper cause, namely, the loss of a sense of community, the loss of the capacity to make community, and these are attributable, at least in part, to the loss of faith in language as a process of genuine communification.[31]

Usually the cause–effect sequence is stated the other way around. It is said that our loss of a sense of community is the effect, rather than the cause, of the conflicts which divide us; and the real causes of those conflicts are found in antagonistic economic and political interests, in racial differences, in technological factors, in the growth of cities, and the like. There is often a strong element of Marxism in such reasoning. Karl Marx postulated an objective economic "base" – the mode of production – upon which is built a social and political "superstructure," and he viewed the ideas which people hold as a superstructural rationalization, reflecting and reinforcing the economic base – not a genuine effort of the human mind to find the truth but an "ideology" (as he called it).[32] This way of thinking leads to the conclusion that those whose material interests coincide will unite and those whose material interests diverge will struggle for mastery.

[30] [See the Conclusion herein, where Berman applies this thesis directly to the Cuban Missile Crisis and Soviet–US relations.]

[31] [See elaboration in Berman, *Interaction*, 122, where this language is repeated nearly verbatim, but the passage ends without attributing the loss of the capacity to make community to a loss in the faith in language. See further ibid., 122–27 and Berman, *Faith and Order*, 324–25 elaborating Rosenstock-Huessy's notion of "Planetary Man," which influenced Berman significantly, both in *Law and Language* and in other work as well.]

[32] [See further, Harold J. Berman, *Justice in the USSR: An Interpretation of Soviet Law*, rev. edn. (Cambridge, MA: Harvard University Press, 1963), 16ff. Under the influence of Marxism, the term "ideology" has come generally to be used to refer to the system of ideas which serves to bolster a particular political and economic order.]

Yet what are these "material interests" other than the values which we place upon our activities? Ultimately, a nation, or a class, or a race, is not defined by "natural" or "material" or "technological" factors but by people's consciousness of those factors and by their response to them. The "mode of production" does not exist independently of the thoughts and feelings of the people who participate in it: a mass of steel and electricity is not a "machine" until it is so perceived by men. Thus we are caught up in another tautology: the "environment" which, according to a materialist philosophy, imposes upon man certain needs called "physical," "economic," or "political" is itself defined by man, as are the needs which it imposes. The history of the past six decades of war and revolution cannot be explained by philosophy which sharply distinguishes between an objective material reality considered to be basic and a subjective realm of thought and emotion considered to be secondary. More than ever before, man has flown in the face of his "environment" and has defied his own "material interests" with myths and dreams. "Objectively," it would appear that the greatest physical, economic, and political need of all countries today is to establish a peaceful world order, and all the "material" conditions necessary for its establishment are at hand; yet that is the thing we seem least able to accomplish.

Marxist and other forms of materialism have themselves contributed to our inability to make peace, and also to our lost sense of community and of the capacity to make community, by subordinating that sense and capacity to external forces. Yet despite its false dichotomies of matter and idea, economics and ideology, power and reason, Marxism does not deny man's capacity, through speech, to express and communicate reality. In this respect, it is less of a threat to the integrity of language than many schools of thought which have prevailed in the West, where for at least four decades writers on semantics have taught us about the tyranny of words, the treachery of words, the inherent ambiguity of words.[33] Political scientists and sociologists have agreed with Humpty-Dumpty that words can mean anything we choose – "it all

---

[33] Much of this teaching owes its inspiration to Ogden and Richards, who made central the distinction between Thought and Things and emphasized the "treacherousness" of language as a means of representing the reality of Things. See Ogden and Richards, *Meaning of Meaning*, 9–10. They proposed to correct language by introducing certain "canons of symbolism," which rest upon the distinction between "symbol and referent," but they failed to recognize that the symbol is what makes the referent a referent.

depends on who is master."[34] Philosophers have said that language is "an irksome constraint for the highest minds," too poor a vehicle for their lofty thoughts.[35] Linguists have sought to create new "scientific" languages. The newer social sciences have invented their own jargons. Even many poets have come to doubt the power of speech to give universal meaning to experience. Indeed, one school of linguistics has gone so far as to state that every person speaks his own language, his "idiolect," with his own private meanings.[36] Thus the possibility of genuine communication is denied altogether.

Against these views stands the obvious fact that, as we have already stressed, we are all the creatures of the language in which we have been brought up. None of us has invented the language he speaks; each of us has been taught it by others, and each of us has only a limited power to change it. The connotations and associations of vocabulary and syntax are a matter of social experience. Individuals may invent particular new words, such as "serendipity" or "gobbledygook," or "speak-listen" or

[34] The famous dialogue is worth reproducing in full:
"I don't know what you mean by 'glory,'" Alice said.
Humpty Dumpty smiled contemptuously. "Of course you don't – till I tell you. I meant 'there's a nice knock-down argument for you!'"
"But 'glory' doesn't mean 'a nice knock-down argument,'" Alice objected.
"When *I* use a word," Humpty Dumpty said in a rather scornful tone, "it means just what I choose it to mean – neither more nor less."
"The question is," said Alice, "whether you *can* make words mean so many different things."
"The question is," said Humpty Dumpty, "which is to be master – that's all."
Lewis Carroll, *Alice's Adventures in Wonderland, and Through the Looking-Glass: And What Alice Found There* (New York: Macmillan & Co., 1897), 124.

[35] The quoted phrase is from Otto Jespersen, *Mankind, Nation and Individual from a Linguistic Point of View* (Oslo: H. Aschehoug, 1925), 131. Jespersen is technically a linguist rather than a philosopher; however, the idea is common enough among philosophers, especially those called logical positivists, who seek to construct a new logically perfect language to replace the faulty language spoken by the rest of us. It is a virtue of the later "Oxford school" of philosophy that it focuses on "ordinary language" as a basis for testing the truth of propositions, rather than constructing a new jargon. By "ordinary language" is meant the way words are used in everyday discourse. Unfortunately, however, this usually leads to analysis of the use of words in relatively trivial situations. See V. C. Chappell, ed., *Ordinary Language: Essays in Philosophical Method* (Englewood Cliffs, NJ: Prentice Hall, 1964). "Extraordinary" language used in everyday discourse – for example, the language of law – is still more revealing. See below Chapters 2 and 3.

[36] Jakobson calls this "a perverse fiction." See his "Results of the Conference of Anthropologists and Linguists," *Anthropology and Linguistics* 8, 15. He points out that for aphasics, however, the single individual's way of speaking at a given time may be the only concrete linguistic reality. It is interesting to note that aphasics tend to become isolated and lose contact with others. Ibid.

"communify," and may give new meaning to old words. But these new words and new meanings enter into the common language and become part of our collective heritage – or else they are not significant. As Roman Jakobson has put it: "There is no such thing as private property in language; everything is socialized."[37] By the same token, no group, be they scholars or politicians, can impose a new language, however great their control over the media of communication, except by persuading the people upon whom they seek to impose it, which means translating it into terms that those people understand and respect. People may be coerced into using certain words and not using others, but they will continue to think in the language they believe in. The manipulators of language – the Goebbelses, the public relations firms, the advertisers – may themselves escape from the power of the words that they abuse (though more often they do not), but they only escape, in von Humboldt's phrase, into another linguistic "magic circle"[38] – whether it be the language of nihilism and war or the language of political or financial success. No man can live only on cynicism; if there are no words he can trust he will break down. In Eugen Rosenstock-Huessy's words, "The same thinker who cries, 'I believe in nothing,' 'I doubt everything,' must always have a reader, a sweetheart, a student, who trustingly says after him, 'He believes in nothing: how splendid! I believe in him,' 'He doubts everything: how clever! I do not doubt him.'"[39]

We need, therefore, a semantics that will explain not only the power of words to distort and oppress and exploit and divide us but also the power to enlighten us, to command our trust, and to unite us. The answer to "the tyranny of words" is not to create a new "scientific" language, be it Basic English or Symbolic logic (though these may have their limited uses), but rather to restore the legitimate authority of the language we have inherited. The word "tyranny" can also be a "weasel word" – and so can the word "weasel." We shall never escape from the abuse of language or from its inadequacies except by strengthening and renewing the language which has been given to us by the communities in which we live – the

---

[37] Ibid.

[38] "Man lives with his objects chiefly – in fact, since his feeling and acting depend on his perceptions, one may say exclusively – as language presents them to him. By the same process whereby he spins language out of his own being, he ensnares himself in it; and each language draws a magic circle round the people to which it belongs, a circle from which there is no escape save by stepping out of it into another." Quoted in Cassirer, *Language and Myth*, 9.

[39] [Source unknown.]

language that has made us what we are – for all artificial languages raise doubts about the validity of language itself.

6

Yet if each community speaks its own language, how is it possible for language to unite different communities; how is it possible to make peace between peoples who speak different languages? Are we not forced back, especially by the anthropological school of linguistics represented by Whorf, Cassirer, and others, to a cultural relativism, and ultimately to its political counterparts, chauvinism and racism, in whose name the communifying power of language has often been invoked?

The answer is that language proves the existence not only of cultural diversities but also of mankind's cultural unity. All men speak. In addition, all people have certain linguistic trains in common. No two grammars are *wholly* different. The statement of Roger Bacon in the thirteenth century that "grammar is, in its essence, one and the same in all languages, although it may vary in accidents" has sometimes been criticized by modern descriptive linguists, but, as Roman Jakobson points out, it is now being proved correct by scientific study of scores of different languages.[40] All languages make some distinction between (what we call) nouns and verbs, and between (what we call) subjects and predicates. All languages have proper names as well as generic terms. All languages have pronouns referring to first and second persons. All languages distinguish between the singular and the plural, and between the plural and the collective.[41] Moreover, and most significant, all languages have the capacity to grow, to develop; and where such development has occurred, it seems to have followed universal laws. Grammatical forms become simplified to enable the language to reduce the number of irregularities, exceptions, and anomalies. Vocabulary develops to permit increased generalization; the concrete image is applied by analogy to a different object or to an idea or attitude or feeling. This, at least, is the way in which all modern languages have evolved.[42]

---

[40] Roman Jakobson, "Implications of Language Universals for Linguistics," in J. H. Greenberg, ed., *Universals of Language: Report of a Conference Held at Dobbs Ferry, New York, April 13–15, 1961* (Cambridge, MA: MIT Press, 1961), 208.

[41] Ibid.; J. H. Greenberg, "Some Universals of Grammar with Particular Reference to the Order of Meaningful Elements," in Greenberg, *Universals of Language*, 58.

[42] See Otto Jespersen, *Language: Its Nature, Development and Origin* (New York: Henry Holt & Co., 1925), 428–32.

In addition, the growth of language involves the capacity to substitute one phrase for another, and hence not only to translate ("carry over") within a particular language but also to translate from one language to another. Many kinds of speech, at least, are susceptible to such translation, although it may require that new words be created or that new meanings be given to old words. Of course, the translation is not the same as the original; inevitably something is lost. But with imagination, the loss can be made up. Even poetry can be translated, although it may take a great poet to do it well.[43]

A leading contemporary writer on language takes a different view. He states that "there is no such thing as universality of grammatic structure." He also denies that there is any "logic" in language, stating that since language "originates as a matter of convention, then chance is uppermost, and it is vain to look for logic in what is arbitrary."[44] This last statement is based on ambiguities in the words "logic," "convention," and "arbitrary." Most linguists say that words are "arbitrary" symbols, in that their sound and structure do not bear any necessary relationship to what they designate. The same animal may be called "bear" in English and *medved* in Russian – the choice of the word is "arbitrary." The significance of calling it arbitrary is to deny the argument of Cratylus,[45] in Plato's famous dialogue, that words are a "natural phenomenon," their form being inherent in the nature of the things to which they refer; the best example is onomatopoeia – we "naturally" say that a bee "buzzes," or a fountain "splashes." Cratylus' opponent Hermogenes argues that words are a matter of social convention; people simply agree to call certain things by certain names, and the particular name chosen is not necessarily inherent in the thing designated. Aristotle later adopted and expanded the position of Hermogenes, and it has been accepted almost universally by modern linguists.

It must be noted, however, that the Greeks were not concerned with the problem of translation; they thought only of their own language. As soon as two languages are juxtaposed, it becomes apparent that both Cratylus and Hermogenes are wrong. Words are not "natural," since different languages have different words for the same thing, but they are not merely "conventional," since the differences reflect historical and social factors

---

[43] See Roman Jakobson, "On Linguistic Aspects of Translation," in Reuben Arthur Brower, ed., *On Translation* (New York: Oxford University Press, 1966 [1959]), 232–39.

[44] Pei, *Voices of Man*, 32.

[45] [See John E. Joseph, "Indeterminacy, Translation and the Law," in Marshall Morris, ed., *Translation and the Law*, 8 vols. (Philadelphia: John Benjamins, 1995), 8:21–23.]

that include but also go beyond agreement, at least in the usual sense of that word. "Bear" comes from the word "brown"; *medved* means "honey carrier." Different peoples have experienced the animal in different ways. This is neither "natural" nor "conventional" in the Greek sense of those terms. Nor is it "logical." Yet it is not unnatural, non-conventional, or illogical. It is not arbitrary. Different peoples had different reasons to give different names to the same creature.

The power to create new words, new grammatical forms, and new meanings is given to us by language itself, and is at the same time limited by language – by the languages we speak and by the universal qualities of all languages. Thus, if we say: "Let us agree to call that round object a ball," we may have agreed upon the word "ball," but the word "us" and the word "agree" are given; there must be a "we" and an "agree" before we can agree. As Whorf says, there cannot be agreement or assent without language. The fact that all languages provide an opportunity to express agreement, and especially to express agreement concerning the meaning of language itself – which is the basis of translation – testifies to the fact that there is such a thing as universality of grammatical structure, despite the "arbitrary" quality of particular linguistic "conventions."

Thus we do not have to live forever in the condition depicted in the biblical story of the Tower of Babel.[46] That story tells us that at one time all men spoke the same language, but because of their pride God "confused the language of all the earth," so that men could not "understand one another's speech."[47] As a result they were "dispersed" upon the surface of the earth, and could no longer make a "name" for themselves as a single universal community. It is significant that the story attributes the existence of separate nations to a breakdown in communications.[48]

Yet implicit in the story of the Tower of Babel is the story of Pentecost, which tells us that at a place where people of different languages had gathered to worship, certain of them were given the power to speak in "other languages," so that all the people of the earth could hear "the mighty works of God," "each in his own native tongue."[49] Thus the story of Pentecost

---

[46] [See later, Harold J. Berman, "Law and Logos," *DePaul Law Review* 44 (1994): 165; "Integrative Jurisprudence and World Law," in Manuel Atienza, et al., eds., *Theorie des Rechts und der Gesellschaft: Festschrift für Werner Krawietz zum 70. Geburtstag* (Berlin: Duncker & Humblot, 2003); "The Holy Spirit: The God of History," *The Living Pulpit* 13(2) (April–June, 2004): 32.]

[47] Pei, *Voices of Man*, 27.   [48] Genesis 11:1–9.

[49] See Helen Silving, "Notes on 'Understanding'; Translation of a Penal Code," *Revista Jurídica de la Universidad de Puerto Rico* 29 (1960): 333–34.

gives hope that the pride of man can be overcome, and that by translation from one language to another we may share each other's experience vicariously and become once again united.

The Judeo-Christian vision of the oneness of mankind, a vision born of faith in one God, the God who speaks,[50] who calls men into being by speech, and who gives men the gift of speech – this vision of human community is realized in part by the power of translation, which enables those who speak different languages to communicate with each other.[51]

Yet, as we have already said, something is usually lost in translation. "Bear" is not quite the same as *medved*. "Law" is not quite the same as either *loi* or *droit*. In addition to translation, however, there are alternative and more effective means of unification of languages – namely, the incorporation of common linguistic expressions. Not by artificial languages such as Esperanto or Idiom Neutral,[52] but through direct common experience, mankind has in fact begun to develop a common language. The roots of that language, as Rosenstock-Huessy has said, are the names of men and events that have universal significance.[53] Such names as Jesus,

---

[50] [See later, Berman, "Law and Logos," 145, where he refers to God as "the Communifier."]

[51] [In his practice and in his academic writings, Tibor Várady, a student of Berman's, has observed the necessity and power of translation in resolving and arbitrating international business disputes. See his Afterword herein and further Tibor Várady, *Language and Translation in International Commercial Arbitration: From the Constitution of the Arbitral Tribunal through Recognition and Enforcement Proceedings* (The Hague: T.M.C. Asser Press, 2006).]

[52] See Otto Jespersen, *An International Language* (London: Allen & Unwin, 1928). In 1880, J.M. Schleyer proposed a new international language called Volapuk, which rapidly collected hundreds of thousands of adherents and just as rapidly died out. Esperanto was invented by a Polish occulist, L. I. Zamenhof, in 1887. Idiom Neutral was invented by W. Rosenberger, a Russian, in 1902. Occidental appeared in 1922 and Latino sine Flexione in 1923. Jespersen proposed something still different, called Novial. The difficulty with all these languages is that they only convey what is cold and clear, and what therefore can easily be translated and can easily wait to be translated. As Jespersen concedes, an interlanguage "must necessarily remain an intellectual language, a language for the brain, not for the heart; it can never expect to give expression to those deep emotions which find their natural outlet through a national language." Ibid., 27.

[53] Acts 2:1–13. See also Roman Jakobson, "St. Constantine's Prologue to the Gospel," *St. Vladimir's Seminary Quarterly* 7(1) (1963): 15–16, referring to a "Canon," called "The Two Teachers of the Slavic Nation," composed by a disciple of the brothers Constantine (better known by his monastic name, Cyril) and Methodius, missionaries to the Slavs who composed the Slavic alphabet and translated the Bible into Slavic. The Canon extols the brothers as illuminated by the Holy Spirit and embraced in the Pentecostal miracle which transmuted the confusion of languages – the punishment at Babel – into a blessed gift of tongues. Professor Silving, in her "Notes," after interpreting the story of the Tower of Babel, states: "Men have sought to remedy this situation by translation. But

Buddha, Galileo, Lincoln, Caesar, Napoleon, Roosevelt, Churchill, Stalin, Mao, penetrate all language barriers. Also Hiroshima is Hiroshima throughout the world, and Berlin is Berlin, although the pronunciations differ. Just as the various national languages continually develop out of common national experiences, embodying the community's memory of those experiences, so intense experiences shared by people of many different countries lead to the formation of new international linguistic symbols – especially names, but eventually other parts of speech as well. Indeed, the international scientific community already has its universal languages of natural science, of mathematics, of medicine, of technology, and to a certain extent of the social sciences as well (including linguistics). Whether one says "electricity" or *electrizität* or *electrichestvo*, the word is the same. And as we shall see in a later chapter, mankind has also begun to develop a common legal language.[54]

Contrary to what is often supposed, the universality of the language of mathematics, physics, medicine, engineering, and other related sciences is not due to the fact that they have a "neutral" subject matter; on the contrary, their "neutrality" is a function of their universality. Soviet experience in the 1930s and 1940s proved this, for once the Soviet leaders decided that science was a class phenomenon, their scientists were required to cut off many, most, or in some cases all of their ties with the "bourgeois" scientists of other countries and to develop a special "social-ist" science with its own terminology and methods. Even apart from this example, history affords abundant proof that science is "culture-bound" – that different civilizations have different number systems, different con-cepts of nature and of the human organism, and the like. Our culture has been able to raise certain sciences to a universal realm of discourse not primarily because of the particular subject matter of those sciences but primarily because the persons pursuing them established links with their fellow-scientists throughout the world and throughout history. They

can translation convey understanding?" Silving, "Notes on 'Understanding'," 334. The significance of Pentecost is that it gives an affirmative answer to that question.

[54] [See below, pp. 85–86, 88 and later elaboration in Berman, *Faith and Order*, 277–83, 323. See also Peter Tiersma, "A History of the Language of Law," in Peter M. Tiersma and Lawrence M. Solan, eds., *The Oxford Handbook of Language and Law*, 2012), 25, and Anne Wagner, Tracey Summerfield, Farid Samir Benavides Vanegas, eds., *Contemporary Issues of the Semiotics of Law* (Portland, OR: Hart Publishing, 2005), 12: "In these times, symbols become global, and the law, as a system of symbols, needs to talk in a global language if it is to achieve its purpose of being obeyed in this wider context. This global language includes symbols of immigration, danger, terrorism, human rights, and constitutionalism."]

created cultural bonds which served to unite all the persons, in all times and places, who would accept them. This was by no means an automatic development. It required great courage and imagination on the part of hundreds of thousands of scientists over many centuries.[55] It required the creation of the university as a community of scholars tied to no single person, no single political system, no single dogma – a *universal* community, where opposing doctrines can be taught. Without a universal community of scientists, speaking a common universal language, there would be only national sciences, racial sciences, religious sciences, class sciences, tribal sciences – in short, not a universal science but only "ideology."

7

If, however, we have the power of translation and, in addition, the roots of a common language in our common experience, why are we not at peace? Why are we not one? Must we conclude that it is not language differences that divide us, and hence not language that can unite us? Is it not a question of interests, rather than of language? Is it not a question of conflicting wills? Do we not *know* how to make peace, and would we not quickly make it if only we all had the *will* to do so?

These questions lead us once again into the trap of a mechanistic theory, and into distinctions between language, on the one hand, and knowledge and volition, on the other, that will not withstand analysis. It is true, of course, that even if all peoples spoke the same language and could communicate with each other without difficulty, that fact in itself would not preclude the possibility of their fighting each other. Before the confusion of tongues at Babel, Cain killed his brother Abel.[56] The long record of civil wars in human history makes it perfectly plain that people who speak the same language may be mortal enemies. Conversely, people who do not understand one another at all may co-exist without fighting.

But these obvious facts, though relevant to the question of why wars break out, do not answer the question of how peace is made. The causes of war are not necessarily the same as the causes of the absence of peace – just as the causes of an illness (say, a virus) are not necessarily the same as the causes of the ill person's failure to get well (say, his refusal to take medication). If we are concerned with finding the causes of conflict in the

---

[55] [Likely referring to Eugen Rosenstock-Huessy, *Out of Revolution* (New York: W. Morrow & Co., 1938), 231.]

[56] Genesis 4:1–8.

factors out of which conflict originates, that is, its *original* causes, we must certainly take into account the political, economic, cultural, and psychological antagonisms which affect the volition to fight – including their linguistic aspects. But if we are concerned with the causes of conflict in another sense of the word "causes," namely, the factors which prevent us from overcoming those political, economic, and other antagonisms, that is, their *final* causes, then language, speech, words, take on a very special significance. We are divided "because" we have not found a common language for overcoming our divisions.

The truth is that we do not really understand how divisions among men are overcome – how peace is made. Most people still think of peace as simply the absence of war, and hope to inhabit the same world with their adversaries without creating bonds of social cohesion with them. Most see the world in terms of the clash of political and economic forces, in terms of the will to power, in terms of the struggle of each against all. Other people who accept a philosophy of reason, rather than a philosophy of will, often tend to make of reason a purely intellectual function and a purely individual one and to ignore its linguistic and social character.

Webster's New Collegiate Dictionary states that the meaning of the intransitive verb "reason," namely "to discourse," is obsolete! But as Rosenstock-Huessy has shown, both *ratio* and *logos* originally meant speech.[57] "In the beginning was Speech!" The Greeks transformed the dramatic narrative and aesthetic representations of Homer into timeless propositions of logic and ethics without, however, cutting off their roots in language.[58] By contrast, the eighteenth-century idealists of Europe divorced reason and will from language and from each other, and the nineteenth-century materialists accepted the divorce and declared the primacy of will.

It is not the lack of knowledge and will, taken separately or together, that is the basic cause of our inability to make peace – internationally or domestically. Mankind has developed to a high degree both the intellectual capacity to live in peace and the desire to live in peace. What is

---

[57] [Likely Rosenstock-Huessy, *Out of Revolution*, 151.]

[58] [Likely, ibid., 428. Rosenstock continues: "Our speech, the Logos of the gospel, leads all of us who are of good will. Anybody who thinks that men invented language as they have invented the making of buttons or coins or stamps, is certainly incapable of understanding one word of mankind. Words are not our tools; since Adam first called things good and evil men have cried, spoken, shrieked, screamed, sung, called and commanded because they *must*, not because they would. Trust language is an expression of necessity, not a tool in a man's hand."]

most lacking is the commitment and the imagination required to *make* peace – above all, commitment to the oneness of mankind, and imagination to develop a common language not only for understanding our conflicts but also for resolving them. What religion and medical science have discovered concerning the therapeutic value of speech for the psychologically disturbed individual has not yet been effectively translated into a speech therapy for a psychologically disturbed world. Scholarship has itself contributed to the disturbance insofar as major schools of thought have failed to see in language the *tertium quid* that underlies and unites reason and will.

Destructive philosophies of mechanism and causality will continue to predominate, and constructive philosophies of organism and purpose will continue to founder, so long as language is seen primarily as a tool of reason and will, and as a means of transferring thoughts about things, rather than primarily as a dramatic expression and fulfillment of man's capacity and craving for association. Living words, words in action, the phrases and sentences that we speak and hear, are not only symbols in the sense of images, or reflections; they are *effective* symbols – that is, they effectuate, bring into being, that which they symbolize. They symbolize not only thought and emotions; above all, they symbolize community.

8

To say that speech – "speaking-listening," language in action – is an effective symbol of community, a process of communification, is certainly not to suggest that a community is made by people sitting around babbling phonemes at each other. We mean, rather, that community is maintained or achieved – social disintegration is prevented or overcome – when men speak words that create bonds of social cohesion; without such words there can be no community.[59] And we mean also that the community itself provides the sources of those words, makes them available to its members, in the language that it transmits. This is the paradox with which we started: that men create community by language, and that the community creates men by language.

---

[59] [A compelling example of this proclamation is found in White, *When Language Meets the Mind*, 27–34, analyzing President Lincoln's Second Inaugural Address, where White says that President Lincoln "imagine[d] North and South, white and black, becoming united in a nation with its own providential history." Ibid., 34.]

The paradox can be resolved if we think of our smaller communities. In a family conversation at the dinner table, for example, it is plain that each person helps to create the family community and that at the same time each is created by it. "Dad," "Mom," "Johnny," "Sue," "What happened in school today, Sue?" "The teacher said she would like to talk to you, Dad": these interchanges are a process whereby each person affirms, sustains, renews, and creates the family, and at the same time they are a process whereby the family gives the character of father, mother, son, or daughter to each of the members.

I contend that the same process of "communification" through language also takes place in the larger "families" to which we belong – the neighborhood, the university, the profession, the factory, the city, the nation, the church, the civilization, mankind. We make these communities by our speech, and they make us by the speech they have taught us.

At this point it may be objected that we are using the word "language" in several different senses. There is: (1) language in the sense of the English language, French, Chinese, Latin, or Sanskrit; (2) language in the sense of the language of worship, the language of scholarship, the language of the factory, the language of politics, the language of law; and (3) language in the sense of dialogue, conversation, "people speaking," the names by which we are called. Are these not three different things?

My answer is that these are *not* three different things but rather three different aspects of the same thing. The English or French or Chinese language is not something apart from what is spoken and heard and written or read by English-speaking, French-speaking, or Chinese-speaking people. If Latin entirely ceases to be spoken, written, or read, it will indeed be a dead language. Once it is granted that language is not merely something on paper, not words in a dictionary, but rather something in people, something alive, then it becomes apparent that the forms a language takes – its sentences – cannot be viewed in isolation from their meaning. Everything we say must mean *something*. If what an American physicist writes is incomprehensible to an American literary critic, or if what an American lawyer says is incomprehensible to an American sociologist, it hardly matters that it is written in English rather than Chinese; it is still a foreign tongue. On the other hand, a non-English-speaking Chinese and a non-Chinese-speaking American traveling together in a railroad train may manage to get along quite well in sign language and by exclamations.

Yet this does not nearly exhaust the matter, since it does make a considerable difference to the American literary critic if the physicist writes in English instead of Chinese. With the help of textbooks, dictionaries, and the like, the literary critic may be able, if he is diligent, to translate the physicist's language into terms somewhat comprehensible, at least, to himself; whereas if the article or book were in Chinese, the literary critic would have to learn Chinese even before he could know what it was about. Moreover, every national language has its own character, its own structure, its own preconceptions, so to speak, and these influence those who know and speak the language. The national language therefore creates some bonds of community among all who speak it – though they may be of different races and nationalities. The English language, for example, helps to preserve links between the most diverse peoples – English, Indians, Americans, Nigerians, and others. It has been amply demonstrated that national languages or language families – English, Russian, or Arabic – cannot be identified with individual nations or with individual races or even with individual cultures. But this does not mean that they do not effectuate any elements of community. On the contrary, the mere fact that peoples of different nations, races, and cultures speak the same national language gives to these diverse groupings certain elements of community.

If we approach language in terms of people engaged in communifying discourse with each other, then we shall be better able to understand the interrelationships of national languages with each other and with the particular types of language of various professions or disciplines or activities. At the same time, such an approach will help us to identify those types of language that are most effective in protecting communities against disruption as well as those types of language that are most effective in creating new communities when old communities have broken down.

One such type of communifying language is that of ceremonies, including both solemn rites and also the rituals of games and other forms of what Michael Polanyi calls "conviviality." In November 1963 the funeral observances for a slain chief of state, President John Kennedy, strengthened, at least momentarily, the unity of the American people, and indeed of many parts of the whole world, at a time of deep distress and fear. Funerals, inaugurations, holiday celebrations, weddings, anniversaries, commencements, dedications, banquets, toasts, office parties – such rituals help to keep us together.[60]

---

[60] See Burke, *A Rhetoric of Motives*, 42ff., which points out that we can reverse this process and look upon narrative expressions as translations of philosophic propositions. The logical idea of a thing's essence can be rendered in terms of the thing's source or beginnings or the terms of the thing's endings (for example, "He's a bastard!" or "He will end on the gallows!"). Ibid., 13ff.

Even faculty meetings serve a necessary function in this respect, and academicians are wrong to disparage them; as Polanyi has suggested, our very scholarship would perish without the conviviality of the scholarly community.[61] Less dramatic than ceremonies but equally important in creating bonds of social cohesion, at least in a society such as ours, is the language of scholarship itself. The historian helps to preserve and renew the group memory of his community. The social scientist helps to preserve and renew the community's common understanding of its social institutions. The literary scholar helps us to select and appreciate the books we read; the natural scientist helps us to find our common bearings in the physical world.

The languages of ceremony and scholarship are only two of the many types of language that we speak. There is also the language of economic activity – of production, technology, commerce, finance, and the like, without which our economy could not function. There is the language of politics – of command, compromise, "deals," regulation, patronage, campaigning, voting, which is essential to the maintenance of governmental authority. There is the language of worship, with its prayers of praise, thanksgiving, confession, repentance, forgiveness, and communion with God. There is the language of poetry, of the visual arts, of music, and many others. Last but not least, there is the language of law, to which subsequent chapters of this book will be devoted.

All of these types of language overlap. We cannot speak one without at the same times speaking others. They all form one language. We may extend Roger Bacon's formula by saying that not only all grammar but all language itself is "essentially" one. Yet particular types of language vary in their "accidents." Each has its own identity, its own time and place. "Man cannot live by bread alone" and "Energy equals mass times the square of the speed of light" are both English sentences. But they also represent two separate types of language, "two cultures," in C. P. Snow's phrase.[62]

Snow was right in calling attention to the great danger that threatens a national community when humanists and natural scientists live in different worlds, so to speak, and are unable to communicate with each other. Yet the problem lies even deeper, for it is not only natural sciences and the humanities (or social sciences) that have developed their own perspectives, their own ways of thinking and speaking. Indeed, *all* the scholarly

---

[61] [See, e.g., Polanyi, *Personal Knowledge*, 224.]

[62] [C. P. Snow, *The Two Cultures and the Scientific Revolution* (New York: Cambridge University Press, 1959).]

disciplines have drifted apart from each other. In many universities today, the classicists do not talk with the sociologists, the economists have no common language with the psychologists, the historians of one civilization have few words to exchange with the historians of another civilization, the legal scholars do not speak with the theologians, and each specialty lives unto itself. In the year 1776, Adam Smith published *The Wealth of Nations*, Edward Gibbon, *The Decline and Fall of the Roman Empire*, and Jeremy Bentham, *Fragment on Government*; each of these great books was addressed to persons learned in history, economics, politics, philosophy, law, and theology, and specialists from each of these fields could read and understand them. Today even a great book addressed to several disciplines is very apt to be either ignored or rejected by all of them. Unless the drive toward specialization in scholarship is complemented by a concerted effort to restore and develop a common language of scholarship shared by all disciplines, we shall see the university disintegrate before our eyes, and with its collapse will come the demoralization of the educated classes of society outside the university.[63]

But the problem lies even deeper. Not only the university world, but the professional worlds of lawyers, doctors, politicians, the clergy, the military, and also the economic worlds of labor, agriculture, big business, small business, and the like, and the racial and regional worlds of white and black, East and West, North and South – all are threatened by a polyglot culture, in which the only words that everybody hears or reads are the slogans of commercial advertisements and of political propaganda. Our common speech is threatened with debasement, and hence with the loss of its sacred character. It is not necessary to say that this has happened, or that it will happen, in order to state the following axiom, on which the argument of this book is constructed: that the health of any society depends upon its ability to maintain and develop its common language without destroying the identity of the separate languages into which the common language is continually being broken.

[63] [See later, Berman, *Interaction*, 18: "the compartments into which we have divided the world are not self-contained units ... if they are not opened up to each other they will imprison and stifle us."]

2

The language of law

1

Surely one of the most important types of language spoken by a community is the language of law.[1] Yet the language of law has been almost totally neglected by most writers on language and either totally neglected or badly mistreated by most writers on law.[2] Such attention as has been paid to the language of law, other than in descriptive works, is devoted largely to its ambiguities, its circularities, its susceptibility to distortion, its excessive technicality, its arbitrariness, rather than to its power to command respect, to resolve conflict, and to establish channels of cooperation.[3] Those who, on the other hand, have written about the role of law in creating bonds of community have seldom emphasized the linguistic aspects of law, except to deplore the difficulties which legal language creates for the establishment of a common legal order.

It is, of course, undeniable that clarity and simplicity are very great virtues in legal language (as in all other kinds of language), virtues which are,

---

[1] [See later, Berman, *Faith and Order*, 49: "Law ... like language itself was ... a matter of holding people together, a matter of reconciliation. Law was conceived primarily as a mediating process, a mode of communication."]

[2] [A notable exception to this point is the hermeneutical philosopher Hans-Georg Gadamer, who uses law-practice and judicial interpretation as an exemplar of a historically aware and contemporarily focused interpretation of texts. See Hans-Georg Gadamer, "The Exemplary Significance of Legal Hermeneutics," in *Truth and Method*, trans. Joel Weinsheimer and Donald Marshall, rev. edn. (New York: Continuum, 2000) (originally published in 1960 as *Warheit und Methode*), 324–41. Gadamer identifies legal hermeneutics as the preeminent form of hermeneutics since legal interpretation is never merely concerned with interpreting legal rules in their historical context, but mediating the meaning of the legal rule and applying it in new contexts. Though Berman knew of Gadamer's work, and had his *Truth and Method* in his library, he evidently did not read him closely because the book, unlike Berman's others, was virtually without any marks. It is likely that Berman would have found much to appreciate in Gadamer's treatment of the open-ended, conversational character of understanding and of Gadamer's emphasis on the role of language in preforming human understanding.]

[3] [See e.g., Mellinkoff, *Language of the Law*, 285.]

indeed, often lacking. It is, therefore, incumbent upon lawyers, judges, administrators, legislators, law teachers, and others to attempt to clarify and simplify the language of law in order that it may be properly understood by those to whom it is addressed.[4] Yet many of the attacks upon the obscurity and technicality of legal language, and many of the proposals to improve it, are based upon a wrong philosophy of language. The critics and reformers have often accepted a mechanistic theory which treats language simply as a tool to be used by reason and will, rather than as an integral part of man's whole personality and hence also a shaper of reason and will. They have accepted a sharp distinction between the language of intellect and the language of emotion. They have started from the premise that words (symbols) are to be distinguished from things (referents), and that words (or at least so-called non-emotive words) have no other proper function than to convey an accurate picture, a photograph, as it were, of the things to which they refer. They have separated the "form" of language from its "content," and both from its "motive." They have failed to give sufficient weight to the fact that words both embody and inspire the traditions and the philosophies of the community which has created them. And they have neglected the communifying character of speech – of prose as well as poetry – that is, the character of all language as a dramatic expression and fulfillment of man's craving and capacity for association.[5]

One of the greatest offenders in these respects, and one who has had a most profound influence, is Jeremy Bentham, famous both as a philosopher and as a jurist, whose works have for almost two centuries been a source of some of the most grievous errors as well as some of the most brilliant insights both in semantics and in jurisprudence. It is worth examining Bentham's theory of language,[6] and his application of that theory to law, in some detail, since his conceptions have become the "common sense" view held by many, perhaps by most, English and American scholars, and because those conceptions are a substantial barrier to the peacemaking, or communifying, character of legal language.

Bentham developed a science of language based primarily on the distinction between (1) real entities, which he defined as objects (whether persons or things) whose existence is made known to us by one or more of our five senses, and (2) fictitious entities, which he defined as objects

---

[4] [See Peter M. Tiersma, *Legal Language* (University of Chicago Press, 1999), chapter 13.]

[5] [James Boyd White has developed similar themes at length, especially in the context of economic language in his *Justice as Translation*, 3–88.]

[6] [See Mellinkoff, *Language of the Law*, 261. See later Berman, *Faith and Order*, 189; Berman, *Interaction*, 112.]

whose existence is imagined – that is, not perceived by any of the five senses. All names, being psychical rather than physical, are thus treated by Bentham as fictitious entities, though they may be used to refer to real entities. We say, for example, that an apple is ripe, as though ripeness were a physical reality like the apple itself, whereas in fact it is a quality ascribed to the apple by our minds.[7] Such a figurative use of language is inherent in the fictitious character of language itself, Bentham said. We cannot help but speak of things which only exist psychically "as if" they existed physically. "To be spoken at all," he wrote, "every fictitious entity must be spoken of as if it were real."[8]

Bentham stated that, although it is impossible to speak without attributing reality to that which is fictitious, nevertheless it is both possible and desirable to reduce the confusion between fact and fiction to a minimum, and to use only those figurative terms which are absolutely necessary to convey the meanings we intend.[9] Further, he contended that this could be achieved by rigorously eliminating all emotion from our language and thereby making it scientific. Thus he argued that we must entirely avoid all "eulogistic" words such as economy, frugality, and thrift, and all "dyslogistic" words such as parsimony, cupidity, and avarice. We should instead, Bentham insisted, use only "neutral" expressions such as desire of subsistence, plenty, profit, acquisition. Similarly, the neutral terms, "curiosity, desire of information," should replace the eulogistic "love of knowledge, passion for literature" and the dyslogistic "impertinence, meddlesomeness."[10]

Bentham made legal language one of the chief concerns of his linguistics, just as he made law reform a chief object of his ethics. His attack on the fallacies of legal language was relentless. He demonstrated the tautology and the circularity of its principal terms. When it is said, for example, that a man has a "right" to something because someone has an "obligation" to transfer it to him, the "right" of the one and the "obligation" of the other are merely two different terms for the same thing. Similarly, the word "crime" and the word "law" itself are only alternative ways of saying

---

[7] [See Jeremy Bentham, "Essay on Language," in John Bowring, ed., *The Works of Jeremy Bentham*, 11 vols. (Edinburgh: William Tait, 1838–43), 8:330–31.]

[8] [Jeremy Bentham, "A Fragment on Ontology," in *Works*, 8:197.]

[9] [Bentham, "Essay on Language," 331.]

[10] [See Jeremy Bentham, "A Table of the Springs of Action," in *Works*, 1:197–205, for Bentham's tables, with columns comparing eulogistic and dyslogistic words with their neutral counterparts.]

"right," "obligation," and the like. "Each of these words may be substituted one for the other," he wrote.

> The law directs me to support you – it imposes upon me the *obligation* of supporting you – it grants you the *right* of being supported by me – it converts into an *offense* the negative act by which I omit to support you – it obliges me to render you the *service* of supporting you ... This then is the connection between these legal entities: they are only the law considered under different aspects; they exist as long as it exists; they are born and they die with it.[11]

But people fail to recognize this circularity, and as a result they ascribe to rights, obligations, and the like an independent existence. "The words rights and obligations," Bentham adds, "have been the foundations of reasoning, as if they had been eternal entities which did not derive their birth from the law, but which, on the contrary, had given birth to it. They have never been considered as productions of the will of the legislator, but as the productions of a chimerical law – a law of nations – a law of nature."[12] In short, Bentham contended that it is not the language of rights and obligations that makes law what it is; those are mere words. It is rather "the will of the legislator," that is, political interests, which, being concerned with things, must seek to eliminate circularity and to make words correspond, so far as possible, to things.

Bentham directed his zeal particularly against that most fictitious phenomenon of law, legal fictions themselves,[13] that is, legal doctrines which state a legal result in terms of assumed facts which are known to be non-existent. To take the most familiar example, it is said that a corporation may sue and be sued because it is "a legal person." If we suppose that the word "person" is really applicable only to individual human beings, it is a fiction to say that a corporation is a person. Indeed, we call it such in order to justify the ascription to it of the rights and duties of "real" persons (such as the right to sue and be sued). Similarly, if we define a "battery" as requiring on the part of the defendant an intent to strike the plaintiff, but we nevertheless hold a defendant liable for battery when he did not intend to strike the plaintiff but a third person, and hit the plaintiff by mistake, we may justify the result fictitiously on the ground that "the law" "transfers" the object of the intent from the third person to the plaintiff. Other examples of fictions, particularly many against which Bentham inveighed, are far less benign both in their logic and in their results.

---

[11] [Jeremy Bentham, "General View of a Complete Code of Laws," in *Works*, 3:159.]
[12] [Ibid., 3:160.]   [13] [See Chapter 3 herein.]

Legal fictions appeared especially venomous to Bentham because they are consciously defended by lawyers on the ground that they accomplish beneficial results. Bentham's whole linguistics, his whole philosophy of utilitarianism, and his whole politics rested on the faith that social utility requires the reduction of the use of figurative speech to the barest minimum. Only if words can be made to correspond, so far as intellectually possible, to things, in Bentham's view, can the legislator be freed from the passions and prejudices of himself and others. Is "[f]iction of use to justice?" Bentham asked. "Exactly as swindling is to trade."[14] "Fiction, tautology, technicality, circuity, irregularity, inconsistency remain (in English law)," he wrote in 1776. "But above all, the pestilential breath of Fiction poisons the sense of every instrument it comes near."[15]

We must admire this great "Scourge of Spellbinders," as he has been called,[16] for his assault upon every kind of fallacy and self-deception. Yet it is important that his own rhetoric be unmasked. He has led us down a dead-end street. He *wants* words to represent things, but he concludes that they cannot, and then he asks us to use them *as far as possible* to represent things, always realizing that we are speaking of fictitious entities "as if" they were real. Thus Bentham set the stage for the "as if" philosophy of the twentieth century, of which C. K. Ogden could write sympathetically in 1932 that it "dominates scientific thought."[17]

The vice in this philosophy is not so much in what it says as in what it fails to say. It fails to say that language is itself as real as the "things" to which it allegedly corresponds – that its reality, its meaning, consists in its power to create relationships, that is in the correspondence of words not to "things" but to the social context in which they are uttered – and that without a genuine (and not merely an "as if") belief in the truth of its own speech, no community, not even that of philosophers, can long survive.

In jurisprudence, Benthamism has found its strongest expression in the twentieth century in various schools of "legal realism," which seek to expose the inherent ambiguities of all words and therefore find the real sources of legal decisions in economic interests, political interests, psychological complexes, personal prejudices, "what the judge ate for

---

[14] [Jeremy Bentham, "Rationale of Judicial Evidence," in *Works*, 7:283.]
[15] [Jeremy Bentham, "Fragment on Government," in *Works*, 1:235 (note "s").]
[16] [Burke, *A Rhetoric of Motives*, 100.]
[17] [C. K. Ogden, *Bentham's Theory of Fictions* (London: Kegan Paul, Trench, Trübner & Co., 1932), cxlviii. See later, Berman, *Interaction*, 112.]

breakfast,"[18] and everywhere else except in the language of law itself. But the rejection of the authority of legal language only results in the effort to substitute new languages, whether of "interests" or of "values" or of "symbolic logic," for a man cannot jump out of his language except into another. And we cannot escape for long from "rights," "obligations," "crime," "property," "contract," and the rest, for they have made us what we are.

The view that words are symbols of things (or of thoughts about things) – rather than symbols of relationships between speakers and listeners – has led many modern jurists, as it led Bentham, to seek to remove from legal language all imagery and emotion and, beyond that, to give to each word a single constant meaning. The focus on things, and the neglect of social context, also leads to an excessive emphasis upon legal nouns and a neglect of verbs. (Bentham, logical to the end, despised poetry altogether.) Yet we have seen in our first chapter that a word does not "have" a meaning. Instead, it *transfers* a meaning; indeed, it *gives* a meaning where there was no meaning before. Therefore, its imagery, and the feelings which give rise to it, are essential parts of the meaning to be conveyed. Nor will that meaning be the same in different contexts; the tone of voice, at least, will vary. And above all, the emphasis upon context, upon the active side of speech, establishes the importance of verbs, and not only of nouns, for the nouns – and this is especially true of law – are always uttered in a context of hearings and of decision.

2

This, indeed, is the clue to the "communifying" function of legal language in all societies where law exists – that it is uttered in the context of legal activities. The vocabulary of law is part of legal syntax, that is, the arrangement of legal terms in phrases and sentences. And legal syntax, in turn, is part of legal proceedings. It is part of our legal system, of pleading, examination of witnesses, advocacy, the rendering of judgments, legislative debates, and legislative investigations. It is part of the drafting of judicial, administrative, and legislative documents as well as commercial and other legal instruments. It is part of interpretation of legal language, of legal counseling, and of "the way lawyers talk."[19] Once the vocabulary of law is put in the context of legal activities, of law-men speaking, it

---

[18] [See Jerome Frank, *Law and the Modern Mind* (Garden City, NY: Doubleday, 1963), 34, where Frank made this famous hypothesis about the role of indigestion in judging.]

[19] [See later, analysis in Judith N. Levi, Anne Graffam Walker, eds., *Language in the Judicial Process* (New York: Plenum Press, 1990).]

becomes apparent that legal words cannot be "neutralized," and that they cannot be assigned single meanings, for their primary function is not to mirror phenomena of the external world but to create social relations.

Traditionally, the "active" side of legal language, the relationship of legal words to the contexts in which they are uttered, has been studied under the heading of legal rhetoric. Rhetoric, however, under the influence of Aristotle, has traditionally been separated from logic, ethics, and politics (as, indeed, each of those three has been separated from the others). Moreover, rhetoric itself has been reduced to a study of the art of persuasion[20] through appeals to emotions, whereas the original Aristotelian conception of it also embraced the art of public deliberation through appeals to reason. Thus rhetoric in its original meaning involves much more than the tricks of argumentation; it is also a mode of reasoning.[21] At the same time, rhetoric is distinguished from logic (in the formal Aristotelian sense), since logic is concerned with declarative (indicative) statements that are considered to be either true or false ("propositions"), whereas rhetoric is concerned with subjunctive, normative, and imperative statements, uttered in order to influence thought or action. The classical formula of logic: "All men are mortal, Socrates is a man, therefore Socrates is mortal" might be rendered in rhetorical form as: "If you would be a man, O Socrates, you must prepare yourself to death!"

Yet the division between rhetoric and logic must not be made too sharp. Neither the persuasive character of language nor the interrelationships of logical propositions can be dissociated from the meanings of the words spoken (semantics) nor from the identification of speaker and listener (communication). Moreover, the Aristotelian distinctions between logic, rhetoric, ethics, and politics must also not be overdrawn. The normative statements of ethics and the imperative statements of politics are closely

---

[20] [See later, analysis in Joanna Jemielniak, "Subversion in the World of Order: Legal Deconstruction as a Rhetorical Practice," in Anne Wagner, et al., *Contemporary Issues of the Semiotics of Law* (Oxford: Hart Publishing, 2005), 139.]

[21] [This connection of logic to rhetoric was part of Sir Edward Coke's description of law as an "artificial reason." Coke claimed that English law had its own rationality based on its long-standing traditions and the experience of its practitioners. Berman credited Coke as one of the progenitors of the historical school of jurisprudence. See Harold J. Berman, "Origins of Historical Jurisprudence: Coke, Selden, Hale," *Yale Law Journal* 103 (1994): 1689–92. Matthew Hale, Coke's protégé, expanded Coke's concept of "artificial reason" to include all historical legal systems: all nations have particular, long-standing legal traditions that have their own rationality irreducible to general or natural reason. Ibid., 1716–17. Berman makes these same points in his history of the German and English legal revolutions. See Berman, *Law and Revolution II*, 242–44, 255–60.]

linked with the subjunctive statements of rhetoric and the declarative statements of logic. These types of statements represent different forms of a single grammar. Unless we can find the relationships between them, we shall not understand law, for every legal utterance contains and combines them all.[22]

The prevailing tendency in Western legal thought in the past 100 to 150 years has been to regard the rhetorical aspect of legal utterances as an emotional and subjective element that only leads to ambiguity and uncertainty. At the same time, the political and ethical aspects of legal utterances have been taken by a great many jurists as "given" – something the politicians or the moral philosophers are concerned with, or something that lawyers "as policymakers" or "as moralists" might be concerned with, but not something that lawyers "as lawyers" are equipped to deal with. The task of the lawyer "as lawyer," many have thought, is to maintain the logic of the law, its internal consistency, given the policies and the moral values of the legislature, administrative agencies, and courts. And for that purpose, the lawyer has sought neutral terms, single meanings, and "lower-order" referents in the world of real life.

This philosophy of law inevitably focuses attention upon that aspect of law that appears to be the most "logical" – namely, its declarative propositions, the formal rules: "If A intentionally causes B to anticipate an unpermitted bodily touching, A is civilly liable to B for assault." "Burglary at common law is the breaking and entering a dwelling in the night season with intent to commit a felony." "A will is invalid unless it is attested by three witnesses." "The Fourth Amendment of the United States Constitution prohibits the unreasonable search of a man's house, and therefore a conviction based upon evidence procured in a search made without a warrant is itself unlawful." Such formulations, purporting to state the legal consequences that follow from hypothetical facts, have been viewed as the principal domain of the lawyer, who has defined law in terms of them. "Law is a body of rules," the legal positivist says; let

---

[22] [In later work, Berman was drawn to the topical method of sixteenth-century Lutheran legal scholars, Philip Melanchthon and Johan Oldendorp as well as the modern German jurist, Theodor Viehweg, *Topik und Jurisprudenz* (Munich: C.H. Beck, 1953). See Berman, *Law and Revolution II*, 77–99, 111–13. For a modern example using the topical method, see Anita Soboleva, "Topical Jurisprudence: Reconciliation of Law and Rhetoric," in Anne Wagner et al., *Interpretation, Law and the Construction of Meaning: Collected Papers on Legal Interpretation in Theory, Adjudication and Political Practice* (Dordrecht: Springer, 2007), 49–64.]

the philosopher or the sociologist worry about where they come from and what they are for.

Especially in the eighteenth and nineteenth centuries, Western jurists sought to make legal reasoning conform to syllogistic logic. The rules of law declared by legislatures, courts, and legal scholars were viewed as major premises, and the fact-situations of particular cases or the terms of particular legal problems were viewed as minor premises. The decision of a case, or the resolution of a legal problem, was thought to follow inevitably from a proper juxtaposition of the major and minor premises. It was supposed by many that if the entire body of law could be summarized in a set of rules, the sole remaining task of law would be to classify particular facts under one rule or another. Thus law could eliminate all "personal" factors, and could become a "science."

If one accepts the idea that the basic unit, so to speak, of legal language is the formal legal rule, the declarative statement of the legal consequences that "flow" from hypothetical sets of facts, then legal decisions – "A is liable to B for assault;" "Jones is guilty of burglary;" "Smith's will is invalid;" "The conviction of Green is hereby reversed" – do indeed appear to be inferences, "conclusions," drawn from the rules. It then appears justified and necessary that "emotional" and "subjective" influences be eliminated both from the statement of the rules and from their application to concrete cases. And indeed, the legal conceptualists, and their successors, the legal empiricists and legal realists, have made a valuable contribution to the formulation of rules and to the systematization of law, that is, to the maintenance of its internal "logical" consistency, by their attack upon the use of figurative words and by their exposure of the ambiguities, emotional overtones, and hidden meanings of legal language generally. It is not surprising that Bentham's major contribution to the law was his insistence upon precision and clarity in the drafting of legislation and his efforts to introduce codification into English law. In fact, the word "codification" was apparently of his invention.

A closer look at legal rules, however, discloses that they are not simply declarative propositions. They are statements made for various purposes, and the purposes add rhetorical, ethical, and political meanings to what first appears as a merely "logical," that is, declarative, statement. The provision of the United States Constitution prohibiting unreasonable searches and seizures, for example, is much more than a declaration of the legal consequences attending such searches and seizures. It is also an expression of a *policy* of protecting citizens against abuses committed by law-enforcement officials, and whether that policy is read broadly or narrowly will in part determine the meaning of the declaration. In addition, it is an expression of a *moral standard*, part of what is called "civil rights," relating to the integrity both of the individual and of the judicial process, and this adds another dimension to the meaning of the declaration. Finally, the provision is intended to *persuade* the law-enforcement officials, the courts, and the American people generally to act in certain ways, to believe in certain principles, to live in certain relationships with each other, and this rhetorical aspect adds a fourth dimension to the rule.

All rules have such political, ethical, and rhetorical aspects, in addition to their logical aspect. The declarative or indicative mood of the rule (its "is-ness") is combined not only with an imperative mood (its "must-ness") and a normative mood (its "ought-ness"), but also with a precative or subjunctive mood its ("would-be-ness.") Therefore a decision that "the conviction must be reversed," "A is liable to B in the sum of $100," "Smith has a right," and the like is not only an inference or conclusion drawn from the declaration of what legal consequences follow from hypothetical facts. Such a decision is also an implementation of policy, a doing of justice, and a response to the rhetorical elements of the language in which the rule is expressed. It is to be justified or criticized in terms of all four of these dimensions, and not in terms of any one alone; for in law (whatever may be the case in philosophy) no one of them exists alone. Thus even if law is conceived as a body (or code) of rules enacted by the supreme law-giver, it would be impossible to make law "scientific" in the emotionally neutral sense of that word adopted by Bentham and his followers.[23]

---

[23] [Berman later added to his analysis: "The mechanical model of the application of rules to facts did not go unchallenged even in its heyday. In Germany, Rudolf von Jhering ridiculed a 'jurisprudence of concepts' (*Begriffsjurisprudenz*) ... However useful syllogistic logic may be in testing the validity of conclusions drawn from given premises, it is inadequate in a practical science such as law, where the premises are not given but must be created. Legal rules, viewed as major premises, are always subject to qualification in light of the particular circumstances; it is a rule of English and American law, for example, that a person who intentionally strikes another is civilly liable for battery, but such a rule is subject, in legal practice, to infinite modification in light of the possible defense (for example, self-defense, defense of property, parental privilege, immunity from suit, lack of jurisdiction, insufficiency of evidence, etc.). In addition, life continually presents new situations to which no existing rule is applicable; we simply do not know the legal limits of freedom of speech, for example, since the social context in which words are spoken is continually changing. Thus, legal rules are continually being made and remade." See Harold J. Berman, "Legal Reasoning," in David Sills, ed., *International Encyclopedia of the Social Sciences*, 19 vols. (New York: Macmillan, 1968), 9:197–204, at 198.]

However, it is apparent that law is much more than rules, for the rules are nothing until they are drafted, debated, voted, published, interpreted, obeyed, applied, enforced – and these activities are surely part of law.[24] As many writers have emphasized, law is an activity, an enterprise – "the enterprise," as Lon L. Fuller puts it, "of subjecting human conduct to the governance of rules."[25] By focusing attention on the enterprise, and not merely on the rules, Fuller has exposed many fallacies of those schools of jurisprudence that treat rules as something given and ignore their purposive character. But just as we cannot, without distortion, abstract the content of rules from the purposes for which the rules exist, so we cannot abstract their purposive content from the processes by which they come into being and are realized; for the purpose, too, receives its meaning in the process.[26] Thus we must consider not only the purposes of a rule, but also the purposes of the persons who made it and of the persons who interpret and apply it. Legal rules are neither self-generated nor self-executing. Statutes, which are a prime example of legal rules, are generally enacted in response to pressures from outside the legislature, and once enacted they require the support of the executive and judicial branches to give them meaning. Moreover, the entire legal profession and, indeed, the entire people, are needed to cooperate in this venture, for if the language of laws is incomprehensible to the legal profession and ultimately to the people, they will become dead letters.[27] Thus to achieve a "neutral" legal language, in Jeremy Bentham's sense, not only the legislatures but the whole community would have to speak a kind of Benthamese. And to achieve a "moral" legal language, or a "purposive" legal language, requires a community which shares a common language of morality and purpose.[28]

Beyond this, it must be stressed that the purposes of the legal enterprise include not only subjecting human conduct to the governance of rules but also establishing human interrelationships that rest on factors other than rules. Even Lon Fuller's definition of law does not go far enough. Rules, even when viewed in their political, ethical, and rhetorical as well as in their logical aspect, and even when interpreted in the light of the

---

[24] [See later, Berman, *Interaction*, 24: "Law is not only a body of rules; it is people legislating, adjudicating, administering, negotiating – it is a living process."]

[25] [Lon L. Fuller, *The Morality of Law* (New Haven, CT: Yale University Press, 1964), 106.]

[26] [See later, Berman, *Faith and Order*, 82: "medieval English law (like any dynamic law, it must be added) was 'not a fact or a collection of rules, but a process'" (quoting Eugen Rosenstock-Huessy). See also Berman, *Interaction*, 85: "Rules of law, like all linguistic utterances, derive their meaning from the context in which they are spoken or written."]

[27] [See later, ibid., 116.]   [28] [See later, ibid., 31ff.]

processes whereby they are brought into being and realized, comprise only one kind of legal utterance, and by no means the only significant kind. At least as important as rules, in law, are decisions: the casting of votes, the issuance of orders, the handing down of judgments. Equally important, also, are agreements, through which parties not only make rules and decisions controlling themselves but also make plans for the future. A legal document such as a contract to manufacture and sell a machine contains a great deal of important legal language that cannot properly be classified as the language of rule or of decision: "The seller agrees to abide by the specifications submitted by the purchaser"; "Inspection shall take place at the seller's plant within ten days after completion" and more. These are, in one sense, rules (or "conditions"), but they are also agreed-upon commitments. Indeed, it has been cogently suggested that the imperative character of law itself rests upon the element of reciprocity that is inherent in agreement. This in turn suggests the "social contract" theories of sovereignty propounded by Locke, Rousseau, and others in the seventeenth and eighteenth centuries. It also suggests the insight expressed in recent studies of the Old Testament, that the Law, including the Ten Commandments, was derived from the covenant between God and Israel and is to be read in terms of the covenant.[29]

In addition to the language of rule, of decision, and of agreement, there is the language of legal argument, a language which weaves rules and facts into a petition or recommendation. And there is the language of legal opinion, and especially the opinion of judges in support of their decisions, in which (in the English and American traditions) arguments of counsel are woven together with rules and facts to explain the decision in a manner satisfactory to the losing side and also to interpret it for those who may wish to rely on it in the future.

The rich variety of forms of legal language, with their various rhetorical, ethical, political, and logical implications, cannot be understood on the basis of the sharp Benthamite distinctions between the physical and the psychical, and between the intellect and the emotions, which continue to dominate much of Western legal thought. Outside of law, these distinctions have generally yielded to various attempts at synthesis. The social sciences and humanities have sought to free language from its bondage either to things or to thought: more and more, language is regarded as shaping (and not merely reflecting) things. At the same time, the dualism of thought and feeling has lost its sharpness. Intellectual efforts are

---

[29] [See later, Berman, *Faith and Order*, 203–4.]

no longer considered to be always so pure, nor the emotions always so deceiving, as it once was supposed. The reason of the heart, to paraphrase Pascal, may be no less persuasive than the reason of the intellect. We do not need to be ashamed of our passions. They create our language, and it is through our language that we respond to each other and to the world around us.

3

As we have seen, a primary function of all language is to influence the listener to make some kind of response. But the language of law accentuates this function of language; law is spoken not only to influence, stimulate, persuade, but also to decide, and by deciding to induce immediate action. Law, like politics, or business, is a language of decisions for action. It is therefore spoken with passion, albeit a controlled passion, and not merely analytically or scientifically. The scholar or scientist, seeking to influence attitudes or incipient actions, describes, infers, analyzes, hypothesizes, and reflects. But the law-maker or judge, responding to the need for immediate action, decides, enacts, rules, orders, decrees, and sentences. And the advocate counsels, negotiates, pleads, moves, argues, and appeals. The scholar is apt to demand that others assume the same objective and detached manner of speech which he prizes in himself. But as Kenneth Burke points out, a cry for help is a very "prejudiced" utterance, and indeed a form of "wishful thinking"! The language of law is closer to the drowning man's cry for help than to the quiet reflections of the ivory tower. It is the language of grievance and remedy, and it is spoken under pressure.

Second, the language of law, like all language, is spoken and heard, written and read, to bring people together, to make community. In the case of legal language, the community is identified as those who are subject to the law – that is, all individuals, groups, classes, and races, living with the same legal order. The law-maker or judge speaks for the entire polity and speaks to the entire polity. Therefore he must speak solemnly, publicly, for all to hear and ponder.[30] His is not the intimate, spontaneous speech of the face-to-face group. His tone of voice, so to speak, as well as his vocabulary and syntax, must rise above the very divisions that have made law necessary. In this, too, the language of law overlaps with the language of high politics.

[30] [See later, elaboration in Solan, *Language of Judges.*]

Third, the language of law is particularly concerned with two kinds of threats to the community: the threat of disorder and the threat of injustice. Law is spoken passionately to bring people together in the name of order and in the name of what is right. It is therefore a language of ordering in the sense of creating order as well as in the sense of giving orders. And it is a language of judgment in the sense of doing justice as well as in the sense of adjudication. In these respects the language of law, once again, is not unique, for ordering and judging are a basic aspect of government, and indeed of all social organization, not confined to law.

Fourth, the language of law is the language of hearing.[31] Indeed, the typical identifying quality of law, in all societies where law exists, is that it responds to social disorder and social injustice by affording a hearing to those who are aggrieved. The law acts passionately, but not impulsively. It takes time to hear and consider the claims of those who resort to it and the contentions of those who are adversely affected by such claims. This is the heart of the law,[32] distinguishing adjudication from vengeance, administration from bureaucratic "red tape," and legislation from despotism.

To say that the hearing is the heart of law is not to deny the importance of types of legal procedure other than adjudication, but only to stress that each of these types also derives from the hearing and is therefore partly adjudicative in nature. Legislation derives its legal character from the opportunity to debate; without such opportunity, one could speak of commands, orders, "ukases,"[33] but not of the kind of procedure that is properly associated with a legislature. Indeed, it is no accident that Parliament was originally called the High Court of Parliament, and that in Massachusetts the legislature is still called the Great and General Court. Also the negotiation of contracts, and even unilateral legal acts such as the writing of a will, inevitably presuppose a consideration of adverse claims and contentions. Moreover, the draftsman of such documents must put himself in the position of a third person who might be called upon to interpret them in the light of a dispute over their validity or their meanings. All the techniques of adjudication, including pleading, advocacy, examination of witnesses, and argument over relevant norms or decisions, are present in

[31] [See later Harold J. Berman, "Epilogue: An Ecumenical Christian Jurisprudence," in John Witte, Jr. and Frank S. Alexander, eds., *The Teachings of Modern Christianity on Law, Politics, and Human Nature*, 2 vols. (New York: Columbia University Press, 2006), 752–64, at 762: "a fair hearing is universally believed in as a sacred instrument of peaceful resolution of conflict."]

[32] [See later, Berman, *Interaction*, 90.]

[33] [Edicts of the Czarist Russian government.]

the mind of the draftsman and are reflected in the terms of the legal instrument. We should avoid the error of stressing the process of adjudication at the expense of legislation, administration, negotiation, and other legal activities, but we should also avoid the error of failing to stress the adjudicative aspects of those other activities.

It is its emphasis on, and institutionalization of, the hearing that distinguishes law from all other political and social activities. The law is supposed always to listen first, and then speak. It is supposed never to pre-judge. At the same time, in law the hearing involves two elements that are not necessarily present in non-legal listening and speaking. The first is formality. The second is categorization. Although these two elements are implicit in the hearing, I shall, for emphasis, list them individually as distinctive features of legal language.

Fifth, then, law speaks formally.[34] There is a deliberate and ceremonial character in legal language that distinguishes it from other governmental utterances, however solemn and public they may be. Such formality is inherent in the hearing, with its formal presentation of claims and defenses, the formal deliberations of the court or other tribunal, and the formal rendering of a decision. The formalities of the hearing help to secure its genuineness – its impartiality, equality, internal consistency, restraint, and authority. And in non-judicial legal proceedings, formalities preserve the adjudicative aspects. Legal grammar is replete with ceremonial utterances, often hoary with age and authority. "Know all men by these presents," "May it please the court," "Do you swear to tell the truth, the whole truth, and nothing but the truth, so help you God?" "The chair recognizes the honorable Senator from Utah" – are a few familiar examples. Legal maxims provide others: "He who comes into equity must come with clean hands," "*De minimis non curat lex.*" The intimate connection between the formal, or ceremonial, quality of legal language and the institution of the hearing is made clear in the famous English saying that "Justice must not only be done but must also be *seen* to be done." We might add it must also be *heard* to be done.[35]

Sixth, and finally, it is a distinctive quality of legal language, proceeding from its growth out of the institution of the hearing, that it speaks in general, or categorical terms. This, too, helps to secure the genuineness of the hearing.[36] John Jones is categorized as "the plaintiff"; Sam Smith is

---

[34] [See later, Berman, *Faith and Order*, 284.]
[35] [See later, Berman, *Interaction*, 32.]
[36] [Ibid., 85.]

categorized as "the defendant"; the defendant is alleged to have broken his "lease" by causing certain "damage" to the leased "premises." These are the "legally operative facts." The "real" facts – Smith's obnoxious personal habits, the neighbors' gossip, the family feud – are excluded unless they can be brought into the relevant legal categories. For the hearing is not to determine who is the better man, Sam Smith or John Jones, but rather to determine whether the rights of a lessor who happens to be Sam Smith, rights established by the community, have been violated by a lessee who happens to be John Jones.

It is Abel's blood that cries to God, but it cries from the earth which received it from Cain's hand. And it is the earth itself that curses Cain, making him a fugitive. For these were not merely two individuals, but brothers.[37] So it is always with law. The matter in dispute, the problem to be resolved, must be defined in community terms, in legal terms, since it is not only the parties but the whole community, its order and its justice, its law, that is involved. The claims and contentions of the parties must be generalized, must be placed in categories which the law recognizes. The defendant's act is alleged to be an "assault" or "a breach of contract." The issue is defined as "whether the right of the accused to confront his accusers requires that the government reveal the sources of its evidence even though they are classified as secret." The problem is stated to be "how to draft an agreement not to compete that will not violate the antitrust laws." However the allegation, issue, or problem may be phrased, it tests, and is tested by, the general category. The question becomes a legal one when it is generalized: "Am I my brother's keeper?" "Who is my neighbor?"

The formulation of the category, and thus the viewing of the concrete facts *sub specie communitatis*, is organically derived from the hearing, though it is logically distinct from it. The dispute or the problem has challenged the existing rules. The parties have invoked a reformulation of them in the light of the concrete facts. And the court (if it is a judicial proceeding) or legislature (if it is a proposed statute) or the administrative agency (if it is a new regulation that is sought) or the lawyers (if it is a contract negotiation) or the testator (if it is a will that is being drawn) is asked to redefine the law, to reinterpret the rules, in the light of the new dispute or the new problem. The reinterpretation is a creative act, which does not follow automatically from the hearing, although it is organically derived from it. The court, or legislature, or agency, or lawyers, or testator must take a second intellectual and emotional step, from the facts of

---

[37] Genesis 4:1–9; see further above p. 57.

the specific situation to the reinterpretation of rules. It is able to take this step only after categorizing, or "characterizing" (to use the legal term for it), the nature of the dispute. Such categorization is an intermediate stage between the hearing of the specific facts and the determination of the applicable rule.

Still another intellectual and emotional step must be taken, from the reinterpretation of the law in the light of the controversy or problem to the application of the law, as reinterpreted, to that controversy or problem. This is, in fact, the most difficult step.[38] It is a veritable leap. For the reinterpretation of the categories and rules in the light of the issues presented at the hearing is not immediately decisive and hence can be carried out more calmly. But the "application" of the law is crucial. Now the chips are down. This step, this leap, is made easier by the fact that there has been a hearing and a reinterpretation of the authoritative legal materials in the light of the hearing. But the resolution is still in doubt. The rules are relatively easy to restate; one gets much help from the books. But the decision itself is one's own unique responsibility. As every responsible judge knows, it is born of anguish. For, in Immanuel Kant's incisive words: "There is no rule for applying a rule."[39]

Thus interpretation of law must be distinguished from application of law, and both must be put in the context of the hearing, with its requirement of generality. There is no "logical," that is, no declarative, no "natural," progression from argument to interpretation to application. It is

---

[38] [See later, Berman, *Interaction*, 35: the "power to interpret the rules and decisions is also the power to remake them." Ibid.]

[39] [This paraphrase is from Immanuel Kant, *Critique of Pure Reason*, trans. Norman Kemp Smith (London: Macmillan, 1929), A133/B172–A134/B174. Berman would later point to Ken Kress, "Legal Indeterminacy," *California Law Review* 77 (1989): 332–33 as an elaboration of Kant's position. See Berman, *Law and Revolution II*, 413, n106. James Boyd White has emphasized the need for judicial responsibility in opinion-writing, in the face of a judicial style that seems to abdicate responsibility for the difficult decision in tired clichés and overbearing oratory. See White, *Justice as Translation*, 92. Concerns about responsibility also arise in the linguistic context. Lawrence Solan has been quite critical of judicial use of rules of grammar and linguistic canons of construction. According to Solan, a linguist, the kinds of ambiguities in language which arise in appellate cases are often hard ambiguities which cannot be resolved. Linguistic canons, which are often applied inappropriately, disguise the real basis for decision. Judges, according to Solan, should be more willing to take responsibility for difficult decisions, which will allow for a candid public discussion of the legal principles which should guide judges in hard cases. See also Solan, *Language of Judges*, 59–62, 96–98, 117, 178–79, 186–87 and further *Language of Statutes*, 223–30, where Solan contends that our legal system works very well most of the time, and linguistic problems can be exaggerated given the rarity of appellate decisions vis-à-vis the totality of cases dealing with statutory interpretation.]

not simply a "calculation." Yet there is a "rational" progression – in the sense that language is itself the primary rationale, in the sense that reason, *ratio*, is itself speech. If the opposing sides are impartially heard, they will invoke the community interests, and the person who hears must also consider, must define, those community interests, and having considered he must sweat out the decision. Nothing else is possible once he is caught up in the hearing, in the judging, in the deciding. It is not "natural"; it is human, it is social.

The hearing, to be a genuine hearing, must result in a decision based on principle, on rule. The principles, the rules, gain their meaning, in turn, from the procedural context in which they are uttered. This is entirely apparent in the case of legislation, for the legislature, although its acts are supposed to be principled, is free to make new principles, new rules. But it is also true of adjudication, where the court's freedom to make new rules is more limited. It is true also of administration and of negotiation. Rules are only the deposit of law, what is left after the legislature, or court, or administrative agency, or contracting parties, or testator, or transferor of property have acted in response to a situation calling for legal action. Rules reflect what has been decided in the past and what will be decided in the future; they are valuable guides to what the law was and to what it will be. But no sentence, as Whitehead said, can give its own meaning. If a rule seems clear at the center, albeit somewhat vague at the penumbra, that is only because at the center the concrete cases and arguments which the rule resolves are apparent: there we can see the rule being invoked, being made, and being applied. At the penumbra, so-called, the leap from the case to the rule and from the rule to the application is a longer, a more difficult one. But the process is the same. I do not argue that rules have no existence, that they are only myths. I argue, rather, that they are treated as myths when they are given a reality apart from their social context. What gives legal rules their reality, their meaning, their vitality, is the invoking and making and applying of them.[40] And that involves hearing and decision, not just rule.

4

If law is seen, in the first instance, not as rules but as the enterprise of hearing, judging, deciding, prescribing, ordering, negotiating, agreeing,

---

[40] [See later, Berman, *Faith and Order*, 292: "the actualizing of law ... is its most essential feature."]

and declaring – it then becomes possible to give a satisfactory explanation
of what Bentham called the tautology and circuity of legal terms, and
what H. L. A. Hart calls the "great anomaly of legal language: our inability
to define its crucial words in terms of ordinary factual counterparts."[41]
It is, of course, true, that legal reasoning is characteristically circular. If
one says that the claimant has a right to a certain tract of land because he
owns it, and that he owns it because it was devised to him by the testator,
the terms "right," "own," "devised," and "testator" all refer to each other,
and each is defined in terms of the other. The legal propositions seem to
have no "empirical referents" – no "things" to which they "correspond."
The statement "A owes B 100 dollars," or "A trespassed on B's land," does
not refer to things, or to acts committed by A, but to liabilities imposed
by "the law." As H. L. A. Hart has shown, they are not to be understood
as descriptive statements but rather as "ascriptive" statements. Each legal
proposition "ascribes" rights and responsibilities. If a lawyer (or a layman
speaking in legal terms) says "A trespassed on B's land," he is not recount-
ing a fact but making a charge. He is ascribing to A responsibility for a
certain type of legally wrongful conduct and to B certain rights against
interference. When a court makes the same statement, the ascription of
such responsibility and right may have the effect of requiring A to pay B a
money judgment.

    Karl Olivecrona carries H. L. A. Hart's analysis further in pointing to
the "hollow" character of legal language, its "magical" effect in accom-
plishing certain results merely by being uttered.[42] If a man, under the
proper circumstances, utters the words, "I take this woman to be my law-
ful wedded wife," she may thereby become, in law, his wife. The statement
"I give and bequeath this watch to my son" – may effectuate the bequest.
A dollar bill is a piece of paper stating that the treasury promises to pay
the bearer – one dollar; legally, a dollar is defined as a dollar, or a right to
a dollar, and nothing more. In the words of the sixteenth-century Russian
economist [Ivan] Pososhkov, "A ruble is not silver, a ruble is the word of
the sovereign."[43] Take another example of legal "magic" from the world of
commerce: a promissory note which states that payment is to be made "to
the order of" the payee is negotiable (that is, it may be transferred to third
persons free of certain defenses, such as the defense that it was originally

---

[41] [H. L. A. Hart, "Definition and Theory in Jurisprudence," *Law Quarterly Review* 70(1)
    (1954): 53. See elaboration in Berman, "Legal Reasoning."]
[42] [See Karl Olivecrona, "Legal Language and Reality," in R. A. Newman, ed., *Essays in
    Jurisprudence in Honor of Roscoe Pound* (Indianapolis, IN: Bobbs-Merrill, 1962), 168.]
[43] [Source unknown.]

procured by fraud). But if the words "to the order of" are omitted, the note is not negotiable, even though the words have no meaning other than to make the note negotiable. Or a still simpler case: to say "you are under arrest" may be to *make* an arrest. Following John Austin, Olivecrona calls such statements "performative utterances," and he rightly notes that they play a decisive part in the law.[44]

We would compare such performative utterances in law with the sacraments of the church, which are called "effective symbols" because they effectuate that which they symbolize. Indeed, there is a sacramental quality to much of the language of law, testifying to its original connection with religion. In English and American law the petitioner still "prays" for relief, and the witness swears an oath. There is a liturgical quality in all judicial procedure.[45]

But to call such legal propositions magical or mystical presupposes a magical or mystical element in all language. All language induces action, if only the incipient action of mental attitudes. To attempt to find an empirical referent for the legal statement, "I give and bequeath my watch to my son," reminds one of the wife who complained that when she asks her husband if he loves her, he thinks she is seeking information. The statement "I love you" is not merely, and not primarily, a descriptive statement; the word "love" in that statement cannot be defined solely in terms of data immediately given by the senses; yet it is not necessarily magic. Indeed, all words are in some sense performative, and all are to some degree circular. Not only the language of law and of love but also the language of military command, of political campaigning and voting, of business deals, even of scholarly analysis – gives meaning where none existed before.

The proliferation of interdependent legal terms to refer to the same thing is due to the fact that the terms are not supposed to "refer" to "things" but instead to regulate a complex interrelationship of people engaged, actually or potentially, in legal activities of various kinds. From the standpoint of the child (to revert to the earlier example of the right to support, given by Bentham), support is a "right" which he possesses: from the standpoint of the parent, it is an "obligation." From the standpoint of the prosecutor, failure to fulfill the obligation may be a "crime." It is true that if there were

---

[44] [Olivecrona, "Legal Language and Reality," 151–91. See later, Sanford Schane, *Language and the Law* (New York: Continuum, 2006), ch. 3, on the speech-act theory of Austin and John Searle in the legal context.]

[45] [See later, Berman, *Interaction*, 31: one of the "principal ways in which law channels and communicates transrational values" is through ritual." See also Berman, *Faith and Order*, 100, 120, 284.]

no right there would be no obligation and no crime, and if there were no crime there would be no obligation and no right (or at least a different kind of obligation and right). But these and many other nouns are needed to identify the complexity of the relationship between the child, the parent, and the state. They are needed especially when the relationship is described in abstract terms, and no legal action is at issue. The decision of the court may be simple enough: "Pay the child $25 a week or go to jail."[46]

What troubles many is the fact that in explaining that decision the court (or legal writers) will often use circular reasoning, going from right to obligation to penalty as if in a logical sequence. Yet what may be senseless as a logical proposition may be sensible as a means of identifying the parties to a dispute and the nature of the disputed issue. A "sale," from the point of view of the seller, is a "purchase," from the point of view of the buyer. To characterize the legal relations of the two parties we must put ourselves first in the position of the one and then in the position of the other. Most legal transactions, like most other human transactions, involve a very complex network of relationships; the fact that behind the legal transaction lies the "hearing" – the consideration of all relevant claims and defenses – requires that the complexities be spelled out.

Law in action, legal language in its verbal aspects, thus involves role-playing.[47] The hearing of opposite points of view, whether in the legislature or the courtroom or in negotiation of a contract, is a process of identification with the interested parties. The rules of law which emerge from this process, or which are presented in the course of it, being stated largely in terms of nouns rather than verbs are often tautological: "The proposed bill would result in a taking of property without due process of law in violation of the Constitution," "Under this contract the seller has the right to repossess the automobile upon default in the payment of any installment." But the tautologies guide the legislator, the judge, the

---

[46] [See Berman, "Legal Reasoning," 51.]

[47] [Milner Ball, a close friend and admirer of Berman, has expanded on this idea of role-playing in the law in his *The Promise of American Law*. In chapters 4 ("Judicial Theater"), 5 ("The Image of Court as Theater of Beginning"), and 6 ("Personae"), Ball suggests that the trial court is stage where litigants should be willing and permitted to play out their stories of injustice before the court ("Judicial Theater"). When citizens engage in the play of the trial, as litigants or jury-members, they affirm their common commitment to the American legal tradition ("The Image of the Court as Theater of Beginning"). Ball agreed with Berman that *when* courts function in this way, they reaffirm the community brought together by the law. Ball would also agree that the "artificial" forms of legal language work to draw citizens into the legal process, establishing and protecting their rights and relationships, and assuring them of their place in the legal system.]

lawyers, the parties, and others, by indicating the complexities of the legal relations and legal interests which are involved. To attack legal propositions as question-begging is itself to beg the question of the function of legal propositions.

It may be objected that we have only resolved the lesser tautologies of the law by substituting an even greater one. We have said "the law is the law," the rules are the decisions. Is not a person who is required by "the law" to perform an obligation entitled to know why? And when he challenges as tautological the terms "rights," "duties," "crime," "contract," or "property," is he not entitled to a better reply than the admission that the terms are indeed tautological but behind them stands "the law" – the responsible legislator, the wise judge, who has heard all the arguments and taken all points of view into consideration?

If one speaks of the universal qualities of law, that which all legal systems have in common, it is by no means clear that a better reply can be given. For in every legal system, the grammar of law, that is, the process by which the language of law is elaborated, makes law what it is and forms the basis of its communifying power. The concepts of law, its noun-filled rules and propositions, derive their meaning from verbs – from the context of hearing, identification of issues, and redefinition of standards – from law in action. Uttered in the context of legal proceedings, of the legal process in all its ramifications, legal language can command respect, can resolve conflicts, can create channels of cooperation – in short, can make community. This, indeed, is their "magic," as it is the "magic" of all communifying speech.[48]

Yet no legal system has been content to rest its authority solely on itself, its own procedures, its own language. Every legal system has relied for its authority also on sources outside the law. A linguistic approach will help us here, too, for it will point us to the sources of legal language in the general language of the community. As we shall see in the next chapter, legal language is not created by law-men out of whole cloth; characteristically, it

[48] [See later, Milner Ball's book *Lying Down Together*. Ball's goal in that text was to critique a fundamental metaphor for law which he identifies as "law as bulwark of freedom," a view of law which emphasizes the individuality and autonomy of citizens and legal persons at the cost of emphasizing social interdependence and community. Ball suggests in its place a metaphor for law as "medium of social relationships." See Ball, *Lying Down Together*, 21–36. According to Ball, this communal vision of law does not preclude serious disagreement: "Argument, as compared with command or propaganda, is a communal act. When we engage in argument, persuading and being persuaded, we practice mutual dignity. The other person must be convinced; the other deserves to be convinced." Ibid., 42.]

is derived from non-legal language. Moreover, once words of general significance are given legal meanings, those legal meanings are themselves subject to change; and the process of the development of legal language, like the process of its creation, imposes limits upon those who would use law arbitrarily for their own special purposes

3

The growth of legal language

1

The language of law, as we have seen, is forged in the fires of legal procedures: of law-making, judging, regulating, negotiating, and other processes of creating, changing, or terminating rights and duties. However, the words used in these processes are historically derived from non-legal speech and usually retain non-legal connotations. The fact that legal terms – "property," for example – have meaning both inside and outside the law gives familiarity to legal language and helps to make it acceptable to the community; but, by the same token, the specifically legal meanings of legal terms may seem all the more strange and unacceptable to the non-lawyer. The strangeness, and often the awkwardness, of legal language has been a source of hostility toward law in all countries. Such hostility is sometimes justified. Where it is not justified, however, it can be reduced by an understanding of (1) how legal terms are derived from the folk language, (2) how legal terms acquire their own technical meanings, and (3) how those meanings change in the course of history. It is to these three matters that the present chapter is devoted.

The derivation of legal terms from the general language of the community is apparent in their etymology.[1] In many Indo-European languages, the word for (what we call) law is itself derived from some word signifying order. In the case of English, the word "law" stems from the Norse *lag*, which means "that which is laid down." The German *Gesetz* has a similar meaning. So does the term "justice" in various languages, as in the case of the German term, *Recht*, the Italian *diritto*, the French *droit*, the Russian *pravo*, all of which mean "right" in the sense of "correct" and in the sense of "the right hand" as well as in the sense of "just." So do the various words for "truth," as in the case of the Hindu *dharma* or the medieval Russian *pravda*. Indeed, the three concepts of order, justice, and truth are

---

[1] [See Mellinkoff, *Language of the Law*, 33.]

suggested in each of these words; that which is laid down or established – *gesetzt* – is identified with that which is normal or straight (not "crooked" or *gauche*) and that which is true ("correct," "right").

Only a relatively few of our modern English and American legal terms are rooted – like "law" itself – in Anglo-Saxon speech, and of these many can no longer be traced to their original meanings. Yet most of them, too, keep non-legal connotations. Such Anglo-Saxon words as "deed," "goods," "guilt," "let," "own," "right," "steal," "swear," "theft," "will," "witness," have significance both within and without the law. Others, like "burglar" (from the Anglo-Saxon "burg" meaning dwelling, possibly combined with the Latin *latro*, "thief"), have retained only legal connotations.

Most of the vocabulary of English and American law stems from Latin roots, brought into English from Roman law and canon law, in most cases via Norman French. Even those terms that derive from Latin, however, often retain the vestiges, at least, of their colloquial origins and generally continue to have non-legal meanings as well. Thus "property" (from the Latin *proprietas*) still has the connotation of "one's own," and may be found outside the law, as when we speak of the "properties" of chemicals or the "propriety" of a course of conduct. "Assault" is from the Norman French translation of the Latin *insultus*, meaning insult, which in turn is derived from the verb *insultare*, to leap at or spring at. "Trespass" is the Norman French for the Latin *transgressio*, sin, which originally meant "stepping across." "Obligation" is from the Latin *ligare*, to bind. "Liability" comes from the same root (through the Norman French *lier*). "Contract" is from the Latin for "draw together" (via the Norman French *contrat*). "Damages" is from the Latin *damnum*, meaning loss, hurt, penalty (like the French *dommage*). The list could be extended a hundredfold.

The Latin derivation of most English and American legal terms is by no means of merely antiquarian interest. As we shall see in later chapters, the terminology of all modern legal systems is to a large extent derived from Latin either by direct descent or by translation; and this fact provides one basis for the development of a common legal language of mankind.[2] Our interest in this chapter, however, is in the origin and growth of legal language.[3] And in that connection, it should not be assumed that the use of Latin terms in English and American law challenges the thesis that legal language is derived from folk language, in the sense of the general body of language of the community. Such an assumption rests on an entirely

[2] [See later, Berman, *Interaction*, 63; *Faith and Order*, 277.]
[3] [See later, Berman, *Interaction*, 23.]

artificial conception of folk language, based on the romantic nationalism of the nineteenth century. In medieval England, when modern English law was being formed, Latin was no "foreign" tongue; it was the language of worship, the language of scholarship, and the language of international relations, as well as the language of much of the law. Also it was one of the main sources of the language which the Norsemen had learned from the people of Normandy, whom they had conquered in the tenth century, and which they brought to their subjects in England in the eleventh. Thus Latin was an integral part of the folk language of the Christianized, Normanized English people. It is usually said that there was no "reception of Roman law" in England as there was on the continent of Europe; but whether or not that is correct, there certainly was a reception of Latin legal terminology in medieval England, and indeed that reception has continued over the centuries down to the present time. Witness, for example, the enormous influence of the Latin phrase *res ipsa loquitur* ("the thing speaks for itself") upon the development of English and American tort law in the twentieth century. Thus Latin remains a source of the development of our legal language even though it has almost died out in many other spheres of our social life.[4]

Etymology thus gives some clues to the origin and growth of legal language, revealing the cross-fertilization of linguistic traditions and also disclosing the ultimate source of legal concepts in concrete images. At some point, the Latin *transgressio*, or "stepping across," became "sin," and at some later point "sin" became "trespass" in the legal sense.[5] At first, the legal concept of trespass was very broad, encompassing violent wrongs inflicted upon the person, the land, or the goods of another. In time, the meanings changed. Today, by a strange reversion, the term "trespass" is usually confined – once again – to the tort of crossing of another's land.

How are we to interpret this development? Did some medieval Norman legal scholar poring over books ask himself, "What word can I find to encompass violent wrongs inflicted upon the person, the land, or the goods of another? Perhaps I should call it 'trespass'?" Occasionally, such deliberate, scholarly inventions of legal terms have occurred. A famous example is the invention of the concept of "right of privacy"

[4] [Berman's historical points are confirmed by Peter Tiersma, who continues the story until the present-day European Union. Tiersma suggests that English may soon function as a unifying legal language, given the problems encountered in the translation of authoritative legal texts by the European Union. See Tiersma, "History of the Languages of Law," 25.]

[5] [See later, Berman, *Faith and Order*, 197.]

by Louis D. Brandeis and Samuel Warren. In an article in the *Harvard Law Review* in 1911 they urged that such a right be recognized, and their proposal was subsequently adopted by many courts and legislatures. The term "privacy," of course, was not new, but it was given a new meaning when it was identified as a legal right not to be exposed to unwarranted publicity.

Usually, however, legal terms are not invented in the quiet of the library but originate in the excitement of live controversy. In this respect, the origin of legal language corresponds to the theory of Hermann Usener and Ernst Cassirer concerning the origins of names generally. Usener writes that the name of a thing is determined not by volition, or by invention of some arbitrary sound-complex, but that "the spiritual excitement caused by some object which presents itself in the outer world furnishes both the occasion and the means of its determination."[6] Thus poetry, according to Cassirer, was the first form of language. This conclusion was drawn largely from primitive languages, without reference to legal institutions. It is supported, however, by studies of the legal institutions of primitive societies. The ancient Irish law-givers were poets. The early law of Greece and Rome, as well as that of the Germanic and Slavic peoples of Europe, was characterized by a heavy emphasis on ritual acts and verbal formulae, often rhymed, with legal words having a highly metaphorical character.[7]

[The early European folklaw introduced trial by ritual oaths ... All the foreoaths, denials, final oaths, and supporting oaths had to be repeated flawlessly, "without slip or trip," if they were to succeed. All were cast in poetic form, with abundant use of alliteration. For example, an oath used in suits affirming title to land reads as follows: "So I hold it as he held it, who held it as saleable, and I will own it – and never resign it – neither plot nor ploughland – nor turf nor toft – nor furrow nor foot length – nor land nor leasow – nor fresh nor marsh – nor rough ground nor room – nor wold nor fold – land nor strand – wood nor water."[8] The expression of legal rules in poetic images helped to stamp them on the memory. Phrases like "unbidden and unbought, so I with my eyes saw and with my ears heard," "foulness or fraud," "house and home," "right and righteous," "from

---

[6] [Hermann Usener, *Götternamen: Versuch einer Lehre von der Religiösen Begriffsbildung* (Bonn: Verlag von Friedrich Cohen, 1896), 3.]
[7] [See later, Berman, *Faith and Order*, 48.]
[8] [Quoted in Francis Palgrave, *The Rise and Progress of the English Commonwealth* (London: John Murray, 1832), part 2, cxxxv.]

hence or thence" – were common. The law was contained in a multitude of proverbs. The earliest Irish law was in the form of poetry.][9]

The poetic quality of legal language in its origins is connected with the sacredness of legal words. As Malinowski stressed in writing of primitive society, the power of speech to bring about cooperation "must be correlated with the conviction that a spoken word is sacred," and this is especially true of law, where "the value of the word, the binding force of a formula, is at the very foundation of order and reliability in human relations."[10] Malinowski writes:

> Whether the marriage vows are treated as a sacrament or as a mere legal contract – and in most societies they have this twofold character – the power of words in establishing a permanent human relation, the sacredness of words and their socially sanctioned inviolability, are absolutely necessary to the existence of social order. If legal phrases, if promises and contracts were not regarded as something more than *flatus vocis*, social order would cease to exist in a complex civilization as well as in a primitive tribe. The average man, whether civilized or primitive, is not a sociologist. He neither needs to, nor can, arrive at the real function of a deep belief in the sanctity of legal and sacred words and their creative power. But he must have this belief; it is drilled into him by the process whereby he becomes part and parcel of the orderly institutions of his community. The stronger this belief, the greater becomes what might be called the elementary honesty and veracity of the citizens. In certain walks of human life speech may develop into the best instrument for the concealment of thought. But there are other aspects – law, contracts, the formulas of sacraments, oaths – in which a complicated apparatus inviolably based on mystical and religious ideas develops in every community as a necessary by-product of the working of legal and moral institutions and relationships.[11]

Even apart from primitive law, in more mature societies, including our own, we find the origin of legal words associated with political and legal contests of an impassioned character. It is no accident that the word "claim" is from the Latin *clamor*, a shout. When a person's rights have been violated, he is hurt, and he shouts, he cries out; the word "violated" itself

---

[9] [Original text breaks off. This text is inserted from Harold J. Berman, "The Background of the Western Legal Tradition in the Folklaw of the Peoples of Europe," *University of Chicago Law Review* 45 (1978): 553, 561–62, reproduced with revisions in Harold J. Berman, *Law and Revolution*, ch. 1.]

[10] [Bronisław Malinowski, *Coral Gardens and Their Magic: A Study of the Methods of Tilling the Soil and of Agricultural Rites in the Trobriand Islands*, vol. 2: *The Language of Magic and Gardening*, (London: George Allen & Unwin, 1935), 234, 235.]

[11] [Ibid., 234–35.]

suggests the use of force (*vis*) and an element of passion. It then becomes necessary to control the conflict through the drama of a trial; and at that point, in the ritual of controversy, the court identifies the rights of the parties, saying "property" (his own) or "contract" (drawn, dragged, together) or "trespass" (sin), or, to take more current issues in our courts, "conspiracy" or "freedom of speech," or "desegregation," or "one man, one vote." These are "fighting words." But when spoken with authority, in the liturgy of legal procedure, they can become pacifying words.

Especially in primitive societies, and in primitive situations in modern societies, that is, when passions run high, the law-speaking authority needs words which characterize the grievance (or the economic or social problem demanding solution) to the satisfaction of both sides and which at the same time command the respect of the community as a whole. Since law always depends for its vitality upon a high degree of acceptance by the community, and since it is always threatened by the possible outrage of those who suffer at its hands, it must seek to develop new legal words out of the general language of the community, a language that is understood and trusted.[12] The trusted language of the community gives law its power – for words that are not believed in lose their power – and at the same time limits the power of the law, restraining it from becoming capricious and arbitrary.

2

When the community language takes legal form, when it is forged in the fires of legal procedures, it inevitably acquires "technical" meanings, that is, meanings specifically related to the legal issues that arose and were resolved in the particular proceedings which gave rise to the words. Such technical meanings must be preserved and guarded against abuse if legal language is to retain its identity and not merge once again into the general folk tongue. Thus a corps of professionals is needed – "medicine men," high priests, or, in our society, lawyers.[13]

[12] [Milner Ball, building on Berman, expresses concern that civil rights litigation, which once was a place where legal language gave expression to concrete injustice, has since lost its creativity in capturing the seriousness of civil rights violations. He thus calls for new and creative ways to represent injustice in legal language. See Milner Ball, *The Word and the Law* (University of Chicago Press, 1995), 136–64.]

[13] [See Mellinkoff, *Language of the Law*, 453. The examples that follow in this section and the next are elaborated in Berman, *The Nature and Functions of Law* (Brooklyn: Foundation Press, 1958).]

Yet the authority to preserve is at the same time an authority to determine when not to preserve. The professionals who are entrusted with the sacred words also have the power to change their meaning. Indeed, the whole of legal history is the story of slow, subtle, and profound changes in the meaning of legal language. In the course of time, the "sin" of trespass became transformed to include a wholly innocent crossing of another's land under the mistaken impression of a privilege – called, indeed, a "technical" trespass. In the past 75 years we have seen the term "contract" expand its meaning to include not only, as before, an arms-length bargain between more or less equal trading partners but also the fine print on the back of an airplane or bus ticket, which the traveler has no time to read in advance and whose terms he could not alter anyway, if only because most of them are set by public agencies. Many similar examples could be given of striking transformations in the meanings of legal terms.

Are the lawyers free, then, to make legal words mean anything they want? In Lewis Carroll's famous passage, Humpty-Dumpty said, "it all depends on who is master." But Alice never got an answer to her next question, "How *can* a word mean so many different things?"[14] The process by which words acquire new meaning is clearer, perhaps, in law than in any other branch of language. For law, at least in our tradition, involves the *deliberate, gradual,* and *explicit* development of new meanings for old words.[15]

One of the best-known modern American examples of this process is the gradual expansion of the concept "inherently dangerous" products, whose manufacturer or distributor is subject to a wider liability for the harm that they cause than in the case of products which are not dangerous in normal use. In the mid-nineteenth century a poisonous drug was classified by the courts as such an inherently dangerous object, and later a 90-foot scaffold; still later various kinds of machines were added to the list; gradually it was recognized that anything may be inherently dangerous if negligently made, and the concept of "inherent danger" receded in importance in cases of negligence. But it later reasserted itself in cases where it was thought that the manufacturer should be liable even if he was not negligent, or if his negligence could not be proved. At all times judges, lawyers, and legal scholars were aware that the term "dangerous" was shifting in meaning as new cases arose to test it. Not only were they aware

---

[14] [See full quote in Chapter 1, at note 34.]
[15] [See later James Boyd White, *When Words Lose Their Meaning* (University of Chicago Press, 1984), 265.]

of the shifts in meaning, but they were called on to explain and justify them against opposition! Linguistic battles took place in the courtroom, in the classroom, and in the scholarly literature, concerning the limits to which such terms as "inherently dangerous," "imminently dangerous," "dangerous to life and limb," as well as other terms such as "negligence," "direct cause," and the like, could and should be extended.

The study of the explanations and justifications given for the changes in the meaning of legal terms by the persons charged with responsibility for declaring their meaning yields unique and significant insights into the process by which language develops. Unfortunately, few professional students of language have availed themselves of the opportunity to make such a study.

Legal scholars speak of four sources of law: (1) *custom*, that is, the norms and patterns of behavior of social groups, giving rise to a sense of obligation and to expectations, (2) *precedent*, that is, decisions of courts in previous analogous cases, (3) *equity*, that is, the sense of equality and fairness derived from the community's highest moral values, and (4) *legislation*, that is, rules of law laid down by legislatures or by other authoritative bodies charged with making legal policy in the form of rules.[16]

From a sociological standpoint, these four sources may be viewed also as four dimensions of law. *Custom* looks *outward* to community practices and community beliefs; it asks what are the standards and usages of people generally with respect to matters such as those now in dispute. *Precedent* is directed to the *past*; it looks to what was done previously. *Equity* looks *inward* to the judge's own conscience; it asks what morality, natural justice, mercy, and fairness dictate in the particular case. *Legislation* (including administrative rule-making) is directed to the *future*; it declares what shall be done from now on. Thus the two-time dimensions of past and future and the two space-dimensions of inner and outer comprise the full four-dimensional reality of legal thought and legal action.

If we apply these legal and sociological criteria to a linguistic analysis of the shift in meaning of legal terms, we see that a judge has four ways of approaching the legal terms that may be applicable to a given case. We may look to the policy implicit in the legal terms, asking what social consequences would flow from various interpretations; insofar as he is

---

[16] [See later, Berman, *Faith and Order*, 292. Berman later developed a course on "Customary Law" with his colleague, David J. Bederman, who distilled some of the learning of that course in a book dedicated to Berman's memory. See David J. Bederman, *Custom as a Source of Law* (Cambridge University Press, 2010).]

not bound by a legislative determination of this question, and is free to make new policy himself, he may indulge in what is sometimes called "judicial legislation." Yet the possibility of expanding or contracting the meaning of legal terms in the light of future consequences is inevitably balanced by the consideration of the meanings given to the terms in the past. Even apart from the English or American doctrine that gives binding force to previous decisions in analogous cases, the nature of language itself compels a judge to examine the historical record of the meaning of legal terms. Yet the problem of interpretation is not exhausted by the inquiry into future and past significance. In addition to "shall be" and "was," the judge must also deal with "is" and "ought": what meaning do the words have in the world around him, and in good conscience what meaning should they have?

Different legal systems, and different branches within a particular legal system, emphasize one or another of these four sources of law, or dimensions of law, or criteria of interpretation of legal language; hence legal discourse is not uniform as between different legal systems or even within a single system. In American law, for example, the legislation-based discourse of a traffic regulation ("Parked cars will be towed away") differs from the precedent-based discourse of a judicial decision ("This court has consistently held that the manufacturer is not liable to the retail purchasers unless he is shown to have been negligent"); and both of these differ from the custom-based discourse of a negotiable instrument ("Pay to the order of John Jones $1000"), or the equity-based discourse of a divorce decree ("The father may have the child visit him four times a year for a week at a time"). It is the possibility of moving back and forth from one type of legal discourse to another – the "is" of custom, the "was" of precedent, the "should" of equity, and the "shall" of legislation – that gives legal language its mobility and provides the criteria by which shifts in the meanings of legal terms may be judged.

3

The criteria for the development of new meanings of legal terms differ from the criteria for the development of new meanings of other kinds of terms principally in the degree of their explicitness. All linguistic change derives from some kind of balance (or imbalance) among the four poles of future and past, outer and inner; in law, however, these four poles are identified and defined. Similarly, the *technique* whereby shifts in meaning are effectuated is the same in all language, but in law that technique is more explicit and more conscious than in other types of language. The technique is that of analogy, that is, of exploring the similarities and differences of words, and, on the basis of similarities, modifying existing words or creating new ones in conformity with familiar word groups. Modification or creation of words by analogy enables us to incorporate new experience into our language. We can say: a 90-foot scaffold is like a poison, in that both are dangerous to life and limb; in time we can say that a defective soda bottle is also dangerous to life and limb. But then the word "dangerous" has shifted its meaning. *Everything* is dangerous if "defective," that is, if negligently made. We can say so with assurance because the word "negligence" means, in part, conduct which creates a danger. The reasoning, Bentham would say, is circular. But the words, interdependent though they be, have shed new light on the matter. They have captured a truth that was formerly obscure. The time was ripe for the obscurity to be removed, but it took a new insight into the meaning of old words to make its removal possible.

Analogy involves exploration of similarities and differences; it also involves transfer of meanings. Such transfer takes two principal forms: metaphor and metonymy.[17] In metaphor, the transfer is from one kind of object or idea to another, the two kinds being physically distinct from each other. We say: "The ship plows the sea" – conveying the image of a seagoing vessel in terms of the action of an agricultural implement. We say, "The defendant, by refusing to pay, broke his contract" – conveying the idea of a financial default in terms of a violent act, a breaking. The implication is that the defendant ought to repair the contract, either put it together again or pay its value.

Students of language have long observed that a very large part of our vocabulary is built on metaphor. The word "language" itself is derived from the Latin word for "tongue" (*lingua*). "Metaphor" is itself a metaphor, being derived from the Greek word for "to carry over" – as "transfer" is derived from the Latin word for "to carry over." As Greenough and Kittredge wrote in 1900: "Language is fossil poetry which is constantly being worked over for the uses of speech. Our commonest words are worn-out metaphors."[18] Law, as we have already indicated, is full of such "dead metaphors," or "faded metaphors," as they are often called. And law, in turn, has been a fertile source of metaphors for non-legal language.

[17] [See Schane, *Language and the Law*, 6.]
[18] [James B. Greenough and George L. Kittredge, *Words and Their Ways in English Speech* (London: Macmillan, 1905), 11.]

Greenough and Kittredge show how the medieval English word for judicial session, "assize," which was derived from the Latin word *assidere*, "to sit by," was used also to mean the judgment or decision of the judges, and then came to mean a determination, then an allotment, then an allotted portion, and then a dimension, which latter meaning it continues to have in the clipped form of "size." The size of a thing, then, is what it is judged to be. Other popular metaphors derived from law include "cheat" (a sixteenth-century slang adaptation of "escheat"), "hold no brief for," "make common cause with," "last resort," "take action," "vouch for," "vouchsafe to," "make a case for," "summing things up," "the verdict of history, or of public opinion," "plead ignorance," "plead poverty," "in rejoinder," "in rebuttal," "give color to," "put in issue," "join issue," "charge with," "indict as," "acquit," "a matter of record," "on record," "have no record of," "by the same token," "bear witness," "swear by," "testify," "take cognizance of," "be stopped from," "burden of proof," "benefit of the doubt," "go through an ordeal, go through fire and water for, sink or swim," "wage war, wage battle, take up the gauntlet, throw down the gauntlet," "law a wager." We shall have occasion to discuss later in this chapter the derivation of the term "fiction," as applied to literature, from the legal fiction (*fictio*) of Roman law and later of English law.

Still more striking is the carry-over from law into science of the basic concepts of scientific method: "cause" (from *causa*, a lawsuit or "case"), "thing" (from the Anglo-Saxon *thing*, or *ting*, meaning judicial assembly; similarly, the French *chose* comes from *causa*, and the German *Sache*, which still means both lawsuit and thing, while the related *Ursache* means cause in the scientific sense), "fact" (originally used procedurally to refer to "matters of fact" as distinct from "matters of law"), "evidence," "prove," "judgment," and, indeed, "law" itself. Owen Barfield has discovered in a passage of Francis Bacon the transition from the legal concept of "law" as an imperative rule of conduct to the scientific concept of "law" as an observed regularity of nature. As Barfield observes: "This is one of those pregnant metaphors which pass into the language, so that much of our present thinking is based on them."[19]

Barfield adds: "It is not by accident that such key words as *judgment* and *cause* have two distinct meanings; the practical task of fixing personal responsibility must surely have been the soil from which, as the centuries

---

[19] [Owen Barfield, "Poetic Diction and Legal Fiction," in *The Rediscovery of Meaning, and Other Essays* (Middletown, CT: Wesleyan University Press, 1977 [1964]), 62.]

passed, the abstract notion of cause and effect was laboriously raised."[20]
Indeed, out of "the practical task of fixing personal responsibility" arose
the generalizations of jurists concerning the circumstances under which
it is proper to impose responsibility, and the systematization of such generalizations – in short, legal science. "The first rule of law," wrote Rudolph
von Jhering, "whatever it may have concerned, was the first onset of the
mind to conscious generality of thought, the first occasion and the first
attempt to lift itself above the sensuously obvious."[21] Thus, as Lon Fuller
writes: "If we define science as the conscious generalization of experience,
then the law was the first of the sciences."[22] With the drastic revision of
concepts of science in the present generation, the metaphorical shift in the
meaning of the word "law" acquires added significance: natural science
itself is exploring the limits of the idea of causal regularities and returning to the idea of judgment, of resolution of alternative claims, and of the
relationship of scientific laws to the procedure in which they are evolved.

In contrast to metaphor, metonymy is the identification of an object in
terms of another object to which it is related spatially, that is, to which it
is physically contiguous. To speak of the highest executive authority of
the federal government as "the White House," or to refer to the emotions
as "the heart," are typical examples. Metonymy transfers to the sign the
meaning of the thing signified; it identifies the contents by the container
or the container by the contents, the whole by the part or the part by the
whole. In law, for example, we speak of "the bench" to refer to the judges;
we identify a certain kind of court order as a "writ"; we speak of the "pure
food laws," or the "rules of the road," or the "dramshop acts," in each
instance referring to a whole body of legal doctrine in terms of a physical
object to which it relates.

Indeed, the characteristic tendency of law to categorize and to classify
involves the abundant use of metonymy. We speak of "the plaintiff," "the
defendant," "plaintiff's counsel," "the trial court," "the court of appeals,"
"breach of contract," "real property," "personal property," and more,
reducing the complex realities of persons, actions, and things to those
particular parts of them that are legally relevant. We are not interested
in the color of John Doe's eyes or in the way he treats his wife; for present

---

[20] [Ibid., 63.]

[21] [Rudolph von Jhering, *Geist des römischen Rechts auf den verschiedenen Stufen seiner
Entwicklung*, 3 vols. (Leipzig: Breitkopf und Härtel, 1869), 2/2:407. Quoted and translated
by Lon L. Fuller in *Legal Fictions* (Stanford University Press, 1967), 132. Berman used an
earlier unpublished manuscript of this Fuller text.]

[22] [Fuller, *Legal Fictions*, 132.]

purposes we are only interested in the fact that he has presented a complaint and we call him, therefore, "the plaintiff." That is not his name; it is the category to which he is assigned. We are not interested in the beautiful landscape or the geological formations that make up the reality of Lot No. 539; we are only concerned with the fact that it is land (real property) and not chattels (personal property). We categorize by combining objects or ideas on the basis of one or more features which they have in common, recognizing that we have characterized each member of the class or category on the basis of only part of its being.

Roman Jakobson has shown that metaphor and metonymy reflect different approaches to life. They are so distinct from each other that victims of aphasia[23] generally can be divided according to whether they are deficient in the power to substitute meanings based on similarity (metaphor) or whether they are deficient in the power to substitute meanings based on contiguity (metonymy). Jakobson also suggests that as metaphor is linked with romanticism and with poetry, so metonymy is linked with realism and with prose. In normal speech, we use both metaphor and metonymy, though poets may be more addicted to the former and lawyers more to the latter. Yet law, too, is rich in metaphor. Metaphor gives law its capacity to select, substitute, interpret, and name. Metonymy gives law its capacity to combine, to "propositionize," to categorize.[24]

Legal language, then, like all languages, grows through the analogizing of one word or group of words to another, and more particularly, through the substitution of meanings on the basis of similarity or the combination of meanings on the basis of contiguity. This process of substitution and combination permits the meanings of legal terms to undergo expansion, but it also sets limits to such expansion.

Paul Freund has given an interesting example of the development of legal concepts on the basis of substitution of meanings of words. He points out that originally the ancient wrong of "eavesdropping" depended on a trespass beneath the eaves of a house to listen to conversation taking place inside. (This, incidentally, is a substitution of meanings partly, at least, on the basis of physical contiguity.) In time, similar offenses, like listening at the window of a house that had no eaves or prying from a distance, were called eavesdropping, and thus the word acquired a metaphorical meaning. Later, shadowing a person, or opening his mail, were

---

[23] [The loss of ability to understand or express speech, because of brain damage.]
[24] [Roman Jakobson, "Two Aspects of Language and Two Types of Aphasic Disturbances," in Jakobson and Halle, *Fundamentals of Language*, 53–82.]

said to be *like* eavesdropping, and thus the metaphor took the form of a simile. Ultimately, Brandeis and Warren, building on the concept of eavesdropping, characterized a variety of different types of unwarranted intervention into, and exposures of, the conversations and activities of others as violations of "the right of privacy," and this concept became widely accepted by American courts. Thus, as Freund points out, the law moved from metaphor to simile (a species of metaphor) and then to a new concept.

Yet we may look at the new concept also in terms of the word found for it, "privacy," which previously meant only "seclusion," "a state of being apart from others." Now it acquired a new legal meaning, derived historically, though not etymologically, from eavesdropping. Etymologically, "privacy" was derived from the Latin *privatus*, which meant apart from the state, and *privatus* in turn was derived from *privare*, to deprive, bereave. What was viewed initially as deprivation came to be seen as separation from the state and ultimately, in the United States, as a right to be let alone. But its etymology and its history are always there, and always available to give it limits.

Such changes in the meaning of words over time are, of course, the rule rather than the exception. What is distinctive about legal language, as I have stated before, is the deliberate, gradual, and explicit character of the changes. This, in turn, suggests both the element of choice: new meanings can be given – and the element of control: not any new meanings can be given but only those which are linguistically acceptable on the basis of analogy, including both metaphor and metonymy.

4

Legal language, as I have said, derives in part from folk language, including the language of political, economic, religious, and other activities. The meanings of legal terms, even the most technical, can never be entirely divorced from their popular connotations. Like any other true speech, the language of law is universal.

This is not the usual view of legal language. On the contrary, laymen have complained for centuries about the obscurity and excessive technicality of legal language. Jonathan Swift ascribed to lawyers "a peculiar cant and jargon of their own, that no other mortal can understand."[25]

---

[25] [Jonathan Swift, *Gulliver's Travels into Several Remote Regions of the World* (London: George Routledge & Sons, 1880), 300.]

The formalism of such legal documents as wills and deeds with their "whereases" and "notwithstandings" and "parties of the first part" and "parties of the second part" has dismayed many generations of testators and landowners. The intricacy of insurance policies, conditional sales contracts, warranties and disclaimers of warranties, and the like, often make them virtually unreadable by the customer. The words "will," "testator," "parties," "insurance," "warranties," and more may indeed be drawn from "real life," but when they are used by lawyers in the context of actual legal transactions they seem to acquire a complexity and prolixity that places them in a heavenly world of their own. "The subject of law," according to *Sheppard's Touchstone*, an eighteenth-century legal treatise (largely of the law of real property), "is somewhat transcendental and too high for ordinary capacities."[26]

To understand the relationship between the "technical" language of complex legal transactions and the popular speech from which it is derived we must consider, first, to whom the language is addressed.[27] So long as legal language is addressed to lawyers, the use of professional refinements does no harm. Every profession must develop its own special language for communication within the profession, partly as a means of "shorthand" expression, but also in order to maintain the identity and fraternity of the profession, in order to hold it together. Usually such special language simplifies intra-professional communication; what looks like complexity and obscurity from the outside ("a peculiar cant and jargon") is often a simplification and a clarification when seen from within. There is no harm in the verbosity of a corporate indenture, for example, which is intended to be read only by lawyers and bankers who are entirely familiar with the significance of every word. The 30 or 40 clauses in fine print in a bill of lading for the carriage of goods by sea only spell out in detail the allocation of risks between the carrier and the shipper, who well understand what it is all about. There is no good reason why the provisions of the law on corporate taxes, as contrasted with personal income taxes, should be written in a language understandable to the man in the street.

The complexity of legal language should not be confused with technicality in the pejorative sense of that word. A legal system that has no professional class of lawyers may have a very simple legal language, which may nevertheless be very "technical" in its operation. In

---

[26] [William Sheppard, *Sheppard's Touchstone of Common Assurances*, 7th edn., ed. Edward Hilliard and Richard Preston (London: J. & W.T. Clarke, 1820), xxiii.]

[27] [See Mellinkoff, *Language of the Law*, 289.]

Germanic and Anglo-Saxon law prior to the twelfth century, law was simple, colorful, and popular. The mode of proof consisted in the giving of an oath by oath-helpers, each of whom had to repeat it "without slip or trip" if the defendant was to be exonerated, or else in ordeals of fire and water, whereby the defendant was found guilty if the burns did not heal within a certain time or if he did not sink far enough below the surface of the water. This was all very simple, but also very "technical."[28]

With the development of a professional legal class, the language of law inevitably acquires a professional character. The danger in this is that professionalism tends to usurp even those parts of legal language addressed to laymen. In the early days of collective bargaining in the United States, lawyers often aroused great resentment among labor union officials by drafting collective bargaining agreements in terms more appropriate to commercial instruments. Such agreements had to be understandable to people not trained in law, and the labor lawyers had to mend their ways or else withdraw.

If law is to command the respect of the community, professional legal language should be addressed by professionals to professionals, or else should either be understandable to non-professional laymen, or else be translated.[29] The technicalities of a check, for example, are probably in the main sufficiently understandable to those millions of Americans who use checks. The concept of negotiation by endorsement, and the consequences of a negligent filling up of the check and of forged endorsements, though not grasped in detail, are probably sufficiently comprehended by laymen so as not to cause difficulty. On the other hand, the technicalities of a jury trial, of the burden of proof in civil and criminal cases, of the rules of exclusion of immaterial or prejudicial evidence, and the like, are poorly understood by laymen. The cure for this may lie partly in simplification of trial procedure,[30] but it must lie chiefly in better education of the public through the schools and colleges as well as through the press, television, and radio. The technicalities of wills, deeds, insurance policies, and conditional sales contracts, to the extent that such technicalities

---

[28] [See later, Berman, *Law and Revolution*, ch. 1.]

[29] [For contemporary criticism of the use of technical legal language in public, lay settings, as well as concrete proposals for change, see Mark Adler, "The Plain Language Movement," in Tiersma and Solan, eds., *Oxford Handbook*, 71–82, and Nancy S. Marder, "Instructing the Jury," in ibid., 439–45.]

[30] [See later, Tiersma, *Legal Language*, 231.]

are necessary, need to be translated for clients and customers by lawyers, insurance agents, bankers, and other professionals.[31]

The language of statutes, on the other hand, should be directly understandable – without the need for an interpreter – by the people directly affected by them. The French Civil Code, or the Soviet Criminal Code, is drafted in terms which an educated layman can understand. It is not uncommon for educated Frenchmen and Russians – not lawyers – to have copies of these codes in their libraries, and to read them. A young middle-class Frenchman contemplating marriage is apt to ask the permission of the prospective bride's father, who in turn may take a copy of the French Civil Code from his shelves and go over with the young man the provisions on marital responsibilities, dowry, and the like. Indeed, the French Civil Code is considered to be a linguistic masterpiece which has contributed to the clarity of French literary style.

In contrast, many of our American codifications lack internal unity of concepts and our statutes are often drafted in a manner hardly comprehensible even to experts. The United States Internal Revenue Code, though admittedly complex and technical by necessity, is so difficult for millions of middle-income individual American taxpayers who wish to itemize their deductions as to drive them almost to distraction. Such language is a threat to the authority of the legal system. For, if the roots of law in the whole body of living language of the community are neglected, the power of law to hold it together is weakened.

To say that legal language addressed to lawyers may be professional language, but legal language addressed to laymen should be translated into lay language, does not, however, solve the most difficult problem; for legal language addressed to lawyers is often meant to be overheard, so to speak, by laymen, and some of it cannot be translated without loss of meaning, or at least of effect. If the origins, the shifts in meaning, and the range of application of professional legal words are explained in "common sense" terms, an illusion of understanding may be created which may be more dangerous than recognized unintelligibility.

For example, the layman is entitled to know, indeed, for the health of the legal system and of the society he should know, in a general way, what negligence means, what contributory fault means, what strict liability means, and what the functions of judge and jury are in a civil case. These are matters which affect his daily life, including his conduct on the highway, the cost of his automobile liability insurance, and his views of proposed

---

[31] [Ibid., 211.]

reforms to introduce strict liability for automobile injuries. Yet no matter how much explanation is given, no matter how many of the interrelated legal terms are translated ("last clear chance," "objective standard," "subjective standard," "ultrahazardous activities," "trier of fact," "trier of law," "directed verdict," "judgment notwithstanding the verdict," and the like), a certain unintelligibility will inevitably remain, unless the layman himself learns to "speak law," that is, unless he becomes, in effect, a professional. But at that point he, too, will want to retain many of the old terms, the professional terms, for once all their ambiguities and ramifications are recognized, they often clarify and simplify rather than obscure or complicate, and, above all, they are the terms that are used in the law; they are the terms that are authoritative.

The lawyer generally likes to translate, if he can get the layman's ear. Indeed, much of his professional work itself requires such translation – to clients, to juries, to legislative committees, and even to judges in oral argument. A good lawyer may argue his case to a judge as though he were explaining it to his wife or sweetheart.[32] But the translation of professional legal language back into the popular speech from which it ultimately derives is not a substitute for the professional language itself. We can unfreeze the legal terms, but we cannot replace them. The pragmatist's view that the particular words do not matter so long as you get the same practical consequences neglects the stubborn fact that you never do get the same practical consequences when you use different words. It also neglects the fact that the legal terms are the language of legal proceedings – legislative enactments, judicial decisions, and other professional activities. Law is not like sociology or philosophy, where the scholar can make up new vocabularies. We can interpret legal language and we can explain it, but to attempt to discard it or to replace it is to challenge the authority of those processes which create it.

Thus the professional as well as the popular sources of legal words help to determine their meaning. Over long periods of time, we may give them new meanings, but we cannot give them any new meanings we choose or any new meanings that suit our immediate interests. The old words are trusted; therefore we can only give them those new meanings which are proper, only those new meanings which the language of the community and the language of the legal profession itself permit. If the old words cease to be trusted, if they cease to have authority, then law loses

[32] [Ibid., 5.]

its communifying power, its acceptability to the losing side, and merges entirely with force.[33] Then the time is ripe for revolution.

5

We have spoken of the origin of legal terms in the general language of the community; their acquisition of technical meanings in the ritual of legal controversy; criteria by which shifts in the meaning of legal terms are explained and justified; linguistic techniques whereby such shifts are accomplished; and problems of interpreting technical legal language to the community as a whole.[34] We turn now once again to a matter discussed briefly in the previous chapter – legal fictions – since an understanding of the nature of legal fictions is essential to an understanding not only of the nature of legal language but also of its processes of growth.[35]

Legal fictions are a special instance of the capacity of all language to grow by substitution of meanings through metaphor and metonymy. What is special about the legal fiction is its professional legal character. A legal fiction involves the use of a term in a purely technical sense, that is, with a meaning which seems at first to conflict with that which the term normally has in other contexts. It is the kind of legal language that should be spoken by professionals to professionals, and where it must be overheard by laymen it should either be translated or else its fictitious character explained. On the other hand, the function of legal fictions in the growth of law should be a matter of interest not only to laymen generally but also, and especially, to students of language.

Some writers have used the term "legal fiction" to designate all metaphorical legal language. Such a broad definition is self-defeating, for it leads to the conclusion that there is nothing else in law but fiction. It may seem fictitious to speak of "breaking" a contract; but as we have seen, the term "contract" – meaning "drawing together" – is itself no less an artifice. Indeed, the "as if" school of semantics reduces not only all law but also all language to fiction, with the consequent absurdity that the phrase "as if" itself becomes suppositious. To point out that some legal terms are fictions is useful only if it is presupposed that other legal terms are not

---

[33] [See later, Harold J. Berman, "The Language of Law: Can Communication Build One World?" *Harvard Medical Alumni Bulletin* 39(2) (Christmas 1964): 29.]

[34] [See later, Heikki E. S. Mattila, "Legal Vocabulary," in Tiersma and Solan, *Oxford Handbook,* 33.]

[35] [See later, Schane, *Language and the Law,* 7.]

fictions. The distinction is between something that is true and something that is "made up."

Yet a legal fiction is not a lie; it is not intended to deceive. To that extent, at least, the term "fiction" is very apt, for it applies equally well to literature and law. In writing *The Brothers Karamazov*, Dostoevsky did not intend to make his readers believe that at a certain time and place a man named Smerdyakov killed his natural father Fyodor Karamazov. The reader is asked, rather, to *imagine* that this happened. We call such novels or stories "fiction" to indicate that they are not meant to be taken as historically true. Similarly a legal fiction is a legal proposition that is not meant to be taken as true.

The term "fiction" derives from the Roman law of procedure, under which certain untrue pleadings could not be challenged. A famous Roman *fictio* was the civil action brought by a foreigner. The older rule had been that only a Roman citizen could bring an action under the Roman civil law. Indeed in Latin, "civil" law literally meant "citizens'" law. Foreigners were governed by the *ius gentium*, the law of (foreign) peoples of the clans or "nations." In time, however, the foreigner was permitted to bring a "civil" action, but only by alleging that he was (or might have been) a citizen, an allegation which the defendant was forbidden to deny. Thus the wording of the rule – that only a citizen could bring a civil (citizen's) action – was maintained, although the meaning of the words was substantially altered.

Another famous fiction from ancient times is that of adoption. In ancient Rome, as in some contemporary primitive societies, adoption was effectuated by a ceremonious simulation of childbirth; that is, the adoptive mother pretended to be in labor and to give birth to the adopted child, who was brought out from her skirts. This ritual enabled family ties to be created despite the absence of blood relationship, while preserving the form of the older tribal rule to the contrary. In the words of Sir Henry Maine, without the fiction of adoption "it is difficult to understand how society would ever have escaped from its swaddling clothes and taken its first steps toward civilization."[36] Although we say that the adoptive mother "pretended" to give birth to the adopted child, it is obvious that the pretense was not intended to conceal the fact that the child was not the biological offspring of the mother. The simulation of childbirth did, however, pay respect to the older rule that only blood relationship could create family ties. The change in the meaning of that rule was clothed in

[36] [Henry Sumner Maine, *Ancient Law*, 10th edn. (London: John Murray, 1906), 31.]

a ritual designed to reconcile the new with the old and to give to the new the authority of the old.

Where continuity in legal development is highly prized, as in the English common law, legal fictions tend to be favored. Instead of openly making new rules, English courts have often adapted old rules to new uses by accepting allegations of fact that are clearly untrue. Thus where the old rule required delivery, and such a requirement no longer made sense, the court spoke of "constructive delivery." Something which was *not* delivery was "deemed to be" delivery. Similarly, the courts have developed doctrines of "constructive notice," "constructive intent," and the like to avoid the consequences of older rules requiring notice or intent without rejecting those rules. In addition, courts have resorted to "conclusive presumptions," which have the effect of excluding from consideration matters that were once required to be proved, or that might be required to be proved by a literal interpretation of existing doctrine. Thus, according to existing doctrine, a gift must be accepted in order to take effect, but it is "conclusively presumed" that property delivered by a donor out of the donee's presence is accepted by the donee. Thus no proof of his acceptance is required, and no evidence of his non-acceptance will be considered.

One of the most notorious fictions of English law was the adaptation of the action of trover to enable it to be used to try the question of title to goods. The action had developed in the late Middle Ages as a means of recovering goods from one who had found them and refused to return them to their owner. In the seventeenth century, the mere allegation of a finding came to be treated as irrebuttable. The defendant might in fact have taken the goods by force; or he might have honestly believed that they were his as a matter of right. Nevertheless, it was sufficient for the plaintiff to allege that the defendant had found the goods in order to raise the question of which of the two owned them. A similar development took place with respect to the action of ejectment. In order to escape from the rigidities of procedural distinctions rooted in the feudal system of medieval English law, without appearing to reject the authority of the older law, English courts ingeniously devised new forms and new concepts framed in the older language.

It is sometimes assumed that legal fictions no longer have a positive role to play in the development of modern law, that they are a thing of the past. Yet as Lon Fuller wrote in 1931, "the age of the legal fiction is not over."[37] He pointed to two important fictions of contemporary law: the fiction

[37] [See Fuller, *Legal Fictions*, 94.]

that a child who enters without permission upon land and is injured – for example, is electrocuted by an exposed wire – is not a trespasser but an invitee, who has been "attracted" by the dangerous condition of the premises, with the consequence that the landowner is liable to the child as he would be to one of his guests. Similarly, the fiction that an out-of-state driver of an automobile "shall be deemed" to appoint the state registrar of motor vehicles as his agent to accept service of a complaint, thus enabling a resident of the state to initiate a civil action against him within the state. Many other such contemporary fictions could be mentioned, both judicial and statutory in origin.

We have suggested that a major function of legal fictions is to give to new law the authority of the older law. This means more than many writers have assumed. It means more than merely paying lip-service to the old while in fact rejecting it. It may be true, as English jurist and historian, Sir Henry Sumner Maine, and others have stressed, that a legal fiction "conceals" the fact that a rule of law has undergone alteration. But that is not the main point. What the fiction accomplishes is to attach the authority of the older words to the altered rule. This was put brilliantly by the great German jurist Friedrich Carl von Savigny, who wrote:

> If a new [legal] form is framed, it is immediately bound up with an old established one, and thus participates in the maturity and fixedness of the latter. This is the meaning of a fiction of the highest importance with regard to the development of Roman law, and often laughably mistaken by the moderns.[38]

It is not enough to say that fictions are a useful way of obscuring the fact that the law is changing, and thus of making change palatable to those who would oppose it if it were openly proclaimed. Nor is it enough to attribute fictions to our inability to grasp the full implications of new situations: a "first step toward the mastery of a new thought" (as Jhering put it) or a means of making "a new situation 'thinkable' by converting it into familiar terms" (as Fuller put it). These justifications of fictions do not exhaust their true nature. Fictions are much more than a convenient necessity when a reform of law cannot be stated in non-fictitious terms. They have, in addition, as Savigny stated, the positive virtue in many instances, of procuring for the reform "the certainty and development of old."[39]

---

[38] [Friedrich Charles (Carl) von Savigny, *Of the Vocation of Our Age for Legislation and Jurisprudence*, 2nd edn., trans. Abraham Hayward (London: Littlewood, 1831), 49; this is the standard English translation and is used herein.]

[39] [Ibid.]

We may better appreciate what fictions may accomplish if we compare them with their nearest relative, the so-called "exception to the rule." Any legal fiction can be restated as an exception to the rule, just as it can be restated as a change in the rule. Given, for example, a rule that only persons can sue and be sued, we can change the rule by saying (1) that a corporation is a (fictitious) person, or (2) that the power of corporations to sue and be sued is an exception to the rule, or (3) that the rule is changed to say that not only persons but also corporations can sue and be sued. None of these propositions is inherently more odious or less odious than the others. Each has its virtues and its vices. Both the fiction and the exception pay respect to the older rule. However, the exception does more violence to the rule than the fiction. The exception raises more sharply the question whether there may not be other situations which also call for exceptional treatment. The justification and the limits of the exception require definition. The third alternative, a reformulation of the rule, goes still farther in opening up new possibilities. May corporations sue and be sued because they are associations of persons? May all types of associations sue and be sued? Should different rules be adopted with respect to the procedural powers and liabilities of corporations from those which are applied to the procedural powers and liabilities of persons? Such questions are avoided when the certainty and development of the rules concerning natural persons are joined to artificial persons – by calling them both persons. Indeed, when the term "legal person" was first used in Roman law, the Latin word for "person" (*persona*) did not refer to natural persons as such but to the facial masks worn on the stage by actors representing the gods.

Over a century ago, Maine advanced the brilliant hypothesis that where social necessities and social opinion are in advance of law, there are three instrumentalities "by which law may be brought into harmony with society … Legal Fictions, Equity, and Legislation." "Their historical order," he wrote, "is that in which I have placed them. Sometimes two of them will be seen operating together, and there are legal systems which have escaped the influence of one or other of them. But I know of no instances in which the order of their appearance has been changed or in inverted."[40]

"It is not difficult to understand why fictions in all their forms are particularly congenial to the infancy of society," Maine wrote. "They satisfy the desire for improvement, which is not quite wanting, at the same time that they do not offend the superstitious disrelish for change which is

---

[40] [Maine, *Ancient Law*, 29.]

always present. At a particular stage of social progress they are invaluable expedients for overcoming the rigidity of law."[41] Equity and legislation come later, Maine insisted. By equity, Maine meant:

> [T]hat body of rules existing by the side of the original civil law, founded on distinct principles and claiming incidentally to supersede the civil law in virtue of a superior sanctity inherent in those principles. The Equity whether of the Roman Praetors or of the English Chancellors, differs from the Fictions which in each case preceded it, in that the interference with law is open and avowed. On the other hand, it differs from Legislation, the agent of legal improvement which comes after it, in that its claim to authority is grounded not on the prerogative of any external person or body, not even on that of the magistrate who enunciates it, but on the special nature of its principles, to which it is alleged that all law ought to conform. The very conception of a set of principles, invested with a higher sacredness than those of the original law and demanding application independently of the consent of any external body, belongs to a much more advanced stage of thought than that to which legal fictions originally suggested themselves.
>
> Legislation, the enactments of a legislature which, whether it takes the form of an autocratic prince or of a parliamentary assembly, is the assumed organ of the entire society, is the last of the ameliorating instrumentalities. It differs from Legal Fictions just as Equity differs from them, and it is also distinguished from Equity, as deriving its authority from an external body or person. Its obligatory force is independent of its principles. The legislature, whatever be the actual restraints imposed on it by public opinion, is in theory empowered to impose what obligations it pleases on the members of the community. There is nothing to prevent its legislating in the wantonness of caprice. Legislation may be dictated by equity, if that last word be used to indicate some standard of right and wrong to which its enactments happen to be adjusted; but then these enactments are indebted for their binding force to the authority of the legislature, and not to that of the principles on which the legislature acted; and thus they differ from rules of Equity, in the technical sense of the word, which pretend to a paramount sacredness entitling them at once to the recognition of the courts even without the concurrence of prince or parliamentary assembly. It is the more necessary to note these differences because a student of Bentham would be apt to confound Fictions, Equity, and Statute law under the single head of legislation. They all, he would say, involve *law-making*; they differ only in respect of the machinery by which the new law is produced. That is perfectly true, and we must never forget it; but it furnishes no reason why we should deprive ourselves of so convenient a term as Legislation in the special sense. Legislation and Equity are disjoined in the popular mind and in the minds of most lawyers; and

[41] [Ibid., 31.]

it will never do to neglect the distinction between them, however conventional, when important practical consequences follow from it.

We have reproduced at some length this famous passage from Maine not for its historical accuracy, which in some respects is doubtful, but because it sheds much light on the process by which the language of law develops in the past and today. Wherever necessary social change is impeded by the rigidity of existing law, and pressure is generated for legal reform, three alternatives are presented: (1) to redefine the existing law, giving the old words meanings that they did not formerly have (fiction), (2) to apply the moral principles and ideals which underlie the existing law and to which the existing law should be made to conform (equity), or (3) to overthrow the existing law and introduce a new law (legislation).

We have already discussed equity and legislation as two sources and dimensions of law, and two types of legal utterance, placing them in juxtaposition with precedent and custom. Precedent, as Maine himself perceived, is closely related to fiction; it presupposes that the old rule has not changed when it is applied to a new case. Maine's insight that fiction (precedent) precedes equity, and equity precedes legislation, permits us to add a historical dimension to our previous discussion. According to Maine, equity, "a set of principles, invested with a higher sacredness than those of the original law and demanding application independently of the consent of any external body," follows fiction because those higher principles "belong[] to a much more advanced stage of thought than that to which legal fictions originally suggested themselves."[42] Legislation, enacted by "the assumed organ of the entire society, is the last of the ameliorating instrumentalities ... distinguished from Equity, as deriving its authority from an external body or person. Its obligatory force is independent of its principles."[43] The balancing of precedent, equity, and legislation tends to proceed in a historical sequence. The pressure of change upon custom – the "is" – is met initially by the attempt to find a solution in terms of precedent, what "was." The custom is restated to respond to the pressure of change without conceding that the older rule has been abandoned. At a later stage, a second response is to apply a subsidiary law of equity, what "ought to be," envisioned as available in exceptional cases when the ordinary legal remedies are inadequate. Here custom and precedent – what "is" and "was" – are bypassed by what "ought to be." When the time is ripe to embark upon a wholly new course, a third

[42] [Ibid., 33.]   [43] Ibid.

kind of response – legislation – may discard the old rule and restate what henceforth "shall be."

Maine's optimism concerning the time in which he lived, coupled with his interest in large-scale legal development viewed over centuries, led him to neglect the fact that the sequence which he discovered is applicable not only historically but also today. Not only "ancient" law but also newly developing law within a "mature" legal system tends to grow through fictions, equity, and legislation – in that sequence. Nor is this accidental, since the human mind, and indeed language itself, proceeds in the same way. We start with the old words, the words we have been taught, the speech that has made us what we are. This is the sacred language. These are the names that create the times and spaces in which we live. When our ideas are challenged by new events, we can only respond at first by investing the new in the language of the old.[44] The familiar names take on new meaning. But later something more may be needed, and may become possible: a bigger, more general name, drawn from outside the existing legal rules. The allegation that the foreigner is, or might be, a citizen, or that the adopted child is "really" the offspring of the adoptive parent, or that the landowner "attracted" the child onto his land by building an electrified wire fence around it, all these fictions fails to satisfy. "Really" it is not so; "really" these are exceptional instances. Equity, fairness, mercy, require that the usual rule be waived. But how to explain the exception? Ultimately, the time may come when a new name is suggested – or shouted. It is not blood relationship but the sacrament of marriage that creates the family. The outsider claims that he has been "naturalized." Landowners are charged with liability to any innocent person injured by defective conditions on their premises, because they can insure against such liability and thus spread the risk among many at low cost. The exception, we now say, has swallowed up the rule, and a new rule is ready to be formulated. New names emerge out of the dialectic of "was," "ought," and "shall be."[45]

---

[44] [See later, White, *When Words Lose Their Meaning*, xii, 4.]

[45] [The text breaks off at this point. Berman repeated this language in later writings, but without any further elaboration. See, e.g., Harold J. Berman, William R. Greiner, and Samir N. Saliba, *The Nature and Functions of Law*, 6th edn. (New York: Foundation Press, 2004), 472–75. Berman will return to Maine in Chapter 4 herein. He also later approved and used my adaptation of Maine's historiography, in John Witte, Jr., *From Sacrament to Contract: Marriage, Religion, and Law in the Western Tradition*, 2nd edn. (Louisville, KY: Westminster John Knox Press, 2012 [1997]). See Berman, *Law and Revolution II*, 184–85, 448. He also would have liked David Bederman's treatment of Maine in *Custom as a Source of Law*, 6, 14, 118.]

4

The development of national legal languages

1

Thus far we have considered language and law in their universal aspects. Men of all races and creeds and classes, men of all times and places, have the power to listen and to speak – a power which, as we have seen, enables them not only to receive and send signals, as the lower animals do, but also to represent their social interrelations symbolically and thereby consciously to create bonds of community. Moreover, men of all races and creeds and classes, men of all times and places, have the power consciously to create, by speech, forms of order and of justice, especially through the hearing of conflicting claims and defenses and the resolution of such conflicts by considered judgment. I have tried to show that the human capacity to hear and to give judgment is the foundation of law, a capacity which, when it is sufficiently developed, finds expression in institutional processes of adjudication, legislation, administration, negotiation, and other forms of legal activity. As language is a universal symbol of community, so law is a kind of language, a universal symbol of two fundamental aspects of community, namely, order and justice.

This, admittedly, is a very long-range view of our common humanity. When we look more closely, we see that mankind speaks many different languages and uses many different kinds of law, each language bearing the stamp of a particular community and each kind of law, each legal system, bearing the stamp of a particular social order and a particular kind of justice. It is important that we recognize that as all language is one, so all law is one. But it is equally important that we recognize the unique qualities of different languages and of different kinds of law, for it is characteristic of our common humanity that it not only permits but also requires a wide range of diversity among the different communities which comprise it. It is the law of a particular community, and not some ideal or transcendental law, which binds the members of that community. This is not merely a reflex of political power, for the law of each community, like its language, is intimately related to the unique history of that community, its unique experiences in the forming of bonds of social cohesion among its members.

Thus when we turn from the universal aspects of language and law to a consideration of particular languages and particular legal systems, we turn inevitably from the study of human nature to the study of history, that is, to the study of the realization of human nature in social experience. The philosopher asks timeless questions: "What is man? What is justice?" But these questions are unanswerable until we have made them timely and specific. Not "What is the nature of man?" but "Who am I, my God? What is my nature?" asked St. Augustine.[1] Similarly, the social scientist must ask: "Who are we? How have we come into being? What experiences have formed our character? In what direction are we heading?" For the "nature" of "man" in "society" is only to be found in the living deposits of remembered social experience, such as language and law. These exist everywhere not in abstraction but in the history of the communities in which men live. It is in this sense that José Ortega y Gasset was right in saying that "Man, in a word, has no nature; what he has is ... history."[2]

---

[1] [See Augustine, *Confessions*, bk. X, ch. 17, trans. Rex Warner (New York: New American Library, 1963), 227: "What am I then, my God? What is my nature? A life various, manifold, and quite immeasurable. Imagine the plains, caverns, and abysses of my memory ... Through all it I range; I fly here and I fly there, I dive down deep as I can, and I can find no end." Augustine's reflections on memory and human identity would later become an important source for Berman's integrative theory of jurisprudence and theology. See Berman, "Toward an Integrative Jurisprudence," 779–801; "World Law," *KOERS: Bulletin for Christian Scholarship* 64(2&3) (1999): 379–84; "The Holy Spirit"; "The Historical Foundations of Law," *Emory Law Journal* 54 (2005): 13–24. In his 1994 article, "Law and Logos," 149, Berman writes: "At least from the time of St. Augustine, Christian theologians have ascribed to the soul of every person the separate but interlocking qualities of the three forms of the tri-une God. For Augustine, these were, respectively, *being* (*esse*, which he also identified with memory, or the experience of time), *knowledge* (*nolle*, which he also identified with reason and understanding), and *will* (*velle*, which he also identified with desire and with love." Berman then argued that this "trinitarian" theory of human nature maps onto a "trinitarian Christian Jurisprudence, that integrates Historical Jurisprudence (based on being and time), Legal Positivism (based on will and desire), and Natural Law Theory (based on reason and understanding)." See further Berman, "Epilogue: An Ecumenical Christian Jurisprudence," 752–62 and "Faith and Law in a Multicultural World," *Journal of Law and Religion* 18 (2003): 297–305, where he combines this trinitarian anthropology and jurisprudence with his late-life interest in the development of "world law."]

[2] [José Ortega y Gasset, "History as a System," in *Toward a Philosophy of History*, trans. William C. Atkinson (New York: W. W. Norton, 1941), 217. This paragraph and the preceding paragraph are repeated nearly verbatim later in Berman, *Interaction*, 50–51.]

A linguistic approach to law is therefore linked inextricably to a historical approach. Law as a spoken tongue means what it has *come* to mean in particular times and places; "usage" is what determines its meaning, just as it determines the meaning of all language; and usage is the record, the memory, of its development.

Here we leave behind, for a moment at least, the common features of all legal systems. We leave behind also the various "types" of law into which scholars have classified legal systems – "primitive law," "democratic law," "Communist law," "Oriental law," the "civil law system of Continental Europe," and the "common law system of the English-speaking world." Common features of legal systems, and even parallel legal terms and concepts, do not comprise a legal history. Even English and American law, despite their use of identical words and despite a historical relationship between them of parent and offspring, are characterized by striking differences which often lurk below the surface of the similarities themselves. Thus the term "crime" is defined similarly in English and American legal dictionaries, but what constitutes a crime is different in the two countries, the procedure for investigating and trying crimes is different, the punishments for crime are different, and the attitudes of society toward crime are different. Likewise, the legal systems of all the countries of the West have come under the strong influence of Roman law, of Greek philosophy, and of Judaic and Christian ethics. Yet the law in action is very different not only as between England and France but also as between France and Germany and Italy and Hungary, and more. A trial in a German court is by no means the same as a trial in a French court or in an Austrian court. In some ways, in fact, there is more difference between German law and French law than between German law and American law. For each of these countries speaks its own language, and each has its own history. And it is out of the distinctive language and the distinctive history of a people that law emerges and develops, and not only out of the universal capacity of all men to have a language and a history.[3]

---

[3] [Berman's purpose in the chapter is mainly expository. Hanneke van Schooten's "Law as Fact, Law as Fiction," provides a concrete example of historical jurisprudence in action, through "institutional legal theory." Schooten shows how Dutch courts relied on unwritten social practices to fill out the meaning of legislative provisions. The Dutch legislators responsible for the provisions had different social practices in mind, but the court relied on both legislators and customary ideas of legality to interpret the statute in question. See Hanneke van Schooten, "Law as Fact, Law as Fiction: A Tripartite Model of Legal Communication," in Wagner, *et al.*, *Interpretation, Law and the Construction of Meaning*, 3–4, 9–20.]

2

In taking a historical approach to law, we follow in the footsteps of two great nineteenth-century jurists, Friedrich Carl von Savigny (1779–1861) and Sir Henry Sumner Maine (1822–1888), whose names are still famous but whose insights are largely ignored or rejected in current English and American legal thought. Before proceeding further with our own exposition of how a legal language develops out of a people's history, and how its validity may be tested in terms of that history, let us briefly retrace the path which Savigny and Maine charted.[4]

Savigny's "historical jurisprudence," as it came to be called, was developed in response to a practical problem, namely, the pressure for introducing into the German states, at the end of the Napoleonic wars, a civil code modeled after the French Civil Code of 1803. Savigny, who was the leading German legal scholar of his time, and whose voluminous writings on Roman law (as received in the German states) remain authoritative to this day, published a short book in 1814, *Of the Vocation of Our Age for Legislation and Jurisprudence*. Second and third editions appeared in 1828 and 1840. There Savigny argued that all existing civil codes, not only the Napoleonic but also the Austrian and the Prussian, were entirely inadequate for German. He argued, further, that the time in Germany was not ripe for codification of the civil law. The booklet was written in the nature of a polemic against legal codes – their gaps, their inconsistencies and ambiguities, their errors. At the beginning, however, in a few pages, Savigny laid down certain propositions about law in general which founded a school of legal thought called the "Historical School of Jurisprudence."

---

[4] [Friedrich Carl von Savigny, Sir Henry Maine, and Edmund Burke were important touchstones for Berman's jurisprudence throughout his life. This book, however, contains Berman's fullest treatment of their work. Few other jurists in recent American scholarship have treated Savigny in the same depth as this work. See Berman's other efforts in *The Nature and Functions of Law*, 13, 23, 390–91; Harold J. Berman and William R. Greiner, *The Nature and Functions of Law*, 2nd edn. (Brooklyn: Foundation Press, 1966), 21, 461, 462–63; Berman, *Law and Revolution*, 79–80, 538–59; *Law and Revolution II*, 280, 381. For other treatments of Savigny in Anglo-American scholarship, on which Berman in part drew, see, e.g., Hermann Kantorowicz, "Savigny and the Historical School of Law," *Law Quarterly Review* 53 (July 1937): 326–43; Peter Stein, *Legal Evolution: The Story of an Idea* (Cambridge University Press, 1980); Stefan Riesenfeld, "The Influence of German Legal Theory on American Law: The Heritage of Savigny and His Disciples," *American Journal of Comparative Law* 37 (Winter 1989): 1–7; Richard A. Posner, "Savigny, Holmes, and the Law and Economics of Possession," *Virginia Law Review* 86 (2000): 542–43.]

The movement for codification, Savigny said, was inspired in the first instance by the desire to "insure a mechanically precise administration of justice; insomuch as the judge, freed from the exercise of private opinion, should be confined to the mere literal application: at the same time they were to be divested of all historical associations, and, in pure abstraction, to be equally adapted to all nations and all times."[5] Secondly, Savigny stated, the movement for codification, was "connected with a general theory of the origin of all positive law, which was always prevalent with the great majority of German jurists. According to this theory, all law, in its concrete form, is founded upon the express enactments of the supreme power."[6] Since, according to this view, legislation is the exclusive source of law under normal conditions, and custom is at best a secondary source, to be resorted to only in case of sad necessity, a comprehensive code was thought to be urgently needed both in order to correct the inadequacies of existing legislation and to act as a brake upon haphazard legislative changes in the future.[7]

Savigny recognized that the two concepts which lay at the roots of the codification movement – the concept of an ideal law, a law of nature or of reason, equally applicable for all peoples and all times, and the concept of law as a product of the will of the legislator – were in some respects mutually antagonistic.[8] However, he opposed them both. He denied that the legal system by which a people is governed – the so-called "positive law," the law that has been laid down, or "posited" – is subordinate to an ideal law of nature or reason, and he denied, on the other hand, that the legislator is free to change the positive law as he wills.[9]

It is worth dwelling for a moment on the two concepts of law that Savigny opposed, for they are the two concepts that still battle for domination of legal thought today. The first, the natural-law theory, stresses the moral and rational elements inherent in law. In the West, this theory dominated social and political thought in the period from the eleventh to the fifteenth centuries. This was the era when Christian jurists and theologians, building partly on Aristotle, partly on Stoic thought, and partly on the Church Fathers (including St. Augustine), but also, and above all, on the new relationship between the ecclesiastical and the secular authorities inaugurated under Pope Gregory VII, developed the idea that the legal ordinances of a society are based on the law of human nature, which

[5] [Savigny, *Vocation*, 21.]
[6] [Ibid., 22–23.]   [7] [Ibid.]
[8] [Ibid.]   [9] [Ibid., 32.]

in turn reflects divine law.[10] Starting from the idea of the lawfulness of all being, of the universe itself, manifested in the creation of the world and in divine revelation, medieval writers saw mankind enveloped in a moral order, a law of nature, that forbids unjustified killing, that commands compensation for harm caused by wrongful acts, that requires promises to be kept, and more. Human law, promulgated by political rulers, must, if it is to deserve the name of law, realize and reflect the law of the universe and the law of human nature. In fact, it is for the purpose of realizing natural justice that men, by the exercise of reason, elaborate rules declaring when homicide is or is not justified, what kinds of acts are wrongful, under what circumstances promises are binding, and the like. Thus St. Thomas Aquinas defined law as "nothing else than an ordinance of reason for the common good, made by him who has care of the community, and promulgated."[11]

With the rise of Protestantism in the sixteenth century, which (in its Lutheran form) rejected the authority of the Catholic Church's canon law, and with the emergence of national legal systems that no longer looked to the Church for inspiration, legal thought began to be secularized.[12] The theory that law is founded on the moral and rational nature of man survived, but without its theological underpinnings. At the same time, a new theory emerged, which saw the origin and sanction of law in the will of the state. Indeed, the word "state," in its modern meaning, was first used by the Italian political writer, Niccolò Machiavelli, in the sixteenth century; he was the first to identify the political organization of society as a single and distinct entity embodying the will of the ruler, the prince. Law, it came now to be thought, is not to be understood as a reflection of human nature but rather as a means by which persons in authority exercise their will over others.[13] In the words of seventeenth-century English political theorist, Thomas Hobbes: "Law properly is the word of him that

[10] [See later, Berman, *Law and Revolution*, 144–47, where Berman goes into much greater detail on the medieval theory of natural law, and *Law and Revolution II*, 71–99, 231–69, comparing later medieval Catholic and early modern Protestant legal theories. See further elaboration in John Witte, Jr., *Law and Protestantism: The Legal Teachings of the Lutheran Reformation* (Cambridge University Press, 2002), chs. 3–4 and *The Reformation of Rights: Law, Religion, and Human Rights* (Cambridge University Press, 2007), chs. 1–4.]

[11] [*Summa Theologiæ*, II–I, q. 90, a. 4, answer, reprinted in St. Thomas Aquinas, *Treatise on Law* (Chicago: Henry Regnery, 1959), 8.]

[12] [See later, Harold J. Berman, "The Spiritualization of Secular Law: The Impact of the Lutheran Reformation," *Journal of Law and Religion* 14 (1999–2000): 313–49.]

[13] [See later, Berman, *Law and Revolution II*, 43.]

THE DEVELOPMENT OF NATIONAL LEGAL LANGUAGES   119

by right hath command over others."[14] The authority of law was now considered by many to lie not in its rationality, morality, or natural qualities, but in the coercive political power that backed it up. At the same time, the laws laid down by the political authority were seen not as a discovery or declaration of moral principles, but as a command expressed in the form of technical concepts and doctrines (legal rules) that might or might not correspond to what is right and good. The believers in a moral law saw in the positive law a manifestation of man's reason; the disbelievers saw in it a manifestation of man's will, his power.[15]

Despite these sharp conflicts, the natural-law and positivist schools of legal thought have something in common as well. The believers in reason do not deny that law is helpless without a political structure to give it reality, and they state that reason itself dictates obedience to the political authority; and the believers in will, or power, do not deny that law must take account of the human need for just and rational solutions of social problems if it is to be politically effective, and they state that political power must be "legitimated" in order to maintain itself. Law is not the word of *any* person in power, according to Hobbes, but only of him who "by right" may issue commands. Thus natural-law theory recognizes the rationality of power, and positivism recognizes the political necessity of reason. The differences between the two schools are not apparent in the middle of the spectrum but only at the outer edges. They are differences concerning the original sources and final sanctions of legal rules – concerning what comes first and what is decisive. Thus, as Savigny saw, they could come together in the late eighteenth and early nineteenth centuries to demand a codification of the laws – the natural-law theorists seeing in such a codification an opportunity to make law conform to reason, the positivists seeing in it an opportunity to make law politically effective.

Savigny, however, in founding the historical school of legal thought, looked for the ultimate origin and ultimate sanction of law neither in right reason nor in political power but in the language, tradition, customs, and character of the community whose law it is. Law, he said, is to be explained in the first instance neither as an expression of man's moral and rational nature, nor as an expression of the will of the political

---

[14] [Thomas Hobbes, *Leviathan, or, the Matter, Form, and Power of a Commonwealth Ecclesiastical and Civil* (London: Andrew Crooke, 1651), ch. xv, 80.]

[15] [See later, Berman, *Law and Revolution*, 12–13, for an expanded historical discussion of natural law theory and historical jurisprudence; *Law and Revolution II*, 96–99, for Berman's discussion of the development of legal positivism in Lutheran political theology.]

authorities, but rather as an expression of the common consciousness of a people as it has developed over a long period of time. The law of a people is no more and no less rational in its origin, and no more and no less political, than its language. Indeed, in the earliest period of a people's development, Savigny wrote, its law is indistinguishable from its language; law, language, custom, and "way of life" are all one.[16] Only in the course of time does law acquire a visible form by which it can be identified. The first incarnation, so to speak, of law is in the form not of developed concepts but of symbolic acts, or symbolic transactions, such as the solemnly repeated ceremonies and formulae characteristic of the early Roman law as well as of the law of the Germanic, Celtic, Slavic, and other tribes of Europe at the time of the introduction of Christianity. "[W]e then find symbolical acts universally employed where rights and duties were to be created or extinguished: it is their palpableness that externally retains law in a fixed form ... In the general use of such formal acts, the Germanic races agree with the ancient Italic."[17]

Such symbolic acts still survive – for example, in wedding ceremonies or in oath-swearing and other procedural formalities in court, and the like; we should not despise them, Savigny said, for our own law, too, often preserves legal formalities without the basis of visibility and of general acceptance that the older legal rituals possessed, so that we only feel them to be arbitrary and burdensome.[18]

In its early stage of visible symbolism, law is the business of the whole community. With the advance of civilization, however, a class of lawyers develops as a distinct profession and then the law begins to develop a special terminology. "[A]s formerly [the law] existed in the consciousness of the community," Savigny wrote, "it now devolves upon the jurists, who thus, in this department, represent the community. Law is henceforth more artificial and complex, since it has a twofold life; first, as part of the aggregate existence of the community, which it does not cease to be; and, secondly, as a distinct branch of knowledge in the hands of jurists."[19] Thus a "technical element," as he put it, is added to the "political element" in law, without, however, severing "the organic connection of law with the being and the character of the community" (*das Volk*).[20] In this respect, too, he

---

[16] [Savigny, *Vocation*, 24.]
[17] [Ibid., 26.]   [18] [Ibid., 27.]   [19] [Ibid., 28.]
[20] [Ibid. 27, 29. As Berman notes in a later essay, the German term *Volk* is difficult to translate: "It means people in the singular, the nation, whereas in English 'people' is usually a plural noun." Berman, "Origins of Historical Jurisprudence," 1737, note 238. See also Stein, *Legal Evolution*, 58.]

added, law is like language: "by saying that all law arises in the same way as what by prevailing but not entirely proper usage is called 'customary law' – that is, it is created first through custom and popular belief, then through legal science, thus always through internal, silently operating forces, not by the arbitrary will of a legislator." "The sum, therefore, of this theory," Savigny concluded, "is that all law is originally formed in the manner, in which, in ordinary but not quite correct language, customary law has been said to have been formed: i.e., that it is first developed by custom and popular faith, next by jurisprudence, – everywhere, therefore, by internal silently-operating powers, not by the arbitrary will of a law-giver."[21]

This was virtually all that Savigny wrote by way of a theoretical foundation for his attack upon the proposed codification of German civil law. The thrust of his argument was that, whether or not codification is a good thing in the abstract, it was a bad thing for Germany at that time because the legal consciousness of the German people and of the German legal profession was not ripe for it. "[T]his opinion, that every age has a vocation for every thing, is a prejudice of the most dangerous kind."[22] Nineteenth-century Germany lacked both the "political" and the "technical" basis for producing a good civil code, in his view.[23] It lacked even an adequate legal language for such an enterprise; indeed, German legal language, he said, was deteriorating. "I know of no German law of the eighteenth century," he wrote, "which, in weight and vigour of expression, could be compared with the Criminal Ordinances of Charles the Fifth."[24]

Savigny's stature as a scholar was so great, and his attack upon the proposed civil code was so powerful, that he is credited with having caused the postponement of the adoption of a German civil code for fifty years. At the same time, his own scholarly systematization of German law was an important factor in the development of a unified legal tradition upon which subsequent codification was based. Thus his historical jurisprudence, as he called it, itself played a practical historical role.

[21] [Savigny, *Vocation*, 30.]
[22] [Ibid., 62.]
[23] [Ibid., 62–65. Savigny used the example of marriage law and property law to illustrate these two inadequacies. As for the political basis, there was no consensus, in German society, on the cultural meaning of marriage, upsetting its legal form. Legislation would undermine any tendency towards a significant consensus on the cultural meaning of marriage. As for the technical basis, while property law does not have the same cultural importance for the "unprofessional public," Germany lacked the juristic expertise and technical skill for law reform, at the present time.]
[24] [Ibid., 68–69.]

In 1815, Savigny founded *The Journal of Historical Jurisprudence* (*Zeitschrift für geschichtliche Rechtswissenschaft*). In the opening article of its first issue Savigny further expounded the ideas which he had stated a year earlier in *The Vocation of our Age*.[25] The Historical School of Jurisprudence, he wrote, teaches "that there is no completely individual and separate human being, but rather that what can be viewed as an individual is, viewed from another side, a member of a greater whole. So the individual person is necessarily at the same time to be considered a member of a family, of a people, of a state, and every age of a people is the continuation and development of all past times."[26] "The subject-matter of law," Savigny wrote, "is given through the entire past of the nation, but not by arbitrariness, so that it could accidentally be one thing or another, but has proceeded from the inner being of the nation itself and its history."[27] On the other hand, he added, "there is a blind overvaluation of the past, which is almost even more dangerous than that empty darkness [into which the 'unhistorical school,' as Savigny called it, has plunged], since it completely cripples the forces of the present: and the historical sense must guard against this, too, if it is to be really practised and not merely verbalized."[28]

Savigny's works helped to produce a profound reaction against both the natural-law and the positivist schools of legal thought. Unfortunately, however, many of his followers, in expanding his views, greatly oversimplified them. They left themselves open to the charge of glorifying the past; of viewing history from such a distance that it appeared to unfold naturally, without purposive effort; and of merely substituting for the idealism of the Enlightenment romantic conceptions of *das Volk* as a "living organism."[29] Savigny himself was not guilty of these charges. He was active in law reform, and he protested against the view that legal institutions originating in the distant past are of a higher order than those of more recent origin and must be maintained against innovation.[30] Nor

---

[25] [*See* Friedrich Carl von Savigny, "Über den Zweck dieser Zeitschrift," *Zeitschrift für geschichtliche Rechtswissenschaft* 1 (1815): 1. All translations from this article are Berman's.]

[26] [Ibid., 3.]   [27] [Ibid., 6.]   [28] [Ibid., 10.]

[29] [For similar criticisms of Savigny, see Roscoe Pound, "The Scope and Purpose of Sociological Jurisprudence," *Harvard Law Journal* 24 (1911): 600–03.]

[30] [See Joachim Rückert, "The Unrecognized Legacy: Savigny's Influence on German Jurisprudence after 1900," *American Journal of Comparative Law* 37 (1989): 124–26; Karl A. Mollnau, "The Contributions of Savigny to the Theory of Legislation," *American Journal of Comparative Law* 37 (1989): 88–89. Both of these articles are critical of Savigny's "bourgeois" commitments, though these criticisms are made from a Marxist

was he a worshipper of the national state; he stressed the European, and not only the national, character of German law, and he had a sense of the corporate character not only of the family, the people, and the state, but also of the human race as a whole. In this he was in the spirit of Edmund Burke, who, in fact, had a very great influence on Savigny's entire circle.[31]

Burke, like Savigny, had a strong sense of the common historical foundations of all Western law. He ridiculed the opinion of English lawyers that English law "was formed and grew up among ourselves; that it is in every respect peculiar to this island; and that if the Roman or any foreign laws attempted to intrude into its composition, it has always had vigour enough to shake them off, and return to the purity of its primitive constitution."[32] The law "of every country of Europe," Burke wrote (and he included England in Europe), "is derived from the same sources."[33] He was, then, no narrow nationalist, and indeed in a letter to the Empress of Russia in 1791 he called himself, in quite modern terms, "a citizen of the world."[34] Yet Burke also stressed the crucial importance of national historical developments upon the general theory and spirit of particular national legal systems, as well as upon their specific institutions and rules. He especially emphasized the peculiar features of English legal history which had resulted in the creation of the distinctive system of English law,

perspective that Berman does not share. See Berman, *Law and Revolution*, 555–57, where Berman takes Marx and Weber to task for discounting the ideological and normative side of law; despite the partial accuracy of socio-economic analysis of law, Berman claims that the history of law following the Papal Revolution is incompatible with a purely socio-economic explanation, given the role of law in limiting the power of the ruling classes. As Berman explains, law reflects cross-pressures in society, the old feudal hierarchies, prescient capitalist business relations, and anachronistic socialist guilds; these cross-pressures belie simplistic socio-economic explanation.]

[31] [In his later article, "The Origins of Historical Jurisprudence," 1737, Berman wrote: "[Savigny] did not cite Burke in his scholarly writings, but was undoubtedly influenced by Burke's political philosophy, which was well known and greatly appreciated in Germany at the time." See also Stein, *Legal Evolution*, 57.]

[32] [Edmund Burke, "An Essay Towards an Abridgement of English History," in *The Works of the Right Honorable Edmund Burke*, 12 vols., 3rd edn. (Boston: Little, Brown, 1869), 7:476.]

[33] [Edmund Burke, "On the Overtures of Peace," in *Works*, 5:319. Berman's quotation represents the substance of Burke's meaning. The letter reads: "It [Europe] is virtually one great state having the same basis of general law ... The whole polity and economy of every country in Europe has been derived from the same sources ... [O]ld Germanic or Gothic custumary [sic] ... feudal institutions ... and the whole has been improved and digested into system and discipline by the Roman law." Ibid., 318–19.]

[34] [Edmund Burke, "A Letter to the Empress of Russia, November 1, 1791," in *Works*, 6:119.]

a system whose principal distinguishing characteristic is its concern with historical continuity. The English constitution, itself a historically evolving set of principles, considers English rights and liberties as an "inheritance" of the people, Burke wrote.[35] Such a conception of inherited law gives stability to political institutions and yet makes it possible to effectuate change. "People will not look forward to posterity," he wrote, "who never look backward to their ancestors. Besides, the people of England well know that the idea of inheritance furnishes a sure principle of conversation, and a sure principle of transmission; without at all excluding a principle of improvement. It leaves acquisition free; but it secures what it acquired."[36]

Though not a systematic scholar, Burke had a strong influence upon scholarship, including legal scholarship, in Europe and America, and the effects of his historical conception of law are evident in the writing of Savigny a generation later. This conception is characterized by a broad view of legal history as the accumulated experience of many centuries, coupled with an emphasis upon the particular circumstances of particular times and places. Thus Burke defined law itself as "the collected reason of the ages, combining original principles of justice with the infinite variety of human concern."[37] Principles in themselves, abstracted from their concrete application, are meaningless, he stressed. "Circumstances," he wrote in a famous passage, "which with some gentlemen pass for nothing, give in reality to every political [or, we may add, legal] principle its distinguishing color and discriminating effect."[38] At the same time, circumstances must be viewed in the perspective of "the collected reason of the ages."

Savigny gave profound scholarly content to Burke's earlier insights. He made four great contributions, both as a historian and as a philosopher. First, he emphasized the intimate relationships between the law of a given people and its whole culture (its language, its customs, its common legal consciousness) viewed in historical perspective, relationships which are most visible in the early stages of a people's legal development but which remain of critical importance in later stages as well. Second, he emphasized the intimate relationships between the law of a given people and the state of its professional legal practice and scholarship (its "legal science"). Third, he emphasized the necessity of weighing both the moral validity and the political effectiveness of legal institutions and legal propositions

---

[35] [Edmund Burke, "Reflections on the Revolution in France," in *Works*, 3:272–75.]
[36] [Ibid., 274.]   [37] [Ibid., 357.]   [38] [Ibid., 240.]

in terms of the extent to which they adequately express both the common legal consciousness of the people and the legal science of the professionals at a given stage of their historical development. Finally, Savigny emphasized the persistence of historical reality, that is, the remembered past, in present legal concepts and institutions.

Thus Savigny called attention to a fatal weakness of the prevailing legal thought of his time – a weakness that persists to this day – namely, a failure to put the morality and the politics of law in the context of legal history. Man is more than the rational, moral being presupposed by natural-law theory, and he is more than the willful master of concepts or of policy presupposed by positivism. The historical experience of particular legal systems provides the context in which legal morality and legal reason, on the one hand, and legal rules and legal policies, on the other, find their times and places. At the same time, history combines normative standards – especially in each society's conception of well-being (and, in the Western tradition, progress) – with factual elements of political power. The "ought" or morality and the "is" (or more accurately, the "shall be") of legal command are brought into focus by the "was" and the "will be" of history. Indeed, once historical jurisprudence is accepted, all three schools can be reconciled, and each can be seen as emphasizing a different side of the same truth. Each school is inadequate in itself. Each asks its own questions, which neither of the other two can answer, but each is a necessary corrective to the others and each needs others to complete it.[39]

3

While Savigny focused attention on the special historical features of a particular national legal system, and especially on the history of Roman law as it was first developed and as it was later received in medieval and modern Germany, a succeeding generation of nineteenth-century legal scholars carried his historical method into the comparison of a wide variety of legal systems. The most important of these were Gaines Post and Josef Kohler in Germany and Sir Henry Maine in England. Perhaps Maine,

---

[39] [See Berman, "Toward an Integrative Jurisprudence"; *Faith and Order*, 289–312 and analysis in Peter R. Teachout, "'Complete Achievement': Integrity of Vision and Performance in Berman's Jurisprudence," in Howard O. Hunter, ed., *The Integrative Jurisprudence of Harold J. Berman* (Boulder, CO: Westview Press, 1996), 75–98; John Witte, Jr., "A New Concordance of Discordant Canons: Harold J. Berman on Law and Religion," in ibid., 99–136; and David J. Bederman, "World Law Transcendent," *Emory Law Journal* 54 (2005): 79–96.]

more than any other, established the comparative-historical method as a precursor to modern sociology of law.

Maine's principal effort was to explain the gradual development of primitive law – ancient Roman law, Anglo-Saxon and Germanic law, Hindu law, early Slavic law – into mature, modern legal systems. With far less reliable historical and anthropological data than we now possess, he sought to formulate some hypotheses concerning the origin and stages of development of law in all societies, or at least in all Indo-European societies. As in the case of Savigny, the subtlety of Maine's historical analysis, and the many qualifications with which he surrounded his insights, often escaped not only his critics but also his followers, with the result that his subsequent influence, though substantial, has not always accurately reflected his true greatness.

We have already examined Maine's theory concerning the role of fiction, equity, and legislation as instrumentalities of law reform in successive stages of legal development.[40] A parallel theory developed by Maine is that law develops first as ad hoc adjudication then, at a later stage, as judicially declared custom (customary law), and finally, as codified law. Maine wrote,

> In the infancy of mankind, no sort of legislature, not even a distinct author of law, is contemplated or conceived of. Law has scarcely reached the footing of custom; it is rather a habit. It is, to use a French phrase, "in the air." The only authoritative statement of right and wrong is a judicial sentence after the facts, not one presupposing a law which has been violated, but one which is breathed for the first time by a higher power into the judge's mind at the moment of adjudication.[41]

The power of judging at this earliest stage of legal history is the prerogative of individual rulers, like tribal chieftains and heroic kings. But in all societies, or at least in all branches of the Indo-European family of nations, Maine wrote, the historical era of heroic kings was succeeded by a historical era of aristocracies, and these aristocracies were the depositaries and administrators of an unwritten law.

> We have in fact arrived at the epoch of Customary Law ... Before the invention of writing, and during the infancy of the art, an aristocracy invested with judicial privileges formed the only expedient by which accurate preservation of the customs of the race or tribe could be at all approximated to. Their genuineness was, so far as possible, insured by confiding them to the recollection of a limited portion of the community.[42]

[40] [See above pp. 109–12]   [41] [Maine, *Ancient Law*, 7.]   [42] [Ibid., 11.]

Finally, ancient law is reduced to writing; the oligarchical monopoly is assailed by a popular element, the plebs, and the era of customary law is succeeded by the era of codes – not in the modern sense, but in the sense of the Roman Twelve Tables, the Attic Code of Solon, the Hindu laws of Menu, and the like.[43]

These historical events, according to Maine, occurred at certain stages in the relative progress of each community. They reflected certain observed regularities of historical developments in all societies.[44] Also, they are the result of certain inherent characteristics of the development of law itself, based on the procedural requirements of adjudication, law-speaking, and legislation. The very nature of legal institutions for decision-making gives rise to changes within those institutions and to changes in the substantive law. In all societies, Maine wrote, the earliest form of law is procedure, and indeed, at early stages of legal development all substantive law "gives the appearance of being secreted in the interstices of procedure."[45]

Finally, mention must be made of Maine's insight that in primitive societies, the individual – as understood in the nineteenth century in the West – had no legal recognition.

> Ancient Law ... knows next to nothing of Individuals. It is concerned not with Individuals, but with Families, not with single human beings, but groups. Even when the law of the State has succeeded in permeating the small circles of kindred into which it had originally no means of pene-trating, the view it takes of Individuals is curiously different from that taken by jurisprudence in its maturest stage. The life of each citizen is not regarded as limited by birth and death; it is but a continuation of the existence of his forefathers, and it will be prolonged in the existence of his descendants.[46]

In the gradual dissolution of family dependency in ancient or primitive societies, and the substitution of the individual as the unit of which civil laws take account, Maine sees the emergence of the modern, civilized legal order. This is his famous "movement of progressive societies from Status to Contract."[47] Individual obligation, Contract, is "the tie between man and man which replaced by degrees those forms of reciprocity in rights and duties which have their origin in the Family."[48]

[43] [Ibid., 12–13. In his *Ancient Law*, Maine used the spelling 'Menu', to refer to 'Manu'.]
[44] [Ibid., 14–15.]
[45] [Henry Sumner Maine, *Dissertations on Early Law and Custom* (London: John Murray, 1883), 389.]
[46] [Maine, *Ancient Law*, 270.]
[47] [Ibid., 174.]   [48] [Ibid., 172.]

Starting, as from one terminus of history, from a condition of society
in which all the relations of Persons are summed up in the relations of
Family, we seem to have steadily moved towards a phase of social order in
which all these relations arise from the free agreement of individuals.[49]

This is not the place to attempt to evaluate the strengths and weaknesses
of Maine's historical analysis. We are concerned, rather, with his method
and especially with his attempt to discover certain observed regularities
in the development of legal systems, what we may call *laws of the history of
law*. Today we are more skeptical about "the movement of progressive societies." Also, we know too much about the diverse peoples of the world to be
comfortable with any broad generalization concerning the remote history
of mankind or the nature of primitive law. Nevertheless, we cannot give up
the struggle for a sociology of law. And any sociology of law must build in
part on the Historical School of Jurisprudence founded by Savigny and on
the Comparative-Historical Method of Law established by Maine.[50]

What is present in their respective approaches, and what is lacking in that of many of their successors, is the emphasis on processes of
growth inherent in law itself. It is, indeed, this very emphasis that probably accounts for the disfavor into which both Savigny and Maine have
fallen in the twentieth century, in "advanced" circles of legal philosophy
and legal sociology. On the law side, neither the natural-law theorists nor
the positivists have been especially interested in the historical development of legal systems. On the sociology side, there has been skepticism
not only concerning the evolutionary theories of the nineteenth century
but also, and more strikingly, concerning the autonomy of legal development. Law changes, many sociologists would say, not because of anything inherent in law but because of external forces, whether economic
and political changes, class conflict, changes in "ideology," or otherwise. There is undoubtedly some value in a "typology" of legal systems,
such as that elaborated by Karl Marx, and, after him, Max Weber and
others. But the existence of different types of law – "feudal law," "bourgeois law," "traditional law," "charismatic law," or "bureaucratic law," – is
viewed by Marx, Weber, and many who have followed their leads, not so
much as a phenomenon of legal history than as a phenomenon of social
and economic conditions.[51] It is supposed that "given a certain stage of

[49] [Ibid., 172–73.]
[50] [Stein shares these criticisms of the Historical School and of Maine, as well as the connection between the Historical School and sociological jurisprudence. See Stein, *Legal
Evolution*, 122–27.]
[51] [See later, Berman, *Faith and Order*, 239.]

economic development," or "given a certain class structure," or "given a certain combination of political, economic, social, ideological, factors," a particular type of legal system will result. Thus law is conceived to be a "superstructure," or a "reflection" of other things. The organic quality of legal history, the inherent capacity of legal institutions to change and develop in the course of time, is denied. Even those who concede that there may be laws of history will usually deny that there are laws of the history of *law*. And those who, on the other hand, often with justification, attack "historicism," neglect the genuine historicity, the time dimension, of legal systems. The Historical School of Jurisprudence asserts that there *are* observable regularities – laws – of legal history, and at the same time refutes a mechanical "historicism" by affirming that we are neither the pawns of history nor its masters; we only help to make it.

It is characteristic of our century that it tends to view the historical school as "reactionary." Looking backward to the past is thought to impede progress. A distinction is made between "traditional" societies, which are thought to be static, and "rational" societies, which are thought to be dynamic. What is neglected is the fact that the ability of a society to maintain traditions is absolutely essential to progress, for it alone makes it possible to introduce changes that will themselves, in turn, have stability. The capacity to change is a negation of progress when it is not linked with the capacity to preserve. For, without the capacity to preserve, there is no change in the sense of taking a new direction but only a perpetual series of changes, each canceling the other. This, indeed, has been the tragedy of many of the underdeveloped countries, which, contrary to what is sometimes taught, are the victims not so much of an inability to change as of an inability to make changes that will *last*. In Edmund Burke's words, a "principle of conservation" and a "principle of transmission" do not exclude "a principle of improvement" but, on the contrary, are necessary in order to "secure" such improvement once it is undertaken.

The validity and importance of the Historical School of Jurisprudence of Savigny and Maine can be demonstrated if we combine their historical insights with an emphasis on the linguistic character of law. Savigny expressly compared legal and linguistic development. For both law and language, he wrote, "there is no moment of absolute cessation; it is subject to the same movement and development as every other popular tendency; and this very development remains under the same of law inward necessity, as in its earliest stages. Law grows with the growth, and strengthens with the strength of the people, and finally dies away as the nation loses its nationality."[52] Yet one does not find in Savigny, as one does in Maine, a systematic explanation of stages of legal development in terms of the institutional and stylistic methods by which law is articulated. And in neither Savigny nor Maine – nor in their distinguished disciple, Eugen Ehrlich, who may be said to have founded modern sociology of law[53] – does one find an explanation of legal development in terms of general principles of linguistic change: the transfer of meanings from folk language to legal language by metaphor and metonymy, the substitution of meanings within legal language by analogical reasoning, the redirection of meanings by grammatical techniques ("was," "is," "ought," "shall be"), the professionalization of legal language, the continual (and not merely "early" or "ancient") development of legal propositions from fiction to exception to reformulation of rule.

In short, the Historical School of Jurisprudence, though recognizing an intimate connection between law and language, has not hitherto attempted to analyze legal history by a linguistic method; nor has it systematically applied a historical method to legal language. A revival of historical jurisprudence is urgently needed today if only as a corrective to the excesses of positivism and natural-law theory. But such a revival must combine historical jurisprudence with linguistics – that is, it must examine the growth of particular legal systems in terms of the growth of the language, the discourse, which is the stuff of which any legal system is made. Such a historical and linguistic analysis of particular legal systems is an essential foundation of legal sociology. Moreover, it is essential to an understanding of the development, which is now taking place, of a common international legal language among peoples who, being governed by different legal systems, speak different legal languages.

4

It is striking that Savigny and his followers on the continent of Europe never attempted, in any thoroughgoing way, to apply a historical method to the systematic analysis of legal rules and concepts; while in England and America, where (despite Maine) historical jurisprudence has been largely neglected, a historical method of legal analysis is almost universally applied in practice. Savigny himself devoted his analytical – as

---

[52] [Savigny, *Vocation*, 27.]
[53] [See esp. Eugen Ehrlich, *Fundamental Principles of the Sociology of Law* (New York: Russell & Russell, 1962).]

contrasted with his philosophical – talents to harmonizing German legal doctrines and to presenting them as a "system." He usually did, indeed, take pains to show how the original Roman meaning of many German legal rules differed from their modern meaning, but he was not generally concerned with the processes by which such meanings gradually (or suddenly) change and continue to change in the course of time. Nor did he attempt to demonstrate in detail how custom, popular belief, and other "internal, silently operating forces" continually find their way into the law. His writings on legal history stop with the Middle Ages, and his writings on modern German law are primarily doctrinal rather than historical.

In England and America, on the other hand, it is quite common for legal scholars, judges, and practicing lawyers, whatever school of legal philosophy they may espouse, to begin – and sometimes to end – the analysis of legal rules and concepts by discussing not only their historical origins but also their shifts in meaning over the centuries. When it comes to explaining or justifying the rules and concepts, historical criteria often give way to moral and political criteria; history is considered merely a necessary "background." Nevertheless, the history is not to be forgotten, and even adherents of the "unhistorical school" of jurisprudence are sometimes forced to treat it as decisive.

Historical continuity is, in fact, built into the English and American legal systems, if only because of the doctrine of precedent, whereby courts are bound – in the absence of weighty reasons to the contrary – by previous decisions in analogous cases. The English or American judge, confronted with a question of law, is required by the legal system itself to ask, in the first instance, "How has this question been answered when it has arisen at various times in the past?" Further, he will seek explanations of past answers, and he will attempt to reconcile his present answer with those explanations. At the same time, he is conscious that his decision will make law for the future: in this sense, the doctrine of precedent is a dynamic, and not a static, principle. Yet the belief in the historical continuity of English and of American law, their growth over generations and centuries, is not due solely to the doctrine of precedent; indeed, viewed historically, the doctrine of precedent is rather a consequence than a cause of the belief in such continuity.[54]

In France, Germany, Italy, Poland, and other European countries, on the other hand, the judge or jurist confronted with a question of law is required by the legal system to ask, in the first instance, "How is this

[54] [See further, Berman, et al., *The Nature and Functions of Law*, 6th edn., 391–518.]

question answered in the code or by other legislation?" His principal task is to achieve doctrinal consistency, rather than historical continuity. Indeed, some European codes forbid judges to cite previous cases. But apart from codes, even the nineteenth-century German Historical School of Savigny and his followers was more concerned with establishing a legal system united by consistency and harmony of rules, concepts, and doctrines, than with maintaining historical continuity. And, in fact, they were confronted with the task of creating a unified legal system in a country whose legal tradition, in contrast with that of England, had been marked with a most striking *dis*continuity: the "reception of Roman law" at the end of the fifteenth and the beginning of the sixteenth century.[55] This was the notorious paradox of German Historical Jurisprudence, which treated law as a product of the developing legal consciousness of the German people: the legal rules in question were derived initially not from the legal consciousness of the German people but from the legal consciousness of the Romans! Moreover, in Savigny's time, German law lacked unity. The various principalities each had their own laws, and it was the declared mission of the historical school to harmonize and unite them.

It is quite possible that historical jurisprudence flourished in Germany just because of the recognized lack of historical continuity and national unity in German legal development. In other words, the historical theory was needed to fill a gap left by history itself. In turn, it is quite possible that historical jurisprudence has *not* flourished in England and America just because the historical continuity of English and American law, and their roots in a national legal consciousness, are taken for granted – and hence other theories (or no theories) are felt to be needed.

---

[55] [See later, Berman, *Law and Revolution II*, 100–30, where Berman treats the "reception of Roman law" more as a "scientization" and "professionalization" of German law, using selected Roman law and canon law teachings among many others.]

5

The development of American law
and legal language

1

A lawyer who is asked, "What is American law?" must begin by saying that, from a strictly legal point of view, there is no such thing as "American law." There is the law of each of the fifty states of the United States of America; and there is federal law – that is, the law of the United States viewed as a governmental entity distinct from the states which comprise it. Massachusetts law is not California law, although there are many similarities between them. Federal law, binding upon all the states, is, of course, in one sense "American"; yet it is by no means the whole, or even the major part, of the law that governs American citizens, for it presupposes the existence of a large body of law within each of the several states.

The dualism of state and federal law does not exhaust the variety of the systems of law under which American citizens live. There is also a dualism of "common law" and "equity"; at one time, these two types of law were divided between different courts, which vied with each other for jurisdiction, and although now they are both applied in the same courts, they remain in some respects distinct legal systems. In addition, maritime law continues to have a separate jurisdiction ("admiralty") and a separate tradition, being linked historically with the law of nations. International law itself is one of the systems of law under which American citizens live, and a considerable number of American statutes and decisions, both federal and state, are derived from international conventions and from international legal doctrine. Indeed, if we look to the historical derivation of statutory and decisional law applied in the United States of America, we shall find that very little of it is purely indigenous. Most of it is derived from English law, and from Roman law, and from the canon law of the Church as it developed in the West from the eleventh century onward.

The ambiguities of the phrase "American law" from a legal point of view are compounded when one adds to them the sociological diversity of American life. Americans are a people of the most diverse ethnic backgrounds, religious faiths, regional cultures, and political and social philosophies. We are all, it is true, immigrants to this continent; the native Indians, too, migrated here from Eastern Asia. But even in our character as immigrants we are divided by the times when we arrived and the places from which we came. There may be less in common between a Daughter of the American Revolution and the daughter of a refugee from Nazi Germany, both living on the same street in a suburb of Chicago, than there is between an Englishman and a German living in London and Frankfurt, respectively.

Must we then abandon the search for an "American law," and possibly even drop the word "American" altogether? We cannot, without being false to history. For history demonstrates that there *is* an American people, and that they are held together in part – and perhaps above all – by their law. American law has developed distinctive features, which reflect, and help maintain, the distinctive qualities of American political, economic, and social life. One of these distinctive features of American law is its very pluralism. At the same time, there is a unity that underlies the variety of legal regimes under which America lives. There is a common American legal language, which differs substantially from the English and other European legal languages from which it is historically derived.[1]

2

Before attempting to identify distinctive characteristics of American legal language, let us trace briefly the principal stages in the growth of American law, and the principal historical strands that make up its unity.[2] The first stage in the development of American law was the colonial period, from 1620 to 1776, when English law was transplanted to the North American continent. The English colonists who came to America in the seventeenth and eighteenth centuries brought their law with them, and ultimately, with some qualifications, the Dutch, French, Irish, Scottish, Spanish, German, Jewish, and other immigrants in those centuries, as well as those of later times, adapted themselves to the English legal tradition. Even the infusion of biblical law into the little "theocracies" of Calvinist New England

---

[1] [See Mellinkoff, *Language of the Law*, 201.]
[2] [See later, Harold J. Berman, "Legal Systems," in Kermit L. Hall, ed., *The Oxford Companion to American Law*, (Oxford University Press, 2002), 507–14.]

was only a reflection of the Puritan movement in the mother countries of England and the Netherlands.

Two features of American colonial law deserve to be singled out, because of their great influence on future development. Both these features were English in origin, but they acquired a new significance in the New World. The first was the English legal doctrine that English law was applicable in the English colonies only insofar as it was suitable to the new conditions in which the colonists found themselves. As William Blackstone stated in his famous *Commentaries on the Laws of England* (1765), a book that was read more widely in the American colonies than in the mother country itself:

> [I]f an uninhabited country be discovered and planted by English sub-
> jects, all the English laws then in being, which are the birthright of every
> subject, are immediately there in force. But this must be understood with
> very many and very great restrictions. Such colonists carry with them
> only so much of the English law, as is applicable to their own situation
> and the condition of an infant colony; such, for instance, as the general
> rules of inheritance, and of protection from personal injuries. The artifi-
> cial refinements and distinctions incident to the property of a great and
> commercial people, the laws of police and revenue (such especially as
> are enforced by penalties), the mode of maintenance for the established
> clergy, the jurisdiction of spiritual courts, and a multitude of other provi-
> sions, are neither necessary nor convenient for them, and therefore are
> not in force: What shall be admitted and what rejected at what times, and
> under what restrictions, must, in case of dispute, be decided in the first
> instance by their own provincial judicature, subject to the revision and
> control of the king in council; the whole of their constitution being also
> liable to be new-modeled and reformed by the general superintending
> power of the legislature in the mother-country.[3]

The principle that the colonial courts could reject those rules of English law that were not necessary or convenient had a profound influence on American law, both in the colonial period and thereafter. The English rule of primogeniture, for example, which resulted in the consolidation of landholdings in the hands of the eldest sons – leaving the younger sons of the landed gentry to go into parliament or the judiciary – made little sense in the backwoods of America, and some colonial courts rejected it. Similarly, the English rule of cattle trespass, which imposed liability on the farmer who failed to fence his cattle in, was hardly suitable on

---

[3] [Sir William Blackstone, *Commentaries on the Laws of England in Four Books* (Philadelphia: J.B. Lippincott Co., 1893), vol. 1, bks. 1–2, sec. 4.]

the prairies of the mid-West, with their huge farms and their scarcity of timber for making fences. After the American Revolution, when new states were formed, they almost invariably adopted the principle that English law prior to the Revolution was to remain in force, but only "so far as the same is applicable." The significance of this doctrine must be measured in terms of the enormous differences between conditions in the well-populated, civilized, and peaceful British Isles and those in the vast, under-populated, uncultivated wilds of the American continent.

A second feature of American colonial law that derived from England but acquired new significance in America was the emphasis upon the law-making power of legislative bodies consisting of representatives elected by the people (or, more accurately, those of the people who owned property). Parliamentary supremacy, and, within Parliament, the supremacy of the House of Commons, which was established in England in the seventeenth century, was a precious part of "the birthright of every subject." However, Parliament was far away from America and the colonists did not send members to it. If they were to have the benefit of the principle of representative government, they had to be permitted to have their own elected legislatures; and indeed, Parliament could not, practically speaking, enact all the laws needed to regulate the diverse conditions of life in America. Conceivably, an attempt could have been made to unite the colonies under a single colonial legislature, instead of establishing thirteen separate colonies with thirteen separate legislatures. It is doubtful that such an attempt could have been successful, however, even if there had been any desire to make it. What happened, in any event, was that each colony was authorized to elect its own legislature, which enacted laws for that colony. Since both the governors and the judges of the various colonies were appointed by the king, the colonial legislatures became, in the course of time, the champions of the rights of the colonists against both the king and the Parliament. One of the chief causes of the Revolution was the king's repeated disallowance of laws enacted by the colonial legislatures.

It would be hard to exaggerate the importance, in the development of American law, of the existence, for over 150 years, of separate law-making power in the hands of each of the legislatures of the various colonies. Our system of state and municipal government, our extensive reliance upon legislative redress of individual and local grievances, our limitations upon the powers of the central federal authority – these and many other lasting features of American public law find their historical roots here.

Let me give one example: in 1660, the Massachusetts Bay Legislature enacted a law giving the elected school committee of each town in the colony the power to establish and maintain public schools within the town and to establish the budget to support such schools; and this is still law in Massachusetts, so that it is not the state, nor even the city council, but the school committee that independently and finally determines this major item of public expenditure and public policy.

Perhaps even more important than its influence on legal institutions was the effect of the colonial system on legal theory. The Hobbesian concepts of law as "the will of the State," and of legislation as the principal source of a nation's law, underwent fundamental changes in a country in which "the State" was not coextensive with the whole political society but was only one of the political units within a larger polity, and legislation was the product not only of a central legislative body but also of a considerable number of legislative bodies in some senses subordinate to, and in other senses independent of, the central legislature.

3

A second stage of development of American law began in 1776, when, on July 2, the Continental Congress, consisting of representatives of the thirteen American colonies, voted that "these United Colonies are, and of right ought to be, free and independent states, that they are absolved from all allegiance to the British Crown, and that all political connection between them and the State of Great Britain is, and ought to be, totally dissolved." Two days later, on the evening of July 4, the Congress agreed to, and fifty-six representatives signed, the Declaration of Independence, which had been drafted by Thomas Jefferson and reported to the Congress on June 28; the purpose of the Declaration was to proclaim to mankind the moral and legal justification for the colonists' revolt.[4]

The American Revolution has two sides to it: on the one hand, it was a secession of the thirteen colonies from the mother country, intended to procure for the colonists "all the rights, liberties, and immunities of free and natural-born subjects, within the realm of England." This was the language of the Declaration of Rights of the first Continental Congress in 1774, in which it was also stated: "That the respective colonies are entitled

---

[4] [All the revolutionary documents quoted hereafter are available online at the Avalon Project – Documents in Law, History and Diplomacy (http://avalon.law.yale.edu/) (visited January 4, 2013).]

to the common law of England" and "That they are entitled to the benefit of such of the English statutes as existed at the time of their colonization; and which they have, by experience, respectively found to be applicable to their several local and other circumstances." As Englishmen, the colonists insisted on the right not to be taxed by a legislature in which they were not represented, on the right of their own legislatures to enact laws that would not be subject to royal disallowance, on the right of their judges to be independent of the king's will for their tenure and their salaries, on the right to trial by jury in all criminal cases, and on many other such rights and freedoms as their brethren in England has possessed for almost a hundred years.

Even in rebelling against England, the colonists invoked English theory and English precedent, proclaiming doctrines of natural rights, and of government by consent of the governed, which were drawn largely from the works of John Locke, written expressly to justify the English Revolution of 1688.[5] The Declaration of Independence listed the illegal acts of the king – his "abuses and usurpations" – in the exact style of the English Declaration of Rights in 1689. In the words of a modern American commentator on the Declaration of Independence:

> To the men of 1776, the "glorious revolution" of 1688 in England was a vivid and thrilling reality. It had occurred less than a century before; it was a living and vital force in their daily conduct and thinking ... Americans resisting what they regarded as infringements of their constitutional rights conscientiously studied the precedents and principles enshrined in English history. They felt themselves to be following in the path of Coke, Pym, Hampden, Eliot, Milton, Algernon Sidney, and the patriots who decapitated Charles I in 1649 and deposed James II in 1689 for violations of the compact between king and people.[6]

Yet there is also another side to the American Revolution. It was a product not only of the ideas that emerged in the English Revolution of 1640–89, but also of the ideas of a century later that ultimately were embodied in the French Revolution of 1789. The American colonists not only seceded from the mother country; they also established a new conception of man and of society. The Declaration of Independence of 1776 reflects not only

---

[5] [See Gary L. McDowell, *The Language of Law and the Foundations of American Constitutionalism* (Cambridge University Press, 2010) for a recent work analyzing the nature of our written Constitution, its linguistic roots, and an originalist method of interpretation.]

[6] [Edward Dumbauld, *The Declaration of Independence and What it Means Today* (University of Oklahoma Press, 1950), 21–22.]

the philosophy of John Locke but also that of Samuel Adams and Thomas Paine – the philosophy of individualism, rationalism, and democracy that exploded full force thirteen years later in France.

With some exceptions, historians have tended to link the eighteenth-century French Revolution with the seventeenth-century English Revolution (whether it be conceived as the "Great Rebellion" of Cromwell or as the "Glorious Revolution" of William and Mary or as a combination of both). Marxists refer to both the English and the French Revolutions as "bourgeois" revolutions. Yet in reality they were fundamentally different from each other, and indeed, the French Revolution, though influenced by English ideas, including those of John Locke, was directed against many of the concepts of institutions identified with the English Revolution.

The English Revolution was waged in the name of restoring – in the words of the 1689 Declaration of Rights – "the true, ancient, and indubitable rights and liberties of the people of this kingdom." The idea of restoration was central even to the Puritan phase of the Revolution: Cromwell's seal was inscribed, "In the first year of freedom restored." The myth of continuity with medieval English public law, interrupted by over 150 years of Tudor and Stuart despotism, was put forth as the principal justification for the new system of Parliamentary supremacy. The landed gentry assumed the role of guardian of sacred English traditions. Thus the Revolution assumed an essentially conservative and aristocratic garb, contrary to the hopes of the radical Levellers. Only after it was over did Locke and others justify it in terms of metaphysical conceptions of a state of nature that precedes society, of the natural freedom and equality of all men, and of a social compact that places limitations upon the powers of rulers.[7]

The *philosophes* of eighteenth-century France divorced Locke's metaphysical ideas from their historical context and carried them much further. They viewed society as a product not of history but of the deliberations of intelligent individuals. The laws of nature, freedom, and the foundation of government in reason, all meant something quite different to men like Voltaire, Rousseau, and Montesquieu from what they had meant to John Milton and John Locke. The differences between 1688 and 1789 are brought out with striking clarity in Edmund Burke's attack upon the French Revolution in the name of the English political conceptions established a century earlier, and in Thomas Paine's reply to Burke. For Burke, a nation

---

[7] [See later, Berman, *Law and Revolution II*, 199–230.]

was a partnership of the generations over time; it was to be governed by the public spirit of its leaders in Parliament and on the bench. For Paine, a nation was an association of individuals at a given moment; it was to be governed by what in 1776 he called "common sense" and what a decade later, in the *salons* of Paris, came to be called for the first time "public opinion."[8]

The American Declaration of Independence reflects the philosophy of the eighteenth-century Enlightenment in its statement that fundamental truths concerning the nature of men are "self-evident" – that is, apparent to naked reason apart from history and tradition; that "whenever" any form of government becomes destructive of natural rights it is the right of the people to alter or abolish it; and that the people have the right to institute a new government on the basis of such principles "as to them shall seem most likely to effect their safety and happiness." Locke had sought to justify a single "Glorious" Revolution in order to perpetuate its principles. Jefferson proclaimed a general right of revolution at any time a people is oppressed. When Locke spoke of a just civil government he had in mind the English Parliament and the English common law. For Jefferson, a just government was one that responded to the will of the majority of the people.[9]

Thus from the very beginning of the American Revolution there was a tension between the rationalist and voluntarist principles that were soon to find drastic expression in the French Revolution and the traditionalist principles of the English Revolution of the preceding century. This tension was later apparent in the conflict between Jeffersonian and Hamiltonian conceptions of government. It is expressed throughout the United States Constitution – for example, in the division of the Congress into a more aristocratic Senate and a more democratic House of Representatives, and in the power of the Supreme Court, our House of Lords, to annul Congressional legislation in the name of the legal traditions established by the Constitution.[10] The Bill of Rights itself is half "English," in its

---

[8] ["Public Opinion" is the title of Berman's College Thesis at Dartmouth, written under Eugen Rosenstock-Huessy. He was proud of this text, referring back to it in a letter to Rosenstock, on April 17, 1966, with a May 28, 1966 supplement: "I have been re-reading Savigny and Burke, and that reminded me of my college thesis on Public Opinion, which, on re-reading 27 years later, still holds up very well (no doubt, owing to the large amount of 'R.H. factor' in it)." He would draw on it heavily again in his 1984 Seegers Lectures at the University of Valparaiso, "Law and Belief in Three Revolutions," reprinted in Berman, *Faith and Order*, 83–140, at 130–39.]

[9] [See later, Harold J. Berman, "The Impact of the Enlightenment on American Constitutional Law," *Yale Journal of Law & the Humanities* 4 (1992): 311–34.]

[10] [See later, Harold J. Berman, "The Religion Clauses of the First Amendment in Historical Perspective," in Dale Bumpers and W. Lawson Taite, eds., *Religion and Politics* (University of Texas Press, 1989), 47–73.]

protection of civil rights (right to jury trial, right to be free from unreasonable searches and seizures, etc.), and half "French," in its protection of civil liberties (right to freedom of speech, separation of churches and states, and more).[11]

Yet the American "half-revolution," with its compromise between the seventeenth-century English Whig traditions and eighteenth-century French ideas of popular democracy, also introduced something distinctively "American." That, above all, was the concept of America itself. The Declaration of Independence created the name "United States of America," and it referred to the separation of "one people" – the Americans – from another, the people of Great Britain. Although it may be argued that each colony individually could be considered as a "People" dissolving the "political Bands connecting it with England," the references in the Declaration of Independence to "the lives of our people," and "the good people of these colonies" leave no doubt that the drafters of the Declaration considered all Americans to be a single people. This is all the more striking because one-third of the signers were of non-English stock.

Connected with the idea of Americans as a single people was the idea of America as one continent. It was the "Continental Congress" which adopted the Declaration, and even before the adoption of the United States Constitution in 1789, while still operating as a loose confederation of states, the Congress enacted ordinances that removed the great expanse of territory west of Ohio from the ownership of the individual Eastern states and established procedures for the carving out of new states across the continent to the Pacific Ocean.

"Nature" to the American of 1776 meant the great American continent from the Atlantic to the Pacific. It meant the wilderness, the frontier, but especially it meant these spaces brought under civil government. When Locke spoke of nature he had in mind human nature, the nature of men living in the universe, their original nature prior to the institution of government. He argued that since it was possible, in the absence of government, for a man to occupy land and to work it, property ownership therefore existed in the pre-social state and should be counted, along with liberty, as "one of the natural-law rights which civil society found already existing when it appeared on the scene, and which it could not touch or

---

[11] [See later, Berman, "Legal Systems," 507–14. Berman would later reject the concept of "separation of church and state" as an adequate description of the First Amendment religious freedom guarantee. See Harold J. Berman, "Religious Freedom and the Challenge of the Modern State," *Emory Law Journal* 39 (1990): 149–64.]

modify."[12] For Locke, the wilderness was an example of nature only *prior* to its being brought under civil government. He visualized a Swiss meeting a native Indian in the backwoods of America, and said they would both be governed by natural law. But once a civil government existed in the backwoods, they would be governed by civil law – which must, however, if it is to be just, protect their "natural" rights. For Americans from the time of the Revolution to the Civil War, however, natural law was not conceived so much in terms of the rights of individuals meeting in the backwoods – certainly not in terms of the rights of Indians. Nor was it conceived primarily in terms of limitations on the powers of rulers. Natural law was conceived chiefly in terms of principles of order for regulating a new and largely unsettled continent.

4

It is from this period of American history, from 1776 to 1861, that America inherited its constitutional system. The state and federal constitutions which were then created and elaborated comprise perhaps the most original and the most important contribution that American law has made to the history of mankind.[13] As soon as the colonies declared their independence, their legislature set about writing constitutions; from 1776 to 1784, eleven of the thirteen new states adopted constitutions. The other two states, Connecticut and Rhode Island, amended their royal charters to fit their new conditions. The importance of these state constitutions can hardly be exaggerated. Not only did they contain many of the basic principles of American law – including, in most cases, statements of individual rights and liberties – that were later reflected in the United States Constitution, they also introduced an entirely new political and legal principle, namely, the supreme legal authority of a written constitution. As Willard Hurst has pointed out, the idea that government owes its moral power to a formal grant from a higher authority was already familiar to the colonists, since the colonial governments had been based on royal charters, trading-company charters, and proprietary grants. Furthermore, the idea that the people and not the rulers are the ultimate source of the grant of governmental authority was derived from the

[12] [Source not found.]
[13] [See later, Harold J. Berman, "The Struggle for Law in Post-Soviet Russia," in Andras Sajo, ed., *Western Rights? Post-Communist Application* (The Hague: Kluwer Law International, 1996), 41–55.]

works of John Locke and other seventeenth- and eighteenth-century writers. But the embodiment of these two ideas in a written constitution, a comprehensive document against which the validity of all governmental action could be tested, was a wholly new development. The colonists had invoked the "unwritten" English constitution as a legal basis for their opposition to the king. Having established new independent states, they put their new constitutions on paper.

The fascination with written constitutions is surely a distinctive feature of American legal life. As new states were admitted to the Union, Congress insisted, as a condition of their admission, that they present a satisfactory state constitution. Since 1776, over 200 state conventions have been held for the purpose of adopting or revising constitutions. This fascination with the United States Constitution is reflected in the extraordinary interest in Supreme Court decisions interpreting it; such decisions have played a role in American political and legal life analogous to that played by the decisions of the highest policy makers in many other countries. Despite many amendments to the state constitutions, their language has remained remarkably stable. The United States Constitution, with its more stringent requirements for amendment, has been amended only fourteen times since 1791, and despite a great many important shifts in its interpretation by the Supreme Court, the original document remains an authoritative statement of American legal realities.

The mere fact that the United States Constitution is in writing is a symbol – indeed, an effective symbol – of its enduring character. America inherited the idea of the historicity of law from England, and ultimately from the Western concept of historical development. But America embodied that idea in a written document, thereby fixing permanently the language of American Constitutional law and at the same time providing an authoritative text for future generations of descendants and immigrants, wherever they might settle in the New World.

The United States Constitution is, in fact, a sacred text. It is to America what the New Testament is to the Christian Church. The devotion rendered to it is similar to that which once was rendered to absolute monarchs and which in the Soviet Union today is rendered to the Communist Party. Americans who are hopelessly divided on critical political and social issues – for example, racial equality – will accept, as morally authoritative, judicial and legislative decisions rendered in the name of Constitutional standards.[14] Such Constitutional phrases as "due process of law," "equal

---

[14] [See later, Berman, *Interaction*, 125.]

protection of the laws," "freedom of speech," "establishment of religion," "unreasonable searches and seizures," "trial by jury," "ex post facto law," "writ of habeas corpus," and many others, are – because they are in the Constitution – an integral part of the American language and of the very concept of what America stands for.

The Constitution, however, is not a code, in the European sense; nor is it a statute, in the English and American sense, to be interpreted according to the "plain meaning" of the words. It states, for the most part, broad legal principles, not detailed rules purporting to control specific conduct. Its language is sufficiently general to be adaptable to changed circumstances. Erwin Griswold has shown the significance of this quality of the American Constitution by contrasting the First Article of its Bill of Rights (the First Amendment) with the analogous provision of the Nigerian Constitution. The First Amendment states:

> Congress shall make no law respecting an establishment of religion, or prohibiting the free exercise thereof; or abridging the freedom of speech, or of the press; or the right of the people peaceably to assemble, and to petition the Government for a redress of grievances.

As Dean Erwin Griswold suggests, if these constitutional rights must be interpreted like statutes, according to their "plain sense," our free speech clause would have to look like Nigeria's. Section 24 of the Nigerian Constitution, relating to freedom of speech, reads as follows:

"(1) Every person shall be entitled to freedom of expression, including freedom to hold opinions and to receive and impart ideas and information without interference.

(2) Nothing in this paragraph shall invalidate any law that is reasonably justifiable in a democratic society –

    (a) in the interest of defence, public safety, public order, public morality, or public health;

    (b) for the purpose of protecting the rights, reputations and freedom of other persons, preventing the disclosure of information received in confidence, maintaining the authority and independence of the courts or regulating telephone, wireless broadcasting, television, or the exhibition of cinematograph films; or

    (c) imposing restrictions upon person holding office under the Crown, members of the armed forces of the Crown or members of a police force."

Dean Griswold comments that this provision has "lost its majesty":

> it may, indeed, have so far become just another statute that will cease to
> be effective just at the time when a provision for freedom of speech and
> the press must be effective if it is worth having such a provision at all ...
> [T]o an outsider it would seem to be a case where the result would have
> been better if it could have been recognized that the task in hand was the
> supremely important one of drafting a Constitution for the ages, rather
> than a statutory provision subject to the detailed supervision of the "plain
> meaning" rule.[15]

The fact that the Constitution is written, coupled with the fact that its
language is relatively broad, makes it not only possible but also inevitable
that those who are called on to interpret it will, in the course of time, give
it new meanings.[16] It is characteristic of law in general that it grows by giving new meanings to old words. But this proposition has a special significance in America, where, for the first time in history, a government was
founded on a written constitution directly binding on all citizens, and on
all branches of government. The survival of the American Constitution
by successive adaptations of its language to new circumstances is central
to the particular style of American legal discourse.

Faith in the Constitution as the highest law – in the words of Article
VI of the Constitution, "the supreme law of the land" – is the foundation of the American doctrine that a court must refuse to enforce a
statute that violates the Constitution. Such a doctrine seems anomalous
to both English and French lawyers: to English because of the belief in
Parliamentary supremacy, to French because of the belief in a strict separation of powers (in contrast to the more flexible American concept of
"checks and balances"). Since the end of World War II, under American
influence, Germany and Italy have adopted the doctrine of judicial review
of the constitutionality of legislative acts. But it was first made a lasting
feature of constitutional law in the United States during the period from
the Revolution to the Civil War.

The fact that the Constitution was in writing contributed to America's
faith in its supremacy over the legislature but it did not in itself create that
faith, as the French example shows: the French Revolution produced a
written constitution but left the legislature free of constitutional control

---

[15] [Erwin N. Griswold, "Two Branches of the Same Stream," Third Maccabean Lecture in
Jurisprudence, British Academy, London, October 18, 1962, quoted in Frederick A. O.
Schwarz, *Nigeria: The Tribes, The Nation, or The Race – The Politics of Independence*, repr.
edn. (Westport, CT: Greenwood Press, 1983 [1965]), 264.]

[16] [See later, Berman, *Faith and Order*, 217.]

by the judiciary. American judges, in contrast, took it for granted that since the judicial power derives from the Constitution and not from the Congress or the Executive, the courts could not do anything which the Constitution does not authorize. This was the reasoning of Chief Justice Marshall in the famous case of *Marbury* v. *Madison*. Marshall's logic has been challenged on the ground that he assumed the conclusion in his premises, but this criticism misses the point. His assumptions were rooted in his conception of the Constitution. Arguably, the courts should bow to a legislative determination of its meaning, as in England or France. But this argument neglects the sacred character of the text, and consequently the secular character of all acts and declarations made by the three branches of government which it has established. The legislature can err; the Constitution cannot ... [17]

5

[The American Revolution profoundly changed the nature of constitutional law in America, reflecting a compromise between American and French ideas and a good deal of innovation, too. The changes were more gradual at the level of common law, where American proved more apt

[17] [The text breaks off after this into a set of notes, some of which are a less developed draft of what is written above, some of which include scattered discussion of and quotes from nineteenth- and early twentieth-century legal developments in America. In a May 28, 1966 letter to Rosenstock, Berman wrote: "My immediate task in completing my book on Language and Law is to write (or finish writing) three (short) chapters: one on the language of American law, one on the language of Soviet law..." The letter breaks off here, too, leaving us to wonder about his plans for the third chapter. I have not found any further chapter drafts on American law or Soviet law. Berman had intended to return to this material in treating the "American Revolution," in the third volume of his *Law and Revolution* series, but he did not get to it. Most of the preliminary material for that third volume is collected in Berman, *Faith and Order*. Berman did continue telling the history of American law after the Revolution in his 1961 chapter, "Historical Aspects of American Law," in Harold J. Berman, ed., *Talks on American Law* (New York: Random House, 1961), 3–17, and I have tipped in a passage from that work, pp. 12–17, to complete this chapter. He included a great deal of teaching material on the development of American law in various editions of his *The Nature and Functions of Law*. And he later wrote a bit more about nineteenth- and twentieth-century American legal developments in several later articles, many with overlapping content. See, e.g., Harold J. Berman, "The Interaction of Law and Religion," *Capital University Law Review* 8 (1979): 343–56; "Religious Foundations of Law in the West: An Historical Perspective," *Journal of Law and Religion* 1 (1983): 3–43; "The Crisis of Legal Education in America," 347–52; "Religion and Law: The First Amendment in Historical Perspective," *Emory Law Journal* 35 (1986): 777–93; "Religion and Liberty Under Law at the Founding of America," *Regent University Law Review* 20 (2007): 31–36.]

to maintain English tradition.] An important part of that compromise was the reception of the English common law by the American states – that is, of the rules laid down by English courts prior to the American Revolution – together with certain English statutes. For the original thirteen American states on the Atlantic seaboard, this meant a continuation of their colonial legal institutions and doctrines. As new states were formed in the westward march across the American continent, it was generally provided in their constitutions that the English common law, as it then existed, should form the basis of judicial proceedings.

In the first seventy-five years of our history as a nation, American judges, jurists, and legislators were able to develop out of the received English law a body of legal institutions and doctrines which reflected the social life of the new American polity – an *American* law. Let me try to state briefly some of the principal characteristics of this new American law which have persisted from the eighteenth and early nineteenth centuries to the present day.

We have seen that a significant feature of English law through the centuries has been the important role of the judiciary in the development of legal doctrine and, consequently, of the lawyers who frame the issues for judicial decisions. In the United States, the role of the judiciary and of the legal profession has been still further enhanced. In part this is due to the existence of written federal and state constitutions, which set limits to the powers of the federal and state legislatures and specifically guarantee certain civil rights and liberties; constitutions whose interpretation, in the last analysis, is in the hands of the courts. In the nineteenth century the doctrine was developed in America that the courts can give no effect to any legislative or executive act which they find to be in violation of the federal or state constitutions.

Also, the existence of a federal structure, in which the individual states have a great measure of independence, made it inevitable that the judiciary play a crucial role in maintaining the constitutional balance between federal and state powers. Federalism, indeed, is one of the basic conditions of American law which has from the beginning influenced the development of all aspects of our system.

In addition, American law from the early nineteenth century on has been characterized by a higher degree of flexibility of judicial decision-making than English law in modern times. While accepting the English doctrine of precedent, whereby a court is bound to follow previous decisions of analogous cases, American courts have generally been more creative in reinterpreting earlier cases in order to adapt the law to changing conditions. American courts also did not accept the English doctrine – finally repudiated in 1966 – that the highest court can never overrule its own precedents; the United States Supreme Court, as well as the Supreme Courts of the various states, have on occasion declared simply that one of their previous decisions was wrong and would not be followed.

Moreover, the American legal profession, although its historical roots are in the English Inns of Court which trained some of the leading American lawyers of colonial times, has developed its own characteristics. The apprenticeship system gradually gave way in the nineteenth century to university education in law; at the same time, the law faculty of an American university is constituted as a professional school, maintaining close connections with the practicing legal profession. Our lawyers have always been very numerous, and from their ranks have come a very large percentage of our presidents, congressmen, state governors, and other leading political figures, both national and local. Moreover, the continental dimensions of our country, and the diverse ethnic backgrounds of our people, have contributed to a tendency to turn to courts and to lawyers for the solution of the widest variety of economic, political, and social problems – problems which in many other countries are solved more informally by private business interests, by government officials, or by custom.

Finally, in the "formative era of American law" prior to the Civil War of 1861–65, courts, lawyers, and legal scholars reshaped and modernized basic legal concepts of property, contract, corporations, negotiable instruments, and other areas of economic law. It would be wrong to suggest that the rules of law worked out in that era were "modern" in the sense that they would correspond to our needs today. Nevertheless, many of the basic concepts of our law were then freed from medieval survivals and put in a form which enabled them to be used more effectively by succeeding generations.

Thus many of the important features of the American legal system were established prior to the great industrial expansion which followed the American Civil War. Of course, the enormous economic, political, and social changes of the past one hundred years have been accompanied by corresponding changes in our legal system. As we became a predominantly industrial and urban society, as the "big business" corporation emerged and labor organized, as communications developed to create a continental market and a continental culture, as our population doubled and quadrupled, our law inevitably became far more complex; and at the same time it became more systematized and more rationalized. Yet it is fair to say that most of our basic legal institutions and concepts antedate these vast changes; and further, that because of that fact, we have been able to assimilate change far more peacefully and efficiently than would otherwise have been possible.

If American law is viewed in the perspective of more than eight centuries, it is justifiable to lay stress on the creative role of the judiciary and of the legal profession, and on basic concepts of civil law and individual rights. In the perspective of more recent generations, the dominant factors seem to be legislative and administrative regulation of private activity. In the 1920s and 1930s, when the judiciary was often hostile to new social legislation, it became fashionable in many circles to advocate the emergence of the "administrative state," which would achieve "social justice" without the need for traditional legal procedures and categories. Yet time has shown that the judicial testing of statutory and administrative regulations by analogy of previous cases has a vital part to play not only in protecting individuals against abuse by officials but also in helping to make the official regulations themselves workable. Beyond this, there are values inherent in the judicial tradition and in the common law which can help us to anticipate and prevent the new barbarism of a technological age. Not the least of these values is that of tradition itself – that is, the vitality of historical experience as a starting point for solving the problems of the present and of the future.

~

Conclusion: Can communication build one world?

1

Language in action is more than a collection of particular sounds, letter combinations, and dictionary meanings. It is a process of creating social relations.[1] The most important aspect of speech is the reciprocal transfer of meanings between speaker and listener. In fact, I feel we need to invent a new term, "speak-listen," to show that we do not speak "to" but "with" each other. Language also involves persons other than the immediate participants in a conversation. By speaking we affirm our membership in the various language communities to which we belong.

If language can be seen as a process of making community, or what might be called "communification," then it clearly has a profound relevance to the tragic disunity that threatens to destroy us – not only to the international disunity of the Cold War and colonial revolutions, but also to national conflicts between races, and even generations and sexes. Behind all these stand the deeper cause, the loss of a sense of community, which is in part attributable to our loss of faith in language as a process of communification.

Usually it is felt that the causes of these conflicts are antagonistic economic and political interests, racial and ideological differences, technological factors, and the like. But a nation, class, or race is not defined by "natural" or "material" or "technological" factors, but by people's consciousness of those factors and by their responses to them. Similarly, it is usually thought that our loss of faith in words is the effect, rather than the cause, of what cynical men do with words to achieve political and economic goals. But if this is so, it only raises, and does not solve, the question

---

[1] [The "Law and Language" manuscript lacked a conclusion. For the first four sections of this conclusion, I have incorporated, with a bit of editing, this text written the same year and published as "The Language of Law: Can Communication Build One World?" 26–31. I have added references to a few of Berman's other writings in the early 1960s when he was working on the "Law and Language" manuscript.]

of how their cynicism can be overcome. The truth is that our own skepticism concerning language antedates the present state of affairs. For at least four decades we have been taught about the tyranny of words, the treachery of words, the inherent ambiguity of words, by political scientists, philosophers, the new social scientists, and even some poets. Against their view stands the obvious fact that none of us has invented the language that we speak, and each of us has only a limited power to change it.

Is it possible, however, to create a language community beyond our own nation or culture? Benjamin Whorf and others have emphasized that each national language reflects a distinct conception of life, and that therefore particular languages are determining factors in our processes of perception. Yet this cultural relativity is not absolute, for all people have certain linguistic traits in common. Moreover, most kinds of speech can be translated from one language into another.[2]

The Judeo-Christian vision of the oneness of mankind can be realized not only by the power of translation but also by the increasing unification of the peoples of the earth through a common vocabulary – not through that of Esperanto or Basic English, but through words from direct and vicarious common experience. Already we have the roots of this language in the names of men and events such as Jesus, Buddha, Galileo, and Lincoln, or, on the other hand, Napoleon, Stalin, Hitler, Hiroshima, and Berlin. The language of science, medicine, and technology is also universal.[3]

If we have the power of translation and the roots of a universal language, why are we not at peace? The answer, I believe, is that we are divided because we do not recognize how divisions among men are overcome. What is lacking is the faith required to begin to make peace, to speak with each other, to develop gradually a common language for understanding and resolving conflicts.

2

Among the words that create social cohesion are the ceremonial ones, such as the language used at inaugurations, weddings, anniversaries, and funerals. Equally important is the language of scholarship, economic cooperation, and political authority. But still another language can do this, the language of law, which has been strangely neglected by both writers on language and writers on law. The social functions of law have in general been found in the authority of legal rules, the morality which

[2] [See above, pp. 52–3.]   [3] [See above, pp. 55–6.]

law reflects, and the nature of legal institutions, but rarely in its linguistic form, that is, its vocabulary, structure, and style. It is the linguistic aspect that is common to all legal systems; on its foundation, rather than on that of uniform legal policies or legal morals, a common body of international law is emerging.

The formality, complexity, and insistence on categorization of legal language tend to make it incomprehensible to the layman. It is important, therefore, to show its relationship to other kinds of language and to improve it, so that it may become one of the community's living languages. There is a school of legal philosophy that would define law as policy, thus removing all restraints from the law-maker or law-interpreter. This definition is not true; the old words are trusted, and if they cease to be, the law loses its acceptability to the losing side, its peacemaking power, and merges entirely with force.

In all legal systems, law begins as a spoken language as a response to social disorder and injustice. Some have found the process of resolving conflict by legal language to be magic, since the terms appear to have no empirical referents. This is because legal statements do not describe what exists; rather they *ascribe* rights and duties and thereby *create* relationships. Legal language is one of ordering, judging, regulating, and negotiating.

As compared to other languages, legal language develops deliberately; it expands or contracts its meanings gradually in the light of new experience. In all mature systems there is a tension created by professionals who would usurp those parts of law to be heard and understood by the laymen. If these roots are neglected, however, the communifying power of law will be weakened.

3

The character of law as a kind of language accounts not only for its universal features but also for the distinctive features of particular legal systems. Let me illustrate by comparisons and contrasts between American and Soviet law. Perhaps 70 percent of the terms of Soviet law are to be found in Western legal systems. These are words such as: civil liability, complaint, jurisdiction, statute of limitations, guilt, negligence, compensation for harm, evidence, administration of evidence, verdict, witness, and many more. Most of these words have been imported into the Russian language from Western Europe, which in turn took them from Latin, directly or indirectly. Thus translation, with or without adaptation to native roots, is a characteristic feature of legal language, and is enhanced by the fact that Soviet and American lawyers share many of the moral principles implicit in these concepts – the right to a hearing, the presumption of innocence in criminal cases, and the proportioning of punishment to the degree of guilt and to the social consequences of the act.[4]

In contrast to the American system, however, most of the present Russian legal terminology has developed only within the past 150 years. Prior to the nineteenth century there was no separate legal profession and only a relatively primitive legal science. Hence legal language has not sunk into the Russian consciousness to the same extent that it has with Western peoples. The roughly 30 percent of Soviet law that is distinctly Soviet stems from such features as the nation's planned economy, which has spawned many new legal terms and concepts, and its one-party state, which has total responsibility for all aspects of social life, including the circulation of thought, the individual's choice of vocation, and a system of informal social pressures such as the "comrades' courts."[5] These features may seem extremely repressive to the individualistic Westerner, yet they serve to organize society for positive purposes as well. Soviet law strongly protects social rights: the right to work, to have an education, to social security, to medical care, to a proportionate share of the limited housing facilities, and to legal services. The key to the differences between Soviet law and ours is its emphasis on the collective, on discipline, and on state protection offered in return for service by the people.[6]

---

[4] [This deep comparative study of the law of the USSR and the West was central to Berman's work from the later 1940s to early 1970s. See esp. his 1963 classic *Justice in the USSR*; see further, Berman, "Soviet Law and Government," 19–26; "Law as an Instrument of Mental Health in the United States and Soviet Russia," *University of Pennsylvania Law Review* 91 (1961): 361–76; "The Comparison of Soviet and American Law," 559–70; "The Dilemma of Soviet Law Reform," 929–51; "Law in American Democracy and Under Soviet Communism," 105–13. See later distillation of his views in Harold J. Berman, "The Rule of Law and the Law-Based State (Rechtsstaat) (With Special Reference to Developments in the Soviet Union)," in Donald D. Barry, ed., *Toward the "Rule of Law" in Russia?* (Armonk, NY: M.E. Sharpe, 1992), 43–60.]

[5] [See Harold J. Berman and James W. Spindler, "Soviet Comrades' Courts," *Washington Law Review* 38 (1963): 842–910.]

[6] [Berman wrote frequently about the contrasts between Soviet and Western ideas of rights. See, e.g., Harold J. Berman, "Human Rights in the Soviet Union," *Howard Law Journal* 11 (1965): 333–41; "American and Soviet Perspectives on Human Rights," *Worldview* 22(11) (November 1979): 15–21; Harold J. Berman, Erwin N. Griswold and Frank C. Newman, "Draft USSR Law on Freedom of Conscience, with Commentary," *Harvard Human Rights Journal* 3 (1990): 137–56; Harold J. Berman, "Freedom of Religion in Russia: An Amicus Brief for the Defendant," in John Witte, Jr. and Michael Bourdeaux, eds., *Proselytism and Orthodoxy in Russia: The New War for Souls* (Maryknoll, NY: Orbis Books, 1999), 265–83; "The Struggle for Law in Post-Soviet Russia,"), 41–55; "Religious Rights in Russia at a

Just as our law has a heritage, so does Soviet law, and the common features of both make it easier to translate into English, and into our own experience, even those parts which seem strange to us. In Russian law, as modified by Soviet law, there is, like ours, the language of advocacy, negotiation, examination of witnesses, and other traditional forms of legal rhetoric.

4

Is this enough to overcome the sharp differences between the two systems so that law can serve as a common language for both countries, or even for all mankind? There also exists the common legal language of international relations, and it is by no means as weak an instrument for maintaining peace as many have supposed. Contrary to what Hans Morgenthau has said, national political interest *has* yielded to international legal obligation on occasion. The withdrawal of British, French, and Israeli forces from the Suez peninsula in 1956 is one example. It is also not true that the Soviet Union has no respect for international law. In the past twenty years, the Soviets have observed fairly rigorously international rules of jurisdiction, freedom of the seas, and other prerequisites of sovereignty, as well as those rules relating to commercial transactions, particularly the exporting and importing of goods.[7] International law has proved its immediate utility to Soviet foreign policy at the time of the U-2 flight, in the conclusion of the test-ban treaty, in United Nations deliberations, and at many other times and places, just as it has often proved its immediate utility to United States foreign policy.[8] Nor does Soviet theory deny that international law is a limitation upon sovereignty, including Soviet sovereignty. G. I. Tunkin, chief legal advisor of the Soviet Ministry of Foreign Affairs, wrote in 1956:

> International law, together with the fact that it represents a combination of principles and norms binding upon states, is, like any law, a weapon of policy: both socialist and capitalist states in carrying out their foreign

Time of Tumultuous Transition: A Historical Theory," in Johan D. van der Vyver and John Witte, Jr., eds., *Religious Human Rights in Global Perspective: Legal Perspectives* (Dordrecht/Boston: Martinus Nijhoff, 1996), 285–304.]

[7] [East–West trade with the Soviets was a central interest of Berman's in this period. See sources in Introduction, herein, note 58.]

[8] [See further, Harold J. Berman, "The U-2 Incident and International Law," *Harvard Law Record* 31(4) (October 13, 1960): 9–12; "Introduction," to *The Trial of the U-2* (Chicago: Translation World Publishers, 1960), i–xxx.]

policy make more or less use of international law. From this, however, it certainly does not follow that international law can be a weapon of any policy. Generally recognized principles and norms of contemporary international law, being in their essence democratic, may be used as a weapon of the foreign policy of states only within the limits defined by the content of these norms.[9]

In addition to traditional international law, the past decades have witnessed the development of a new body of international law, exemplified by the United Nations, with its many specialized agencies and its broad multilateral arrangements for resolving conflict – a body of law to which both the Soviet Union and the United States are committed.

Nevertheless, it is obvious that existing international law is not highly enough developed or powerful enough to bind the world, and especially the Soviet Union and the United States, into a unified legal order capable of withstanding serious political conflict and creating a positive peace. Some people believe that this kind of peaceful collaboration is impossible in the foreseeable future, and that we are destined to live in the Cold War indefinitely. Others answer that peace can only be made by strengthening the United Nations into a kind of supranational government that will enforce order in a disarmed world. A third answer is that we may look forward to the increasing acceptance by all states, including Communist states, of certain principles of order, certain shared legal values; and that the existence of common principles among the various legal systems of the world already forms an empirical base for a uniform system of world law, an emerging "common law of mankind," as Wilfred Jenks has called it.[10] All of these answers, however, rest on traditional philosophies which in my view neglect the linguistic and historical aspect of law. All of them conceive of law in terms of will or reason, or both, of policy or morality, or both, without taking into account the creative and therapeutic power of language itself.

[9] [I have not found this exact quote, but this is a central theme of Tunkin's work in this period and thereafter. See, e.g., Grigorii Ivanovich Tunkin, *The Tunkin Diary and Lectures: The Diary and Collected Lectures of G.I. Tunkin at the Hague Academy of International Law [1958-1986]*, ed. and trans. William E. Butler and Vladimir G. Tunkin (The Hague: Eleven International Publishing, 2012); *Theory of International Law* (Harvard University Press, 1974); *Contemporary International Law: Collection of Articles* (Moscow: Progress Publishers, 1969); *Law and Force in the International System* (Moscow: Progress Publishers, 1985).]

[10] [C. Wilfred Jenks, *The Common Law of Mankind* (New York: Praeger, 1958). See Berman's development of this theme in his "Religious Foundations of Law in the West," 42–43; "Law and Religion in the Development of a World Order," 35; *Faith and Order*, 307–10.]

A similar legal philosophy leads to the error of proposing a centralized world government for the near future. It is argued that since law depends on the existence of a state apparatus, international law needs only an international political organization, with an international legislature, an international judiciary, and an international police force. However, drafters of these plans do not tell us how we are to take the first steps necessary to establish the kind of understanding essential even to consider such proposals, much less the kind of common loyalties necessary to make them work.

Similarly premature is the effort to establish moral-legal principles or values to which all governments would adhere. Those are important as criteria for testing and reforming an existing body of law, but if the law does not yet exist, agreement on principles is only a basis for disagreement concerning their specific application. The only way to move from the existing coincidence of broad moral and legal principles to world law[11] is to view its development in terms of a development of a common legal language.

The United States must learn to sacrifice its idea – adopted from the Soviets – that speech is an instrument of ideological warfare. In the propaganda fight, we have everything to gain and nothing to lose by unilateral disarmament. Let us speak only with the truth and only in the interest of peace. We must seek to develop, together with the Russians, a common legal language of rights and duties, of contract, property, and crime, adjudication, administration and legislation, negotiation and advocacy. Such language will develop out of the application of legal techniques and legal science to common problems, in accordance with the legal ideals of both countries.

A striking example of how speech, including legal speech, can help to make peace, is that of the Cuban crisis of October 1962. Many Americans,

---

[11] [The development of a "world law" would become a major theme in Berman's later work, especially in the last decade of his career, when he developed a "World Law Institute" at Emory Law School, and convened conferences at Emory, Central European University, Moscow State University, and elsewhere. See, e.g., "Introduction to the World Law Institute." Speech delivered at the World Law Institute Inaugural Conference entitled: "World Law and World Health: Especially the Health of Women in Least Developed and Developing Countries," on March 22–24, 2007, *Emory International Law Review* 22 (2008):1–6. For his later writing on this topic see: "Law and Religion in the Development of a World Order"; "Law and Logos"; "World Law in the New Millennium"; "World Law," 379–84; "Integrative Jurisprudence and World Law"; "Faith and Law in a Multicultural World," 69–89; "World Law: An Ecumenical Jurisprudence of the Holy Spirit," 365–74. See further above, introduction, p. 12; chapter 4, n. 1.]

perhaps most, have drawn an entirely wrong lesson from that experience. They have viewed it as an example of the supremacy of force in international relations. The Soviets are said to have shown their respect for force. We were ready to fight if they would not withdraw their missiles, so they withdrew their missiles. But this interpretation is only half the truth. President Kennedy made it clear on many occasions that he did not accept the view that the Cuban experience teaches us only that the Soviets will always back down if confronted with our superior force and our determination to fight for what we want. President Kennedy was convinced in October 1962 that the Soviets would not go to war with us *provided* that we spoke softly and did everything possible not to say anything to humiliate them. Indeed, we made a bargain with them: we said that if they would withdraw their missiles we would agree not to invade Cuba. This was a substantial commitment. Also, we took care not to flaunt our blockade but to attempt to disguise it as a "quarantine," thereby paying lip-service at least, to international law. It is because our force was backed by the language of peace, by a bargained promise not to commit aggression against Cuba, and by the invention of an ambiguous legal term, "quarantine," that Krushchev could treat it at home as a victory and abroad as a basis for further cooperation, including the negotiation of the test-ban treaty and also that of a consular treaty.

This is an example from high international politics. It is offered in order to illustrate the point that our communicated experience can be a source of development of legal relations, out of which can grow, in turn, a common legal language and a more peaceful international community. But in the long run, the more important examples must come from levels of experience less highly charged with tension. We need to ratify the consular treaty with the Soviet Union. We need a civil air agreement that would permit American planes to fly to Moscow and Soviet planes to fly to New York. We need not 40 Soviet graduate students in American universities each year but 140, indeed 1,400, with or without reciprocity. We need a trade agreement with the Soviets of the type the British, French, Italians, West Germans, and dozens of other countries have. We need to expand scientific and technological cooperation in a hundred areas.

Given the common experience of two world wars, of a worldwide economy, of a universal technology which has reached even into outer space, and of the anticipation of the possible destruction of the entire human race, mankind is ready to begin to develop a common law. Such a common law cannot develop, however, out of the efforts of each major power to project its own will and reason upon the rest of the world.

Our hope is rather in a restoration of the power to speak and listen, the power to find the words to identify areas of agreement, and the power to develop – by all the arts of legal rhetoric – the language of agreement into a language of law which will ultimately serve to command respect, to reconcile conflict, and to communify the nations.

5[12]

For the first time in history, mankind is united in a practical sense. It is united by its capacity to destroy itself. It is united by communications systems that bring every part of the world in almost immediate contact with every other part. It is united by worldwide science and technology, by worldwide trade, by a worldwide system of diplomacy. It shares some features of a common culture. It has the rudiments of a common law.

The idea of the unity of mankind is, of course, not new: it is implicit in the biblical story of creation, and it found its greatest expression in the lives of the great Hebrew prophets, in Jesus Christ, who died for all men, in St. Paul, who taught that God made of one blood all nations of the earth, and in the lives and teachings of such great personalities as Buddha and Lao Tzu. What is new is the manifestation of this idea in the gradual emergence of world institutions of a political, economic, and cultural character. These institutions are being forged in the midst of wars which continue to be, for the most part, international in form but which in substance are civil wars, revolutionary wars, precisely because they are being fought within the community of a mankind that is seeking to create for itself a common process of establishing order and justice and a common system of ultimate values.

Mankind already has, of course, the rudiments of a law of international relations, including the law of diplomacy, the law of treaties, the law of international organizations, the law of international trade and finance, the law of conflicts of laws, and other branches of public and private international law. Originally derived from the Western legal tradition, modern international law is now developed by all countries of the world. It is true that states violate international law when they believe it is in their overriding interest to do so; nevertheless, it is important to recognize that without a common legal language the major powers might well have been at full-scale war with each other at any time during the past twenty-five

---

[12] [Section 5 is drawn from Berman, *Interaction*, 122–25 (a subsection entitled "The Communification of Mankind").]

years. Moreover, the fact that governments, groups, and individual persons from all different countries of the world speak with each other in terms of internationally accepted legal norms – negotiate, settle disputes, and jointly regulate their affairs – unquestionably reflects a common legal consciousness and also strengthens, renews, and indeed helps to create that consciousness.

Yet the community of mankind needs much more law. It needs arms reduction agreements. It needs a willingness on the part of the wealthy countries of the world to finance, through the United Nations, substantial economic development among the poor countries. It needs a willingness on the part of the great powers to submit their disputes to impartial adjudication. It needs the expansion of treaty relations, especially of an economic character, between the countries of Western Europe and the United States, on the one hand, and the countries of Eastern Europe and the Soviet Union on the other. Also, much remains to be done to bring Communist China into full participation in the international legal community. These and other measures must be taken to strengthen international law if the community of mankind is not to dissolve into anarchy.

If the common law of mankind is rudimentary, its common religion is almost non-existent. Indeed, it is precisely in its fundamental beliefs that mankind is most divided. Of course, just as a common religion or ideology does not guarantee peace, so religious or ideological differences are not necessarily divisive, provided that a basic humanism and tolerance and respect for law are maintained. Yet the lack of a common religious, racial, and cultural consensus among the peoples of the world places a substantial burden on the unifying role of law – as is shown by the experience of the United States, where we have had to rely very heavily on our faith in the Constitution and the courts to unite us just because of our religious, racial, and cultural diversity.

Looking at the world as a whole, it seems apparent that humanism and good will and respect for law cannot alone overcome the gods of Nation and Race and Class, and that some elements of a common universal religion are necessary to give mankind a sense of direction and the courage to face the future. The world needs a radical vision of a common destiny, and common convictions for which people of different nations, races, and classes are willing to make sacrifices; and it needs common rituals and traditions that embody its vision and its convictions.

And so mankind lives on its planet, like the two men under a tree waiting for Godot in Beckett's play – with means of communication but little to say, with some rules to go by but with no assurance they will be followed. Yet it is mankind, planetary man – a new creature. The new law that he needs will come – if at all – from a reconstituting of preexisting concepts and processes, "a universalizing and intensifying of them until they are reborn."[13] The new religion will come – if at all – from the prophets, saints, and heroes of the new era.

6[14]

[Let me conclude with a brief reflection on the distinct role that Christianity, among other world religions, has to play in this process of peace-building, of communification.[15]] In the real world, Christianity often has precious little to do with peace. Of course, if Christianity were really taken seriously by those who profess it, there might not be any wars, because true Christians would never fight in wars and by their example they might convert the war-makers. But most Christians, not being pacifists, do fight in wars, on whatever side they happen to be. Furthermore, people who really believe in peace, that is, true pacifists, are not necessarily Christians. But even apart from pacifism, the way to build world peace is to develop friendly relations among the different peoples of the world, to develop political institutions through which international conflicts can be resolved, to solve the problems of poverty in the underdeveloped countries, and in general to take the humane steps toward building a healthy world order. All decent people agree that these steps are necessary, though, because of human selfishness and prejudice, they do not always find concrete reflection in international society. Again, Christianity is not really necessary here either, though it can be helpful.

---

[13] Cf. Edward Le Roy Long, *A Survey of Christian Ethics* (New York: Oxford University Press, 1967), 34.

[14] [Section 6 is drawn from an unpublished sermon by Berman, "Peace and Security: World," A Lenten Talk on March 5, 1969 in an ecumenical series at First Church Congregational in Cambridge.]

[15] [Berman converted from Judaism to Christianity as a young adult. See his own stirring account of his conversion in Harold J. Berman, "Judeo-Christian Versus Pagan Scholarship," in Kelly K. Monroe, *Finding God at Harvard: Spiritual Journeys of Christian Thinkers* (Downers Grove, IL: IVP Books, 1996), 291–95. Berman, however, retained a deep attachment to his Jewish roots. He often read the "Old Testament" passages of the Bible in Hebrew. In other contexts, Berman also liked to read the Qur'an and some of the writings of Confucius. His colleagues took note of his embracive religiosity. See, e.g., the two responses to Berman's 2005 essay "The Historical Foundations of Law," 13–24; Abdullahi An-Na'im, "Globalization and Jurisprudence: An Islamic Law Perspective," *Emory Law Journal* 54 (2005): 25–52; Michael J. Broyde, "A Jewish Law View of World Law," *Emory Law Journal* 54 (2005): 79–96.]

Where does this leave Christianity? Christianity is the set of beliefs, attitudes, feelings, which each and every Christian has in relationship to God. It's up to the individual – some choose Christianity, others choose some other philosophy of life. The Christianity of some is much worse than the humanism of others – though the "true" Christian, of course, has hold of the greatest philosophy of life that mankind has ever produced, even though it is incapable of creating peace in the world (because very few people are capable of living up to it).

My idea is that Christianity is not so much a personal philosophy of life, not so much a religion in that sense, as it is an explanation of the history of mankind. Christianity rather takes the form of a dialogue between God and man – a kind of Socratic dialogue. God explains the human situation by putting questions to us. He asks us, "Won't you agree to this?" "Don't you want that?" "Do you realize the danger you are in if you ignore these commandments?" "Do you fully appreciate how right it is to sacrifice yourself for others?" "Look around you – do you see how dependent you all are on each other?" If we see Christianity as a dialogue which God has initiated with man, I think we can see that Christians are called to transform this dialogue into a dialogue also among men, in which we are brought into relationships with each other, so that we share common convictions, undertake common tasks, and recognize a common authority. All life is a great conversation, a discourse, a speaking together, which goes back to the very beginning, to God Himself.

Now what has this to do with peace? In the first place, the Bible tells us that all mankind forms a single community – that we have a common ancestor in Adam and that we have a common destiny to live ultimately in a universal peace, or else a universal destruction. This *idea* of the community of mankind found its supreme expression in Jesus Christ, who died for all mankind, and in whose spirit St. Paul taught that God made of one blood all nations of the earth. We sometimes forget that at that time the world consisted of a great multiplicity of wholly separate communities, most of which had never heard of each other. Jesus stood in total defiance of the political and economic environment in which he lived when he taught that all men everywhere could be united through love of God and of each other. In fact, his followers did spread to virtually all countries, and ultimately it was their faith in the oneness of mankind – and their betrayal of that faith – that brought into being the one world we now live in, united not by love but by technology, by trade and investment, by political, economic, and cultural strife.

This physical, or material, unity of mankind is, of course, new. Every people of the world is directly involved politically and economically and technologically in the fate of every other people; and that is a phenomenon of the past two generations. Two world wars, and the threat of a third, have joined all mankind in a common destiny. We are all in contact with each other. Paradoxically, the human race is becoming unified by its capacity for mutual self-destruction.

So one explanation of human history, given by Christianity, is the oneness of mankind, that is, the supremacy of the human spirit – the supremacy of faith, hope, and love – over all physical, racial, geographical, economic, and political boundaries. This is not a personal philosophy I am speaking of but a social philosophy. Socially, all people are brothers and sisters, and they will either love each other or they will hate each other – they will either make a real peace or they will make a real war.

Now, the community of mankind, and the various sub-communities of nations, races, classes, cities, corporations, universities, and the like into which it is divided, has the choice to live by faith or cynicism, hope or despair, love or hate. That is the choice that God gives the human race viewed in social terms. This gives us a clue to the relationship between our social life and our individual life, or rather our macro-social life as Americans or capitalists or professionals, and our micro-social life as husbands, sons, neighbors, or classmates.

What Christianity says, it seems to me, is that the same rules apply to our personal lives as to our social lives: not the same rules of morality, necessarily, but the same rules of the human spirit. The same rules of faith, hope, and love. The same rules of sacrifice and of imagination and of putting yourself in the place of others. In other words, it seems to me that Christianity, says, quite simply, that all mankind is a single family, and that the little families in which we live are models and training grounds for the bigger universal human family. Peace is indivisible in this sense: peace in our personal relations with God, peace in our interpersonal relations with our neighbors, and macro-social peace among classes, races, and nations. All are made out of the same stuff.

~

Afterword: On Harold Berman, law, language, the Tower of Babel, and Pentecost

TIBOR VÁRADY

1

At the opening of Chapter 3 of this volume, Harold Berman writes: "The language of the law, as we have seen, is forged in the fire of legal procedures: of law-making, judging, regulating, negotiation, and other processes of creating, changing or terminating rights and duties."[1] This language relies on words derived from non-legal speech; but what is "forged in the fire of legal procedures" becomes a distinct domain, and it becomes "strange and unacceptable to the non-lawyer."[2] A rift has been created between the legal language and the layman's language. (More or less the same applies to the juxtaposition of any professional language and layman's language.) This creates a need for translation. Translators can only be those who speak both languages. This limits the circle of potential translators from legal language to lawyers. As Berman points out:

> The lawyer generally likes to translate, if he can get the layman's ear; and much of his professional work itself requires such translation – to clients, to juries, to legislative committees, and even to judges in oral argument … But the translation of professional legal language back into the popular speech from which it ultimately derives is not a substitute for the professional language itself. We can unfreeze the legal terms, but we cannot replace them.[3]

Thus, there is both a need and a possibility to build bridges between legal language and layman's language. Yet these bridges yield no merger; they merely allow communication between distinct domains.

---

[1] See above, Chapter 3, p. 87.   [2] Ibid., 87.
[3] Ibid., p. 104.

The problem also has a further dimension, which creates an even more pressing need for bridges (that is, for translation). Let me quote Berman again:

> When we look more closely, we see that mankind speaks many differ-ent languages and uses many different kinds of law, each language bear-ing the stamp of a particular community and each kind of law, each legal system, bearing the stamp of a particular social order and a particular kind of justice. It is important that we recognize that as all language is one, so all law is one; but it is equally important that we recognize the unique qualities of different languages and different kinds of law – for it is characteristic for our common humanity that it not only permits but also requires a wide range of diversity among the different communities which comprise it.[4]

Legal language relies on terms and notions that are not only profession specific, but also culture specific – and which find different expressions in different languages. Within the process of international dispute reso-lution (which has a constantly and rapidly growing share within dispute resolution in general) translation is a multidimensional problem – and also an everyday problem.

Berman captures both the problem and the solution in terms of a bib-lical metaphor. The problem is encapsulated in the story of the Tower of Babel, in which God prevented men from erecting a city and a tower that would reach the sky. A handicap was imposed on men to make them unable to accomplish their God-defying project. This handicap was a newly born multitude of languages and inability to understand each other. In the words of Berman: "That story tells us that at one time all men spoke the same language, but because of their pride God 'confused the language of all the earth' so that men could not understand one another's speech."[5] While the metaphor for the problem is the Tower of Babel, the metaphor for the solution is Pentecost, "[w]hich tells us that at a place where people of different languages had gathered to worship, certain of them were given the power to speak 'in other languages', so that all the peoples of the earth could hear 'the mighty works of God', 'each in his own native tongue'. Thus the story of Pentecost gives hope that the pride of man can be over-come, and that by translation from one language to another we may share each other's experience vicariously and become once again united."[6]

---

[4] See above, Chapter 4, p. 113.

[5] See above, Chapter 1, p. 54, with reference to Genesis, 11:2–9.

[6] Ibid., pp. 54–55, with reference to Acts 2:1–13.

It is interesting that – according to the Bible – when Parthians and Medes, residents of Mesopotamia, Judea and Cappadocia, Pontus and Asia, Phrygia and Pamphylia, Egypt, Jews and Proselytes, Cretans and Arabians, visitors from Rome, and others, asked themselves, "How is it that we hear, each of us in his native language?" one emerging explanation was: "They are filled with new wine."[7] But Peter lifted his voice and explained that "these people are not drunk, as you suppose," and offered a more dignified explanation of the miracle of translation, hinting at illumination by the Holy Spirit.[8]

One may add here that the need to reach people in a variety of languages – and an awareness of the importance of translation – has also received recognition in other holy books that have established religions. For example, it is stated in the Qur'an that:

> And among His Signs
> Is the creation of the heavens
> And the Earth, and the variations
> In your languages
> And colors;[9]

To take another example, the origin of the Book of Mormon is tied to a tale of translation. As stated in the introduction of the Book, when Joseph Smith was 21 years old, an angel named Moroni gave him the gold plates on which Mormon wrote/engraved his book by his own hands. Joseph had little formal education and was unfamiliar with the ancient language used by Mormon, but he was able to translate it because God gave him the power to do so. The translation took less than three months, and in 1830 the book – and a new religion – appeared.

2

Translation may be a blessing, but it is also a momentous task. How can you, for example, translate "certiorari" into various languages, when other legal cultures do not have an identical institution? This also applies to legal cultures based on the English language, which have not adopted a writ of certiorari as a possible remedy. At such a juncture, translation by way of finding a matching word in another language is

---

[7] Acts 2:8–13 (English Standard Version)
[8] Acts 2:14–21 (English Standard Version)
[9] The Holy Qur'an, trans. Abdullah Yusuf Ali (Brentwood, MD: Amana Corporation, 1989), Sūrah 30.22.

simply not a solution. In these situations, the substitute for translation is explanation.

Or let us take an example mentioned by Berman. Speaking of the development of legal concepts based on the substitution of meanings of words, he takes the example of "eavesdropping" (referring to Paul Freund).[10] Originally, the ancient wrong of "eavesdropping" depended on trespass beneath the eaves of a house with the aim of listening to what people were saying inside. Later, "eavesdropping" gained a much broader meaning, but retained a distinct touch of history. Can one translate history-transmuted-to-flavor? Unfortunately not. But one can find in most languages a more or less matching term that will translate the present notion and connotations of "eavesdropping."

Let me add that documents that are the focus of a lawsuit will typically offer cause for dispute because they are ambiguous and are thus understood differently by different parties. Can translation mirror the same ambiguity, and will it offer the same chances as the original? In other words, will the likelihood of an interpretation in favor of the seller (or of the buyer) be the same as it would be on the basis of the original?

To continue the list of limitations to the blessing of translation, let me mention that translation of advocacy, of pleadings, may amount to a daunting (and not always possible) task. The advocate will try to make an impression with logic, and this is usually translatable. But persuasion has other elements, too, which may not be reproduced in an adequate translation. There are words that are very well suited for emphasis in one language, but not in another. A play on connotations may or may not be reproduced effectively in translation.[11]

The point is not that we should abandon or disparage translation. Translation is, indeed, a blessing, but it will produce better results if one is aware of its limitations. As a matter of fact, we have witnessed a dramatic increase in the importance of translation during the past several decades. This increase is due to a most consequential upsurge in dispute settlement without an anchor in one specific language. During the past decade, the International Court of Justice (ICJ) and the Permanent Court of Arbitration (PCA) have been joined by international criminal courts, like the International Criminal Court (ICC), and specialized international

---

[10] See above, Chapter 3, pp. 99–100.
[11] See the subchapter on limitations of translation in Tibor Várady, *Language and Translation in International Commercial Arbitration* (The Hague: T.M.C. Asser Press, 2006), 85–90.

criminal courts, like the International Criminal Tribunal for the Former Yugoslavia (ICTY) or the International Criminal Tribunal for Rwanda (ICTR). None of these tribunals has one official language only; and practically all cases before the ICTY and ICTR involve the translation of documents and witness statements from the languages spoken in the area of the conflict. Let me add that during the past decades international commercial arbitration has become mainstream; it is no longer just an alternative but has become the dominant method of settling international commercial disputes. This dominant option does not have an official language (as courts do); it has instead various rules on determining the language of arbitration[12] – and translation has become an element of the environment of international commercial arbitration.

In order to bring closer the present-day mission of bridging language differences, I would like to offer in this essay some illustrations indicating the complexity of the problem in real legal life.

First, can there be full equality in a multilingual setting? Building bridges and crossing bridges between languages takes time. The time factor leaves an imprint on cases in which translation is needed and used. It is commonly accepted that one of the key purposes (and results) of translation is equality. Someone who does not speak the language of the proceedings, or the language of a witness, will nevertheless become an equal participant by way of translation. But the time factor also emerges, and the question arises whether it might taint equality – and if it does, whether remedy is justified.

Let me bring this problem closer through an illustration from the practice of the ICJ. Oral pleadings before the ICJ sometimes have quite a tight schedule. This is particularly true for shorter hearings devoted to one specific issue – like pleadings on jurisdiction. Let me mention a possible schedule with which I have had personal experience: one party presents its pleadings between 10 a.m. and 1 p.m.; the other party will have to respond the next day starting at 10 a.m. (and will have to submit to the Secretariat the written text of its response an hour earlier). Between 10 a.m. and 1 p.m. the Pentecost miracle is in full operation. One advocate speaks in French, and others hear him/her in English (via earphones, thanks to the translating service); then, another advocate speaks in English, while others hear him/her in French. But the response has to be formulated between 1 p.m. and 9 a.m. on the next day, and, at this point, some limitations of the

[12] See Várady, "Language-Related Strategies in Preparing Arbitration," *Across Languages and Cultures* 7 (2006): 209–23.

miracle come to the fore. Often, as a gesture of mutual courtesy, the parties will present to each other copies of the text of their oral presentation after the pleadings are completed at 1 p.m. In most cases, presentations are in two languages: French and English. At 1 p.m. the party rushing to prepare its rebuttal will have the originals (in English or French). Around 6 p.m. the Secretariat of the ICJ will deliver translations as well. This means that a counsel or advocate who speaks (or at least reads) both English and French can start working on the basis of the full text already at 1 p.m. (or, say, half an hour later, because he or she has to get from the Peace Palace to a working room in a hotel or in an embassy). Those who do not speak both languages will be in the same position five hours later – and these daytime five hours are significant, considering that one has less than twenty hours altogether (including the night) to prepare a rebuttal. Thus, translation does not yield equal arms in every respect. The counsel who speaks both languages will have a certain tactical advantage against the counsel who is relying only on translation. And there is no remedy here, just as there is no remedy if one of the opposing counsels needs less time because he or she thinks more quickly.

A similar problem arises in international litigation and arbitration cases in which one of the advocates is relying on translation. Suppose that one of the parties is Polish and the other party is German. The language of arbitration is Polish. The arbitrators invite (or allow) an exchange of arguments. The Polish attorney speaks both Polish and German, the German attorney does not speak Polish. The solution is in translation. During the oral hearing, the German attorney will rely on the services of an interpreter for his pleadings, rebuttals, or surrebuttals. If there is simultaneous translation, it will bring about a balance regarding time as well. If there is consecutive translation (which is also fairly common), the Polish attorney will hear (and understand) the arguments of the German opponent twice. Hence, he or she will have more time to prepare responses. The German attorney will first hear each argument in Polish, but he or she will only become alerted to some arguments after hearing the German translation. Again, we have a certain imbalance in favor of the attorney who does not need translation – and again, it would be difficult to find (and to justify) some remedy.

Let me add at this point that arbitrators – who are typically free to set time limits – will often set adjusted (longer) time limits for submissions when translation of documents is implied. But what about time limits that are judicially created or set by statutes? In a 1989 decision, the United States Court of Appeals for the First Circuit considered a request to set aside an arbitral award. The US District Court for the District of Puerto Rico had dismissed the action as time barred. One of the principal issues brought before the First Circuit was whether the Puerto Rico 30-day judicially created time bar also applied when translation was implied (the original documents were in Spanish). The First Circuit held: "We are unpersuaded by appellant's plea that the necessity of translating Spanish documents into English warrants a more protracted interval within which to sue in Puerto Rico's federal courts." One of the arguments explaining this position was that "[t]ranslations can be made after the fact; verbatim transcripts and elaborate documentation are unnecessary for filing of a complaint, which under the Civil Rules ought only to contain a 'short and plain statement' of the claim."[13] It remains an open issue whether a more consequential and persuasive burden of translation would have prompted a different position. It is not easy to modify deadlines while maintaining principles and predictability. (With statutory time limits this is probably even more difficult than with judicially created time limits.) The question also arises whether time limits adjusted to the needs of translation would impair equality from another angle. Translation should – and normally does – establish a basic balance of fairness. It cannot completely eradicate a certain competitive advantage on the part of those who do not need translation.

Second, who is (and what causes are) entitled to translation? In *Dominique Guesdon* v. *France*,[14] the Human Rights Committee had to face some specific language issues that were not mainstream, but not insignificant either. Guesdon was accused of painting over some road signs (which were in French only) in order to manifest his desire that road signs on the territory of Bretagne be henceforth bilingual (French and Breton). Guesdon denied personal involvement, but expressed sympathy and understanding for those who painted over the road signs. The procedural problem arose when Guesdon indicated to the French court that he and his twelve witnesses wished to give their testimonies in Breton (with translation into French). Guesdon stated that he and the witnesses did speak French, but that they were more at ease with Breton. This request was denied by the French courts, including the *Cour de Cassation*. The question arose whether this amounted to a violation of the right to fair trial. According to the view[15] expressed by the Human Rights Committee,

[13] *Posadas de Puerto Rico Associates Inc* v. *Asociation de Empleados de Casino de Puerto Rico*, 873 F.2d 479, at 485.

[14] *Dominique Guesdon* v. *France*, considered by the Human Rights Committee established under Article 28 of the International Covenant on Civil and Political Rights. Communication No. 219/1986 – Report of the Human Rights Committee, Vol. II GAOR Forty-fifth Session, Supplement No. 40 (A/45/40), pp. 61–68.

[15] The conclusions of the Human Rights Committee are stated in the form of a "view."

the requirement of a fair hearing does not mandate state parties to make available to a citizen whose mother tongue differs from the official court language the services of an interpreter, if this citizen is capable of expressing himself adequately in the official language.

Two interesting issues are highlighted in the Guesdon case. First, the question arises of how one should come to a conclusion whether translation is really needed for the purpose of understanding. The second question is how to deal with situations in which the main purpose of translation is not understanding but recognition of contested identities. In the Guesdon case, the French courts did not really consider whether translation was needed for the purpose of understanding, assuming (probably rightly) that Guesdon had other reasons for requesting translation. This approach was essentially approved by the Human Rights Committee. In a number of interesting (and somewhat similar) cases, different positions were taken.

In a high profile case before the ICTY, the issue arose whether Slobodan Milošević should be entitled to translation. Submitting that Milošević had a good command of English, the prosecution wanted to present to him witness statements in English. This position of the prosecution was challenged by three *amici curiae*. It was not contested that Milošević spoke English (he actually spent some years of his career as a banker in London). The objection against the position of the prosecution may have been inspired by defiance, but it is also a fact that Milošević was certainly more at ease in his native Serbian. The court did not try to weigh linguistic skills, and – probably in order to avoid potential problems – Judges May, Robinson, and Fihri rejected the prosecutor's motion, stating that the "demands of justice outweigh the prosecution pleas for judicial economy."[16]

Let me also mention a case in which the Supreme Court of Bronx County, New York, undertook some linguistic analysis. The issue was whether Krio, a language spoken in Sierra Leone, is or is not a separate language – and, hence, whether translation to and from Krio was needed. In *The People of the State of New York* v. *G. Smith*,[17] the services of an interpreter were used, but the defendant moved for a mistrial on the grounds that Krio did not require the services of an interpreter, and that the interpreter relayed the testimony inaccurately. The defense counsel submitted that Krio is not a separate language, that it is "nothing more than

---

[16] See IWPR Tribunal Update No, 236, Part I, September 17–22, 2001.
[17] 195 Misc.2d 434, 759 N.Y.S. 2d 315, decision of April 4, 2003.

a Patois [and] ... English with a bad accent."[18] The court first stated that, as a matter of principle: "In dealing with the question of whether Krio is in fact a language separate and distinct from English, the court is compelled to examine the nature of Krio and how it evolved into a language in the context of the history of Sierra Leone."[19] Having opted for this point of departure, the court undertook an investigation, and established, among other things, that "In sociolinguistic terms, Krio is a derivative of Creole English and had its source in native contact with speakers in English. Historically, it became a makeshift form of speech called Pidgin. Eventually it evolved into a distinct language of its own."[20] After the analysis, the New York court came to the following conclusion: "The court finds that Krio, although related to English, is a separate and distinct language that cannot be readily understood without an interpreter."[21]

3

The dissolution of the Soviet Union had linguistic consequences as well. Newly created states wanted to reinforce new – and somewhat still frail – identities, and this resulted in the establishment of new official languages as well. In a number of cases, Russian ceased to be an official language. In the beginning of the 1990s, the question arose as to what the impact of these changes would be on communication with authorities of the newly emerging states. It is known, for example, that Article IV of the New York Convention on Recognition and Enforcement of Foreign Arbitral Awards requires the submission of the original award, and – if the language of the award is not the same as the official language of the recognizing court – an authenticated translation into the official language of the recognizing court. Does this mean that English or French awards will have to be translated to Tadjik, or Uzbek, or Kirgiz – or will translation into Russian suffice? It is safe to assume that judges who spoke Russian and performed their official duties in Russian a year or two ago would understand perfectly a Russian document.[22] But the point I am making is that there are various reasons for seeking translation – and confirmation of identities is one of them.

---

[18] 759 N.Y.S.2d 315, at 316.
[19] 759 N.Y.S. 2d at 316. One may note that the Supreme Court of Bronx County did not devote separate attention to the allegation that "the interpreter relayed the testimony inaccurately."
[20] 759 N.Y.S.2d 315, at 316.   [21] 759 N.Y.S.2d 315, at 317.
[22] Or, at least, this was the case in the beginning of the 1990s.

In *Finamar Investors Inc.* v. *The Republic of Tadjikistan*,[23] Finamar sought an order to compel the foreign government to submit to arbitration. One of the key issues before the New York District Court was whether the petitioner had effected proper service under the Foreign Sovereign Immunity Act (FSIA). Subsections 1608(a)(3) and (4) of the FSIA clearly require the petitioner to translate summons, complaint, and notice of suit into the official language of the foreign state. Documents were first served in English – which was evidently inadequate. Later, however, the petitioner obtained translations and served the process in Russian. Tadjikistan objected, stressing that Tadjik, not Russian, was the only official language of Tadjikistan. The District Court held that the requirements of the FSIA were not met. It pointed out: "Petitioner details the difficulty in ascertaining the official language of a nation recently separated from the former Soviet Union. Such difficulty, however, does not absolve petitioner of its responsibility to follow the requirements of §1608(a)(3) and (4) which specify that the summons and complaint must be translated into the official language of the foreign state."[24] Let me add that the District Court did not dismiss the complaint, but allowed rectification of service "within reasonable time."

In another case, the Commercial Court of Tashkent City (Uzbekistan) refused to enforce a GAFTA award[25] in favor of Romak S.A. from Geneva because the award presented to the Uzbek court was not translated into Uzbek, the official language of Uzbekistan – as required by Article IV of the New York Convention. Again, translation into Russian was held not to be adequate.

One may characterize the position taken in these two post-Soviet cases as inflexible – but it would be difficult to justify an opposite holding. Language is a tool of understanding – and it is also an important symbol. It may be true that in both Soviet cases the main motive behind the request for translation was pride rather than the need for understanding. Nevertheless, it would be difficult to depart from the (rather unequivocal) provisions of the FSIA, or of the New York Convention, on the ground of an analysis of the motives behind the assertion of an unconditional statutory right. Moreover, it may indeed be difficult to provide translation into Tadjik or Uzbek, but the problem is clearly not

---

[23] 889 F. Supp. 114 (SDNY, June 20, 1995).

[24] 889 F.Supp. 114, at 117.

[25] Award of the Grain and Feed Trade Association, London, between Romak S.A. Geneva and FTC Uzdon Tashkent, Reported in 16–10 Mealey's International Arbitration Report (2001), 2.

insurmountable – particularly not for a company doing business with Tadjikistan or Uzbekistan.

4

What we have had to face in the post-Soviet cases is the growing relevance of a number of clearly distinct languages. Within the setting of the dissolution of the former Yugoslavia we have experienced a phenomenon much more reminiscent of Babel, namely the dispersion of one language into several.

Let me try to explain this. The official languages of the former Yugoslavia were Serbo-Croatian, Slovenian, and Macedonian. The languages of the two most sizable minorities (Albanian and Hungarian) also had a semi-official status at the federal level, and the *Official Gazette of the SFRY* was published in these languages, too. There was a lingering debate whether there was indeed a Serbo-Croatian language, or whether instead there existed a Serbian, a Croatian, and a Bosnian language. The additional claim emerged that Montenegrin, too, was a separate language. It is common ground that Serbs, Croats, Bosnians, and Montenegrins do not really have difficulty understanding each other (at least, not language-wise). It is also clear that one can tell whether a person is speaking Serbian, Croatian, Bosnian, or Montenegrin. The dividing line between the *very similar* and the *identical* is subtle. One might add that the differences between dialects within Serbia (or Croatia) may be greater than the differences between literary Serbian and literary Croatian. When new states emerged from the dissolution of the former Yugoslavia, we witnessed a drive to identify and acknowledge symbols of distinct identities. Language has always represented a strong symbol of identity. In this context it is understandable that with the emergence of new states the concept of a Serbo-Croatian (or Croato-Serbian) language was abandoned, and the new constitutions of the new sovereign states established Serbian, Croatian, and Bosnian as distinct official languages. Soon after Montenegro separated from Serbia in 2006, the Babel syndrome continued, and Montenegrin became the official language of Montenegro.

The question has arisen how this reality (or quasi-reality) should be heeded in the process of international decision-making. I would first like to mention an arbitration case from my own experience. One of the parties was from Croatia, the other was from Serbia. Earlier, there would have been no problem in agreeing on the language of arbitration – the obvious choice would have been Serbo-Croatian. This was, however, no longer a possible choice. Choosing Serbian (or Croatian) would not have jeopardized understanding, but it would have offended sensitivities by granting recognition to one identity over the other. Thus, a more balanced and circumspect solution was needed – and actually this was not difficult to find. Both parties and all three arbitrators easily agreed to identify both Serbian and Croatian as the languages of the arbitral proceedings, allowing all participants to use one or the other, without requiring translation. In this way, in addition to choosing language(s) which allowed the participants to understand each other, a balance of symbols and identities was also respected.

The arbitration case mentioned above shows that common sense may transcend Babel-type problems. But what if common sense is lacking? In some cases before the ICTY – and in the Šešelj case in particular – the problem appeared in a rather odd setting. Let me first mention that the ICTY has accepted the fact that Serbo-Croatian is no longer an official language, and therefore it has been using separate names (Serbian, Croatian, Bosnian), but it also accepted as a fact that these languages can be used interchangeably. This is how the S/C/B (or C/S/B, or B/C/S) language was established. The crux of the solution is that a Croat, a Serb, or a Bosniac is entitled to translation, and will receive a B or C or S translation depending on the availability of the translator.

The case of *Prosecutor* v. *Vojislav Šešelijk* trial has put on record a long list of endeavors by Šešelj to defy, disparage, or obstruct the ICTY. In 2003, some of the translations that reached Šešelj were in Croatian, and this provided a new opportunity. He claimed that he could not understand a "C" translator, and thus his due process rights were violated. Šešelj pointed out several (rather unconvincing) examples, stating, for instance, that he did not understand what "Zapadni Srijem" might mean. (This is a geographical region with which some of Šešelj's activities were linked, called "Zapadni Srijem" in Croatian, and "Zapadni Srem" in Serbian.) The problem had to be addressed, because Serbian, Bosnian, and Croatian have indeed become separate official languages. In *Prosecutor* v. *Vojislav Šešelj*, Trial Chamber II rendered a specific Order on Translation of Documents.[26] In reaching its decision, the Trial Chamber relied on Article 21 of the Statute of the ICTY, which guarantees to the accused information "in a language which he understands" … In the concluding sentence of the Order of March 6, 2003, it is stated that the Trial Chamber

---

[26] *Prosecutor* v. *Vojislav Šešelj*, Case No. IT-03–67-PT, Order on Translation of Documents of March 6, 2003.

"FURTHER ORDERS the Registry to provide the Accused with translations of any future motions filed by the Prosecution (without attach-
ments) in B/C/S ... thereby guaranteeing the right of the Accused to be
heard in a language he understands." Later during the trial, on March 25,
2003, Judge Schomburg responded to Mr. Šešelj endeavoring to return to
common sense:

> Dr. Šešelj, we are here in a tribunal where we use the – all three variants
> of the same common Serbo-Croatian language, and everybody is treated
> equally ... So you have to accept and you have to show some tolerance.
> Language is a tool bringing persons, bringing people together, and to make
> us understand each other, but we can't expect that everybody speaks the
> same variant or, even worse, the same dialect. In this Tribunal, for example,
> we have English as one of the official languages. Sometimes also for us it
> is difficult to understand a person speaking Irish English, French English,
> German English [meaning English spoken by a Frenchman or by a German
> person], American English, but we have to live with this in the spirit of
> tolerance and trying to understand each other ... And to be honest, we
> don't care about this from where a person comes, be it Zagreb, Novi Sad,
> Belgrade, or wherever. The main point is that it's translated into a language
> you understand, and there should be not the slightest problem with this.[27]

As this case nicely illustrates, it is not always easy to decide upon entitlement to translation. There is, of course, an obvious and straightforward
justification: the need to understand. Yet claims for translation are sometimes based on different concerns, such as the assertion of sovereignty or
of a distinct identity. Translation may very well be perceived as a tribute
to sovereignty or distinct identity. Such claims might be asserted directly
(like in the post-Soviet cases), or under the guise of the mainstream justification (the need to understand a different language). In my opinion,
as a rule of thumb, one should recognize entitlement to translation if the
target language is the official language of a sovereign country. Even if one
assumes that Uzbek or Tadjik officials and judges speak Russian as well,
this does not supersede the entitlement to receive submissions in their
official language. Flexibility is possible – particularly if such flexibility is
exercised by those courts whose official language is at issue[28] – but the entitlement remains.

[27] ICTY, Transcript of the Šešelj trial of March 25, 2003, available at www.un.org.icty/
transe67/030325IA.htm, at pp. 76–77.
[28] Such flexibility was exercised in a few cases by Norwegian and Dutch courts, which recognized arbitral awards written in English, without requesting translation into Norwegian
or Dutch. See e.g., *Pulsarr Industrial Research B.V. (Netherlands) v. Nils H. Nilsen A.S.*

Minority rights could also conceivably justify an entitlement to translation – but a scrutiny of this issue would take us beyond the boundaries of this chapter. The situation is particularly sensitive when the asserted justification is the need to understand, but the circumstances indicate other concerns. Faced with this quandary, the solution might be to stay on the track of understanding, and to establish whether translation is really needed for the purpose of understanding. (One has to mention, though, that this might sometimes take us to the uncertain ground of linguistic controversies with regard to closely related languages.)[29] Faced with a real dilemma as to whether the request for translation is prompted by an actual need for understanding or by other concerns, one should keep in mind that it is a lesser error to allow unnecessary translation than to disallow translation when it might really be needed. Unfortunately, the blessing of the obvious does not always provide a solution regarding the issue of entitlement to translation.

5

Staying with the example of the ICTY, I would like to draw attention to some further risks built into the process of multilingual proceedings. The ICTY has two working languages: English and French (as provided by Article 33 of the Statute). In practice, the dominant language is English. However, most of the accused, most victims, and most witnesses do not speak either French or English. This poses a host of logistical problems, and it has an impact on the quality of the proceedings as well. The prosecution is shaping a picture relying at least in part on witnesses. These witnesses speak another language. Doubts or confidence are first of all triggered by the allegations themselves – and these can be mirrored in an accurate translation. But can translation fully substitute for direct communication? Speaking a language is not only important in order to understand what the witness is saying. Being at home with a language also offers an added opportunity to be able to make an educated guess whether the witness is telling the truth. Prosecutors, advocates, and judges who are themselves part of a given language culture are in better position to fully

---

(*Norway*), Judgment of July 10, 2002 – reported in Yearbook Commercial Arbitration Vol. XXVIII (2003), 821; or Southern Pacific Properties (Middle East) Ltd. and the Arab Republic of Egypt, decision of the District Court of Amsterdam, decision of 12 July 1984, reported in 24 International Legal Materials 1040 (1985).

[29] See on this problem Várady, *Language and Translation*, 140–56, dealing with closely related languages in the context of international commercial arbitration.

understand and also to screen what the witness is saying. They can recognize and discern familiar patterns of exaggeration, and patterns of telling the truth, patterns which are different in different cultures. Newly formed international criminal tribunals have offered an opportunity to gain more insight into both the capacities and the limitations of translation.

Focusing on accuracy, it deserves to be pointed out that the ICTY adopted rules that are clearly mindful of priorities (as well as nuances) with regard to accuracy. In Article 10(1) of the "Code of Ethics for Interpreters and Translators Employed by the ICTY"[30] it is stated:

> Interpreters and translators shall convey with the greatest fidelity and accuracy, and with complete neutrality, the wording used by the persons they interpret or translate.
>
> Interpreters shall convey the whole message, including vulgar or derogatory remarks, insults and any non-verbal clue, such as the tone of voice and emotions of the speaker, which might facilitate the understanding of their listeners.
>
> Interpreters and translators shall not embellish, omit or edit anything from their assigned work.
>
> If patent mistakes or untruths are spoken or written, interpreters and translators shall convey these accurately as presented.

Article 10 offers a thoughtful and well-balanced definition of the goal. Attention has been devoted to the issue, and results have been achieved. However, there have been failures as well. I would like to highlight the problem through a rather bizarre episode, in which the source of the problem was a translation crafted by secret services outside the ICTY. The process of clarification was burdened by the classified character of the information – and the admissibility of the information was also an open issue.

In order to make the plot understandable, let me make some preliminary remarks on the expression (*ribanje*) which became a challenge. In all post-Serbo/Croatian languages (Serbian, Croatian, Bosnian) *riba* means "fish." From fish (*riba*), however, you do not get to "fishing" the same simple way as in English. It may be enticing to add just the *–nje* ending (which does mean "–ing") and to come up with *ribanje*. But there also exists a verb *ribati*, which means "to scrub," and "*ribanje*" actually means scrubbing. What is even more important, in a figurative sense, *ribanje* means scolding or slating or dressing-down. In other words, translating *ribanje* as "fishing" is about as adequate as if one were to translate "giving

---

[30]   See www.un.org/icty/basic/codeinter/IT144.htm.

someone a good dressing-down" as "assisting someone in strip-tease." In B/C/S languages "fishing" is actually *ribolov* (literally "fish hunt") or *ribarenje* (built on the word *ribar*, i.e., "fisherman").

And this is where the problem started in the ICTY case against Radoslav Brđanin. The prosecution presented as evidence an intercepted 1992 phone conversation between Radovan Karadžić and Nenad Stevandić. The interceptors had to translate. They did. The transcript mentions Mr. Brđanin "being taken fishing up to Jovica's" ("Jovica" was Mr. Jovica Stanišić, then head of the Serbian secret service). In the original Serbian text it was stated that Mr. Brđanin was summoned to Jovica (Stanišić) for *ribanje* (scolding, dressing-down). Western intelligence forces came up with a translation stating that Mr. Brđanin went fishing with Jovica (Stanišić). The context raised doubts, and prompted a discussion which takes thirteen pages(!) of the transcript of the hearing on July 3, 2003.[31] The dialogue is at some points reminiscent of Ionesco or Beckett – and, in line with patterns of absurd drama, there is no clear unbinding; the knot remains.

The main focus is on the following part of the intercepted and translated conversation:

> STEVANDIĆ: But, I wanted, no, as concerns Brdjo [nickname for Brđanin], there are no problems there. Miroslav and I have hold of Brđanin. Last time we took him fishing up to Jovica's.
> KARADŽIĆ: Yes.
> STEVANDIĆ: And he scared him a little so that stupid things shouldn't be done and so on and we have hold on Brdjo now ...[32]

Had *ribanje* been translated by the CIA as "scolding, dressing-down," the picture would have been quite clear. Brđanin was sent to the head of the secret police, where he was subject to scolding or dressing-down, and after that it could have been expected that he would no longer dare to oppose Karadžić and Stevandić. In other words, after Brđanin had been subjected to some harsh words by the head of the secret police, Karadžić and Stevandić had a hold on him. The situation is different, however, if one were to assume that Brđanin was not scolded by the head of the secret police, but went fishing with him (which might indicate a friendly relationship with the strongman). Judge Agius sensed the inconsistency, and a probing dialogue developed. Here are some typical fragments:

---

[31] IT-99-36-T, *The Prosecutor* v. *Radoslav Brdjanin*, 3 July 2003, pp. 18761–73.
[32] Ibid., p. 18767.

JUDGE AGIUS: But my – why I wondered yesterday and why I wonder still today, how you came to your conclusion at the time that you could take it literally is that how can two persons have on hold or keep on hold or have a hold on someone simply because they took him fishing at Jovica's?

THE WITNESS: Well, what I think is going on here is –

JUDGE AGIUS: I can assure you that I have a lot of friends with whom I have gone fishing but none of them have any hold on me.[33]

The rumination continued, and on the thirteenth page a solution was suggested. The emerging proposition was, however, still somewhat foggy, and eventually Judge Agius proposed to move on towards other matters:

MR. ACKERMAN: Your Honour, I'm told that there is another interpretation of the word *ribanje* [...] which is brainwashing, which may be what was meant here. I don't know.

JUDGE AGIUS: Let's – if you were following what the interpreter, one of the interpreters said at one moment, she said that the word "fishing" could actually mean something else, and that's sort of convincing or I forgot exactly.

JUDGE JANU: Task.

JUDGE AGIUS: I understand your point here. Let's go ahead because we have – I anticipate – a lot of problems in the course of today's sitting so let's proceed.[34]

At the end, the meaning set by the mistranslation got loosened up, became volatile, but was not really replaced. (Fortunately, this did not really have an impact on the conviction.) One is prompted by such episodes to wonder what happens to mistranslations in the files of various secret services that never see the daylight of court proceedings.

6

It is a fact that nowadays we have a dominant language at the global level. This language is English. It follows that in a considerable number of cases the use of English may represent at least a partial substitute for translation. If a party from Hungary and a party from Belgium conduct their correspondence in English, if they execute their contract in English, and if they agree on an arbitration clause which sets English as the language of arbitration, translation is avoided (except maybe for witnesses who might testify before the arbitral tribunal if a dispute arises – or except for purposes of contact with Hungarian and Belgian authorities if the contract were to need government approval or registration). To a lesser extent, some other "world languages" (like French or German), or languages

[33] Ibid., p. 18772.   [34] Ibid., p. 18773.

widely spoken in a region (like Russian) may also serve as a bridge between parties from different countries with different languages. As English has been gaining more and more ground on territories where it is not the first language, we have witnessed an interesting turnaround. Normally, translation follows the original. An interesting trait of our time is an increased frequency of the reversed sequence, in that translation precedes the original. In the domain of international transactions, for example, contracts are often drafted in a language that is not the native language of any of the parties to the contract (typically in English). In such situations, the original signed by the parties is actually a translation, and the language from which this translation was made remains hidden. This raises some quite fascinating questions.

I remember an arbitration case in which the bone of contention was an exchange of letters in connection with a contract. The contract was executed in English; the letters were also written in English. The first letter was written by a party from Bosnia, who proposed "to put the contract to peace." The other party (from a different country, whose native language was not English either), agreed "to put the contract to peace." The problem was that while the party from Bosnia thought that they had agreed to *suspend* the contract, the other party took a position that they had agreed to *terminate* the contract. The Bosnian party was in all likelihood shaping his thoughts in Bosnian, and tried to find an adequate English expression of the Bosnian words. In Bosnian (just as in Croatian or Serbian) *mir* means "peace." *Staviti* [putting] *u mirovanje* (derived from *mir*) is being used as a legal term, meaning suspension. This is what the Bosnian party must have meant, when he translated *staviti u mirovanje* as "putting to peace." The other party, on the other hand, may have understood the expression as indicating termination. It is also conceivable that there was no real misunderstanding, but the other party wanted to get out of the contract anyway (rather than just to postpone contractual obligations), and used the imprecision molded by the literal translation as an opportunity to turn things in this direction. What makes this problem-pattern specific is that mistranslation (or ambiguous translation) is part of the *original*. It is true that there is a deeper layer below the text which is formally the original, but this deeper layer (which I call "anchor language"[35]) is not on record, it is invisible. The question is whether one could and should reach

---

[35] See Várady, *Language and Translation*, 133–40; and also "The Anchor Language – When the Original is Actually a Translation," in Andrew Wilson, ed., *Translators on Translating: Inside the Visible Art* (Vancouver: CCSP Press, 2009), 144–48.

towards the anchor language (in this case, the language of the Bosnian party who coined the contested phrase) in deciding whether the contract was suspended or terminated.

Staying with the issue of the hidden anchor language, the original may also remain hidden when the language of the contract is not a third language but is the language of one of the parties, and the draft is prepared by the other party. For example, the contract is concluded between a US and a Finnish party, and the Finnish party is the one that submits the draft. (In such situations, it also matters how much negotiation will actually take place and how much effort will be invested by the native-speaker party in scrutinizing the language of the contract.) Again, the question arises whether the anchor version of a contract (or of a phrase in a contract) may gain relevance before the arbitrators (or before a court).

This was the issue in a case between a Hungarian and a UK party who agreed on an arbitration clause which read: "In case of controversial matters the parties determine the selected court, which operates next to the Chamber of Commerce in Budapest." What became a bone of contention here was a literal translation of the Hungarian term for arbitration. In Hungarian, arbitration is called *választottbíróság*, which means literally "selected court" or "chosen court."[36] The case reached the Budapest Court of Arbitration. An oral hearing was held, but the UK respondent failed to appear (although duly notified). The absence of the UK party made it more difficult to clarify the intentions of the parties. As stated in the English language award, the claimant offered the following explanation: "[t]he designation 'selected court which operates next to the Chamber of Commerce in Budapest' is a literal translation. The Hungarian term 'választottbíróság' means arbitration, but its literal translation is 'selected court.'"[37]

The arbitrators raised the question whether a valid arbitration agreement existed, and stated: "Scrutinizing the wording of the 'Mutual Agreement' the arbitrators were faced with another example of clauses falling into the category labeled *'clauses pathologiques'* by Eisemann. This leads to the difficult question of the limits of the power of the arbitrators in seeking the 'true intent' of the parties beyond (or even in spite of) what the parties actually wrote. It is the opinion of the arbitrators, that

---

[36] Some other languages follow the same logic. In Croatian and Serbian, for example, the term for "arbitration" is *izbrani sud* or *izabrani sud* – which also means "chosen court" or "selected court."

[37] Award of May 21, 2002 in Case No. Vb/01181 (unpublished).

the arbitration agreement must possess in itself a minimum level of co-herence in order to serve as a foothold for a search after the true inten-tions of the parties."[38] Referring specifically to the phrase "selected court," the arbitrators stated further on: "The wording of the arbitration clause does not make much sense otherwise but on the assumption that this is a translation of a Hungarian draft – which translation actually conveyed the words, more so than the meaning." Eventually, the arbitrators found that they had no jurisdiction, but for reasons other than the imperfect reference to the arbitral institution.[39] It appears from the wording of the award that the phrase "selected court" may not in itself have justified re-fusal of jurisdiction.

The intriguing question (which remained unanswered) was what the intentions and the perception of the UK party were. It is quite obvious that the English native-speaker party did not devote much attention to the language of the contract. It happens – unfortunately with some frequency – that contracts are concluded without sufficient scrutiny. Normally, the party that failed to devote attention to the wording but signed the contract will be bound. Will the party also be bound by an arbitration agreement which refers to a "selected court"? Let us repeat that a party is normally bound by what is written in a clause, even if he or she failed to scrutinize it (though having had the opportunity to do so). The situation is somewhat different when one has to reach towards an anchor language in order to establish the proper meaning of a contractual provision. If the literal translation offers a plausible option as it stands, the party that has no command of the anchor language may possibly insist on this option, arguing that he or she was misled (led to trust the mean-ing flowing from the literal translation). *Bona fide* reliance on the literal meaning may block an examination of the anchor language. In the case referred to above, however, it would have been difficult for the UK party to argue that it did not know that "selected court" meant arbitration. In the given context, this argument would not have been persuasive. It would also be quite difficult for the English-speaking party to explain what it did have in mind. In the case, which ended with the May 2002 award, the English party did not show up at the oral hearing, and thus could not

---

[38] Award of May 21, 2002, No. Vb/01181, at p. 4 (unpublished).

[39] The dispute was between two companies, while the "Mutual Agreement" containing the arbitration clause was signed by two natural persons, without indicating the names of the legal persons they represented; furthermore, the "Mutual Agreement" was an agency agreement, while the subject matter of the dispute arose from a sales contract.

offer any explanation. Had the party appeared, it might have confirmed that both parties meant arbitration. Explaining any other meaning would have been quite difficult: it just would not sound plausible to argue that by saying that "[t]he parties determine the selected court, which operates next to the Chamber of Commerce in Budapest," the parties actually meant to submit disputes to a court which is identified by being in the proximity of the Budapest Chamber of Commerce. Reaching after the hidden anchor language mandates caution, but it is a rational device of contract interpretation when contracts are being shaped in a multilingual environment.

In Chapter 1 of this book, Berman writes that "we are all creatures of the language in which we have been brought up."[40] This is a most apposite remark, which also explains the role of the anchor language. There are, however, some ramifications of this truth as stated by Harold Berman. There are people whose life is marked by transitions – including transitions between languages. There are persons whose identity is denoted by changeovers. Can such an identity be considered as the anchor, as the hidden layer behind the formal original? In most cases probably not – but there are exceptions.

I would like to refer here to an award of the Iran–United States Claims Tribunal, in which transition between identities served as (added) guidance in interpreting the text of a letter.[41] Professor Dadras wrote his letter in Persian (Farsi), and dated it according to the Persian calendar. Persian was the native language of Professor Dadras, this was the language in which he had been brought up; but he left Iran, and he had been living in the USA for almost thirty years.[42] The date of the letter was indicated according to the Persian calendar, and corresponded to September 11, 1978. Professor Dadras asserted, however, that he got confused, and actually wrote his letter on August 21, 1978. The date of the letter was important. Endeavoring to establish which date was accurate, the arbitrators relied on indications in the text of the letter, but they also relied on the circumstance that behind the original (which was Persian/Farsi) there was another layer. In this case, it appeared that this hidden original was actually not English as a newly acquired anchor, but rather the perplexity

---

[40] See above, Chapter 1, p. 50.
[41] *Dadras International and Per-Am Construction Corporation* v. *The Islamic Republic of Iran, and Tehran Redevelopment Company*, Award No. 567–213/215–3, of November 7, 1995.
[42] It is not clear from the award whether thirty years were counted up to the year of the award (1995), or up to the year of the contested letter (1978).

yielded by transition. The arbitrators captured this with the following words:

> The third and particularly significant factor is that the letter was written in Persian, a language in which Prof. Dadras was no longer comfortable after having lived in the United States for almost thirty years during most of which time he was married to a non-Persian speaker. As discussed above, the letter contains dates written in three different calendars, namely the Gregorian, the Iranian Hejri-Shamsi and the Iranian Imperial calendars. The necessity of making date conversions in or between three different calendars therefore would have added to the stressful situation in which Prof. Dadras found himself, and would have significantly increased the likelihood of making faulty conversion.[43]

7

The idea of Pentecost may have been bestowed on us by God, but its implementation is left to humans. People who have the courage to sail between languages, however, have a patron saint in Saint Jerome. It is interesting to consider the character of the person who received the quite peculiar status of the patron saint of translators. Saint Jerome was born in 347, and lived until 419 (or 420). He was born in Stridon,[44] lived in Rome, Trier (Germany), Constantinople, Bethlehem, Antioch, the Desert of Chalcis, and many other places. His most important achievement is the translation of the Holy Script from Hebrew and Greek to Latin and thus the creation of the Vulgate, the official version of the Holy Bible for more than a millennium. He was a brilliant intellectual. In a number of his writings he gave a subtle (and still relevant) analysis of many intricate problems of translation. Let me cite one of the many subtle elucidations one can find in the writings of Saint Jerome. In his letter to Pammachius he states:

> It is difficult in following lines laid down by others not sometimes to diverge from them, and it is hard to preserve in a translation the charm of expressions which in another language are most felicitous. Each particular word conveys a meaning of its own, and possibly I have no equivalent by which to render it, and I make a circuit to reach my goal, I have to go many miles to cover a short distance. To these difficulties must be added the windings of hyperbata, differences in the use of cases, divergencies

---

[43] Iran–United States Claims Tribunal, Award No. 567–213/215–3 of November 7, 1995, para. 210.

[44] It is not clear where Stridon was exactly. It is assumed that it was on the present-day territory of either Croatia or Slovenia.

of metaphor; and last of all the peculiar and if I may so call it, inbred character of the language.[45]

In the same letter, Saint Jerome quotes Horace, who gave the following
advice to the skilled translator:

> And care not thou with over anxious thought.
> To render word for word.[46]

Of course, Saint Jerome and Horace were focusing on literary translation, and one cannot equate literary translation with legal translation. But
the basic problem-pattern is the same, and the guidance of Saint Jerome
remains relevant. Saint Jerome's main focus is not on strengthening faith
in the miracle of translation. Unqualified faith is actually more often
characteristic of people who do not really have experience with multilin-
gualism, who have not seen things from inside, do not have a realistic picture of the task, and tend to believe that translation is bound to produce
an identical twin of the original. Saint Jerome did not try to offer protection and encouragement by way of eliminating doubt. He tried instead to
throw light upon on various sources of doubt and difficulties in order to
enable the translators to cope with them. The more we are aware of inside
structure, layers, intricacies, limitations, traps, and jargon, the closer we
can get to the spirit of Pentecost.

---

[45] Saint Jerome, "To Pammachius on the Best Method of Translating," Letter LVII, available at: www.newadvent.org/fathers/3001057.htm (formatted by the Christian Classics
Ethereal Library, 1996).

[46] Ibid.

BIBLIOGRAPHY

Adler, Mark, "The Plain Language Movement," in Peter M. Tiersma and Lawrence M. Solan, eds., *The Oxford Handbook of Language and Law* (Oxford University Press, 2012), 67–83.

An-Na'im, Abdullahi, "Globalization and Jurisprudence: An Islamic Law Perspective," *Emory Law Journal* 54 (2005): 25–52.

Atienza, Manuel, et al., eds., *Rechtstheorie: Theorie des Rechts und der Gesellschaft: Festschrift für Werner Krawietz zum 70. Geburtstag* (Berlin: Duncker & Humblot, 2003).

Augustine, *Confessions*, trans. Rex Warner (New York: New American Library, 1963).

Ayer, Alfred Jules, *Language, Truth, and Logic* (London: Victor Gollancz, 1936).

Ball, Milner, *Lying Down Together: Law, Metaphor, and Theology* (University of Wisconsin Press, 1985).

The Promise of American Law: A Theological, Humanistic View of Legal Process (University of Georgia Press, 1981).

The Word and the Law (University of Chicago Press, 1995).

Barfield, Owen, "Poetic Diction and Legal Fiction," in *The Rediscovery of Meaning, and Other Essays* (Middletown, CT: Wesleyan University Press, 1977 [1964]), 49–74.

Barry, Donald D., ed., *Toward the "Rule of Law" in Russia?* (Armonk, NY: M.E. Sharpe, 1992).

Barry, Donald D., F. J. M. Feldbrugge, and Dominic Lasok, eds., *Codification in the Communist World* (Leiden: A. W. Sijthoff, 1975).

Bartmanski, Dominik, "How to Become an Iconic Social Thinker," *European Journal of Social Theory* 15 (2012): 433–36.

Bastarache, Michel, "Bilingual Interpretation Rules as a Component of Language Rights in Canada," in Peter M. Tiersma and Lawrence M. Solan, eds., *The Oxford Handbook of Language and Law* (Oxford University Press, 2012), 159–74.

Bederman, David J., *Custom as a Source of Law* (Cambridge University Press, 2010).

"World Law Transcendent," *Emory Law Journal* 54 (2005): 79–96.

Bentham, Jeremy, *The Works of Jeremy Bentham*, 11 vols., John Bowring, ed. (Edinburgh: William Tait, 1838–1843).

Berman, Harold J., "American and Soviet Perspectives on Human Rights," *Worldview* 22(11) (November 1979): 15–21.

"The Background of the Western Legal Tradition in the Folklaw of the Peoples of Europe," *University of Chicago Law Review* 45 (1978): 553–97, at 553.

"Book Review of Mikhail Gorbachev, *PERESTROIKA: New Thinking for Our Country and the World* (1987)," *The Atlanta Constitution* (December 13, 1987): 12J.

"The Challenge of Christianity and Democracy in the Soviet Union," in John Witte, Jr., ed., *Christianity and Democracy in Global Context* (Boulder, CO: Westview Press, 1993), 287–96.

"The Challenge of Soviet Law," *Harvard Law Review* 62 (December 1948 and January 1949): 220–65, 449–66.

"The Comparison of Soviet and American Law," *Indiana Law Journal* 34 (1959): 559–70, at 559.

"The Crisis of Legal Education in America," *Boston College Law Review* 26 (1985): 347–52.

"The Crisis of the Western Legal Tradition," *Creighton Law Review* 9 (1975): 252–65.

"The Current Movement for Law Reform in the Soviet Union," *American Slavic and East European Review* 15 (April 1956): 179–89.

"The Devil and Soviet Russia," *The American Scholar* 27 (Spring 1958): 147–52.

"The Dilemma of Soviet Law Reform," *Harvard Law Review* 76 (March 1963): 929–51.

"Divorce and Domestic Relations in Soviet Law," *Virginia Law Weekly* 2(2) (April 1950): 28–33.

"Epilogue: An Ecumenical Christian Jurisprudence," in John Witte, Jr. and Frank S. Alexander, eds., *The Teachings of Modern Christianity on Law, Politics, and Human Nature*, 2 vols. (New York: Columbia University Press, 2006), 752–64.

"Faith and Law in a Multicultural World," *Journal of Law and Religion* 18 (2003): 297–305.

"Faith and Law in a Multicultural World," in Mark Juergensmeyer, ed., *Religion in Global Civil Society* (Oxford University Press, 2005), 69–89.

Faith and Order: The Reconciliation of Law and Religion (Atlanta, GA: Scholars Press, 1993).

"Foreword," to Michael W. McConnell, Robert F. Cochran, Jr., and Angela C. Carmella, eds., *Christian Perspectives on Legal Thought* (New Haven, CT: Yale University Press, 2001), xi–xiv.

"Freedom of Religion in Russia: An Amicus Brief for the Defendant," in John Witte, Jr. and Michael Bourdeaux, eds., *Proselytism and Orthodoxy in Russia: The New War for Souls* (Maryknoll, NY: Orbis Books, 1999), 265–83.

"The God of History," *The Living Pulpit* (July–September 2001): 27.

"Gorbachev's Law Reforms in Historical Perspective," *Emory Journal of International Affairs* 5 (Spring, 1988): 1–10.

"The Historical Foundations of Law," *Emory Law Journal* 54 (2005): 13–24.

"The Holy Spirit: The God of History," *The Living Pulpit* (April–June 2004): 32–33.

"Human Rights in the Soviet Union," *Howard Law Journal* 11 (1965): 333–41.

"The Impact of the Enlightenment on American Constitutional Law," *Yale Journal of Law & the Humanities* 4 (1992): 311–34.

"Impressions of Moscow," *Harvard Law School Bulletin* 7(3) (December 1955): 7–8.

"Integrative Jurisprudence and World Law," in Manuel Atienza et al., eds. *Rechtstheorie: Theorie des Rechts und der Gesellschaft: Festschrift für Werner Krawietz zum 70. Geburtstag* (Berlin: Duncker & Humblot, 2003), 3–16.

The Interaction of Law and Religion (Nashville, TN: Abingdon Press, 1974).

"The Interaction of Law and Religion," *Capital University Law Review* 8 (1979): 343–56.

"Introduction," to *The Trial of the U-2* (Chicago: Translation World Publishers, 1960), i–xxx.

"Introduction to the World Law Institute," *Emory International Law Review* 22 (2008): 1–6.

"Judeo-Christian Versus Pagan Scholarship," in Kelly K. Monroe, *Finding God at Harvard: Spiritual Journeys of Christian Thinkers* (Downers Grove, IL: IVP Books, 1996), 291–95.

Justice in Russia: An Interpretation of Soviet Law (Cambridge, MA: Harvard University Press, 1950).

Justice in the USSR: An Interpretation of Soviet Law, rev. edn. (Cambridge, MA: Harvard University Press and New York: Random House, 1963).

"The Language of Law: Can Communication Build One World?" *Harvard Medical Alumni Bulletin* 39(2) (Christmas 1964): 26–31.

"Law and Logos," *DePaul Law Review* 44 (Fall 1994): 143–65.

"Law and Religion in the Development of a World Order," *Sociological Analysis: A Journal in the Sociology of Religion* 52 (Spring 1991): 27–36.

Law and Revolution: The Formation of the Western Legal Tradition (Cambridge, MA: Harvard University Press, 1983).

Law and Revolution II: The Impact of the Protestant Reformations on the Western Legal Tradition (Cambridge, MA: Harvard University Press, 2003).

"Law as an Instrument of Peace in US–Soviet Relations," *Stanford Law Review* 22 (1970): 943–62.

"Law as an Instrument of Mental Health in the United States and Soviet Russia," *University of Pennsylvania Law Review* 91 (1961): 361–76.

"Law in American Democracy and Under Soviet Communism," *New Hampshire Bar Journal* 5(3) (April 1963): 105–13.

"The Law of International Commercial Transactions (*Lex Mercatoria*)," *Emory Journal of International Dispute Resolution* 2 (Spring 1988): 235–310.

"The Law of the Soviet State," *Soviet Studies* 6 (January 1955): 225–37.

"The Legal Framework of Trade Between Planned and Market Economies: The Soviet–American Example," *Law and Contemporary Problems* 24 (Summer 1959): 482–528.

"Legal Reasoning," in David Sills, ed., *International Encyclopedia of the Social Sciences*, 19 vols. (New York: Macmillan, 1968), 9:197–204.

"Legal Systems," in Kermit L. Hall, ed., *The Oxford Companion to American Law* (Oxford University Press, 2002), 507–14.

Letter to Eugen Rosenstock-Huessy (April 17, 1966), unpublished.

"Limited Rule of Law," *Christian Science Monitor* (April 29, 1958): 9.

"A Linguistic Approach to the Soviet Codification of Criminal Law and Procedure," in Donald D. Barry, F. J. M. Feldbrugge, and Dominic Lasok, eds., *Codification in the Communist World* (Leiden: A. W. Sijthoff, 1975), 39–52.

"The Moral Crisis of the Western Legal Tradition and the Weightier Matters of the Law," *Criterion* 19(2) (1980): 15–23.

The Nature and Functions of Law: An Introduction for Students of the Arts and Sciences (Brooklyn, NY: Foundation Press, 1958).

"Negotiating Commercial Transactions with Soviet Customers," *Aspects of East–West Trade, American Management Association Report No. 45* (1960), 68–75.

On the Teaching of Law in the Liberal Arts Curriculum (Brooklyn, NY: Foundation Press, 1956).

"Origins of Historical Jurisprudence: Coke, Selden, Hale," *Yale Law Journal* 103 (1994): 1651–1738.

"Principles of Soviet Criminal Law," *Yale Law Journal* 56 (May 1947): 803–36.

"The Problems that Unite Us," *The Nation* 192 (February 18, 1961): 132.

"The Prophetic, Pastoral, and Priestly Vocation of the Lawyer," *The NICM Journal* 2 (1977): 5–9.

"Real Property Actions in Soviet Law," *Tulane Law Review* 29 (June 1955): 687–96.

"Recollections of Eugen [Rosenstock-Huessy], 1936–1940," March 29, 1999, unpublished.

"Religion and Law: The First Amendment in Historical Perspective," *Emory Law Journal* 35 (1986): 777–93.

"Religion and Liberty Under Law at the Founding of America," *Regent University Law Review* 20 (2007): 31–36.

"The Religion Clauses of the First Amendment in Historical Perspective," in Dale Bumpers and W. Lawson Taite, eds., *Religion and Politics* (University of Texas Press, 1989), 47–73.

"Religious Foundations of Law in the West: An Historical Perspective," *The Journal of Law and Religion* 1 (1983): 3–43.

"Religious Freedom and the Challenge of the Modern State," *Emory Law Journal* 39 (1990): 149–64.

"Religious Freedom and the Rights of Foreign Missionaries Under Russian Law," *The Parker School Journal of East European Law* 2 (1995): 421–46.

"Religious Rights in Russia at a Time of Tumultuous Transition: A Historical Theory," in Johan D. van der Vyver and John Witte, Jr., eds., *Religious Human Rights in Global Perspective: Legal Perspectives* (Dordrecht/Boston: Martinus Nijhoff, 1996), 285–304.

"Renewal and Continuity: The Great Revolutions and the Western Tradition," in M. Darrol Bryant and Hans R. Huessy, eds., *Eugen Rosenstock-Huessy: Studies in His Life and Thought* (Lewiston, NY: Edward Mellen Press, 1986), 19–29.

The Role of Law in Trade Relations Between the United States and Japan, a talk given to the Industrial Association in Osaka May 23, 1981, and to the Industrial Law Center in Tokyo May 27, 1981, unpublished.

"The Rule of Law and the Law-Based State (Rechtsstaat) (With Special Reference to Developments in the Soviet Union)," in Donald D. Barry, ed., *Toward the "Rule of Law" in Russia?* (Armonk, NY: M.E. Sharpe, 1992), 43–60.

"Soviet Education," *Atlantic Monthly* (April 1953): 16–19.

"The Soviet Family," *Atlantic Monthly* (February 1952): 18–20.

"Soviet Law and Government," *Modern Law Review* 21 (January 1958): 19–26.

"Soviet Law Reform and its Significance for Soviet International Relations," in Edward McWhinney, ed., *Law, Foreign Policy and the East–West Détente* (University of Toronto Press, 1964), 3–17.

"Soviet Legal Reforms," *The Nation* 182 (June 30, 1956): 546–48.

"The Soviet Peasant," *Atlantic Monthly* (March 1953): 15–18.

"Soviet Perspectives on Chinese Law," in Jerome A. Cohen, ed., *Contemporary Chinese Law* (Cambridge, MA: Harvard University Press, 1970), 313–28.

"Soviet Planning," *Atlantic Monthly* (December 1951): 11–12, 14.

"The Soviet Soldier," *Atlantic Monthly* (September 1952): 4, 6, 8.

ed. and trans., *Soviet Statutes and Decisions: A Journal of Translations* 1–5 (Fall 1964–Spring-Summer 1969).

"Soviet Trade," *Atlantic Monthly* (August 1954): 14–17.

"The Soviet Worker," *Atlantic Monthly* (July 1952): 8–10.

"The Spiritualization of Secular Law: The Impact of the Lutheran Reformation," *Journal of Law and Religion* 14 (1999–2000): 313–49.

"The Struggle for Law in Post-Soviet Russia," in Andras Sajo, ed., *Western Rights? Post-Communist Application* (The Hague: Kluwer Law International, 1996), 41–55.

"Suggestions for Future US Policy on Communist Trade," *Export Trade and Shipper* 35 (July 16, 1956): 11–12.

ed., Symposium, "Soviet-American Trade in a Legal Perspective: Proceedings of a Conference of Soviet and American Legal Scholars," *Denver Journal of International Law and Policy* 5 (1975): 217–370.

ed., *Talks on American Law* (New York: Random House, 1961).

"Thinking Ahead: East–West Trade," *Harvard Business Review* 32(5) (1954): 147–58.

"Toward an Integrative Jurisprudence: Politics, Morality, History," *California Law Review* 76 (1988): 779–801.

"The Tri-Une God of History," *The Living Pulpit* (April 1999): 18–19.

"The U-2 Incident and International Law," *Harvard Law Record* 31(4) (October 13, 1960): 9–12.

"The Weightier Matters of the Law," *Royalton Review* 9(1 & 2) (1975): 32.

"The Weightier Matters of the Law," in Ronald Berman, ed., *Solzhenitsyn at Harvard* (Washington, DC: Ethics and Public Policy Center, 1980), 99–113.

"World Law," *KOERS: Bulletin for Christian Scholarship* 64(2 & 3) (1999): 379–84.

"World Law: An Ecumenical Jurisprudence of the Holy Spirit," *Theology Today* 63 (October 2006): 365–74.

"World Law and the Crisis of the Western Legal Tradition," *The William Timbers Lecture, Dartmouth College, Hanover, NH*, April 21, 2005 (unpublished).

"World Law in the New Millennium," *Twenty-First Century* 52 (April 1999): 4–11 (in Chinese).

Berman, Harold J., and George L. Bustin, "The Soviet System of Foreign Trade," in Robert Starr, ed., *Business Transactions with the USSR, The Legal Issues* (Chicago: ABA Press, 1975), 25–75.

Berman, Harold J., Susan Cohen, and Malcolm Russell, "A Comparison of the Chinese and Soviet Codes of Criminal Law and Procedure," *The Journal of Criminal Law and Criminology* 73 (Spring 1982): 238–58.

Berman, Harold J., and William R. Greiner, *The Nature and Functions of Law*, 2nd edn. (Brooklyn: Foundation Press, 1966).

Berman, Harold J., William R. Greiner and Samir N. Saliba, *The Nature and Functions of Law*, 6th edn. (New York: Foundation Press, 2004).

Berman, Harold J., Erwin N. Griswold and Frank C. Newman, "Draft USSR Law on Freedom of Conscience, with Commentary," *Harvard Human Rights Journal* 3 (1990): 137–56.

Berman, Harold J., and Donald H. Hunt, "Criminal Law and Psychiatry: The Soviet Solution," *Stanford Law Review* 2 (1950): 635–63.

Berman, Harold J., and Miroslav Kerner, "Soviet Military Discipline," *Military Review* 32(3) (June 1952): 19–29.

"Soviet Military Discipline," *Military Review* 32(4) (July 1952): 3–15.

Soviet Military Law and Administration (Cambridge, MA: Harvard University Press, 1955).

Berman, Harold J., and Peter B. Maggs, *Disarmament Inspection Under Soviet Law* (Dobbs Ferry, NY: Oceana Publications, 1967; 2nd edn., 1972).

Berman, Harold J., and John B. Quigley, Jr., eds. and trans., *Basic Laws on the Structure of the Soviet State* (Cambridge, MA: Harvard University Press, 1969).

Berman, Harold J., and James W. Spindler, "Soviet Comrades' Courts," *Washington Law Review* 38 (1963): 842–910.

eds. and trans., *Soviet Criminal Law and Procedure: The RSFSR Codes* (Cambridge, MA: Harvard University Press, 1966).

Berman, Harold J., and Van R. Whiting, Jr., "Impressions of Cuban Law," *The American Journal of Comparative Law* 28 (Summer 1980): 475–86.

Berman, Ronald, ed., *Solzhenitsyn at Harvard* (Washington, DC: Ethics and Public Policy Center, 1980).

Binder, Guyora, and Richard Weisberg, *Literary Criticisms of Law* (Princeton University Press, 2000).

Bishin, William R., and Christopher D. Stone, *Law, Language, and Ethics: An Introduction to Law and Legal Method* (Mineola, NY: Foundation Press, 1972).

Black, Max, ed., *The Importance of Language* (Englewood Cliffs, NJ: Prentice Hall, 1962).

Blackstone, Sir William, *Commentaries on the Laws of England in Four Books* (Philadelphia: J.B. Lippincott Co., 1893).

Britton, Karl, *Communication: A Philosophical Study of Language* (London: K. Paul, Trench, Trübner & Co., 1939).

Brower, Reuben Arthur, ed., *On Translation* (New York: Oxford University Press, 1966 [1959]).

Broyde, Michael J., "A Jewish Law View of World Law," *Emory Law Journal* 54 (2005): 79–96.

Brunt, Lodewijk, "Thinking About Ethnography," *Journal of Contemporary Ethnography* 28 (October 1999): 502.

Bryant, M. Darrol, and Hans R. Huessy, eds., *Eugen Rosenstock-Huessy: Studies in His Life and Thought*, (Lewiston, NY: Edward Mellen Press, 1986).

Buber, Martin, *Between Man and Man* (New York: Macmillan, 1947).

Bumpers, Dale, and W. Lawson Taite, eds., *Religion and Politics* (University of Texas Press, 1989).

Burke, Edmund, *The Works of the Right Honorable Edmund Burke*, 12 vols., 3rd edn. (Boston: Little, Brown, 1869).

Burke, Kenneth, *A Rhetoric of Motives* (New York: Prentice Hall, 1950).

Butler, William E., Peter B. Maggs, and John B. Quigley, Jr., eds., *Law after Revolution: Essays on Socialist Law in Honor of Harold J. Berman* (Dobbs Ferry, NY: Oceana Press, 1988).

Cardozo, Benjamin N., *Law and Literature, and Other Essays and Addresses* (New York: Harcourt, Brace & Co, 1931), 3–40.

Carroll, John B., *The Study of Language: A Survey of Linguistics and Other Related Disciplines in America* (Harvard University Press, 1953).

Carroll, Lewis, *Alice's Adventures in Wonderland, and Through the Looking-Glass: And What Alice Found There* (New York: Macmillan & Co., 1897).

Cassirer, Ernst, *Language and Myth*, trans. Susanne K. Langer (New York: Dover Publications, 1946).

The Philosophy of the Enlightenment, trans. Fritz C.A. Koelln and James P. Pettegrove (Princeton University Press, 1951).

Chappell, Vere Claiborne, ed., *Ordinary Language: Essays in Philosophical Method* (Englewood Cliffs, NJ: Prentice Hall, 1964).

Clark, Robert C., "The Interdisciplinary Study of Legal Evolution," *Yale Law Journal* 90 (1981): 1238–74.

"Preface to A Conference on the Work of Harold J. Berman," *Emory Law Journal* 42 (1993): 428.

Cohen, Jerome A., ed., *Contemporary Chinese Law* (Harvard University Press, 1970).

Cohen, Saul, "Book Reviews," *UCLA Law Review* 11 (1964): 461–64, at 461.

Cotterill, Janet, ed., *Language in the Legal Process* (New York: Palgrave Macmillan, 2002).

Currie, Brainerd, "Book Reviews," *Journal of Legal Education* 17 (1964): 227–30.

Dewey, John, *Experience and Nature* (London: George Allen & Unwin, 1929).

Dufrenne, Mikel, *Language and Philosophy*, trans. Henry B. Veatch (Indiana University Press, 1963).

Dumbauld, Edward, *The Declaration of Independence and What it Means Today* (University of Oklahoma Press, 1950).

Duncan, Hugh Daziel, *Communication and Social Order* (New York: Bedminster Press, 1962).

Edwards, Harry T., "The Growing Disjunction Between Legal Education and the Legal Profession," *Michigan Law Review* 91 (1992): 34–78.

"The Growing Disjunction Between Legal Education and the Legal Profession: A Postscript," *Michigan Law Review* 91 (1993): 2191–219.

Ehrlich, Eugen, *Fundamental Principles of the Sociology of Law* (New York: Russell & Russell, 1962).

Engberg, Jan, "Word Meaning and the Problem of a Globalized Legal Order," in Peter M. Tiersma and Lawrence M. Solan, eds., *The Oxford Handbook of Language and Law* (Oxford University Press, 2012), 175–86.

Fisher, William W., Morton Horowitz and Thomas Reed, eds., *American Legal Realism* (New York: Oxford University Press, 1993).

Frank, Jerome, *Law and the Modern Mind* (Garden City, NY: Doubleday, 1963).

Fuller, Lon L., *The Anatomy of the Law* (New York: Praeger, 1968).

Legal Fictions (Stanford University Press, 1967).

The Morality of Law (New Haven: Yale University Press, 1964).

Gadamer, Hans-Georg, *Truth and Method*, trans. Joel Weinsheimer & Donald G. Marshall, 2nd rev. edn. (New York: Continuum, 2000).

Warheit und Methode (Tubingen: J.C.B. Mohr, 1960).

Girdansky, Michael, *The Adventure of Language* (London: Allen & Unwin, 1963).

Greenberg, Joseph Harold, "Some Universals of Grammar with Particular Reference to the Order of Meaningful Elements," in *Universals of Language: Report of a Conference Held at Dobbs Ferry, New York, April 13–15, 1961* (Cambridge, MA: MIT Press, 1961).

ed., *Universals of Language: Report of a Conference Held at Dobbs Ferry, New York, April 13–15, 1961* (Cambridge, MA: MIT Press, 1961).

Greenough, James B., and George L. Kittredge, *Words and Their Ways in English Speech* (London: Macmillan, 1905).

Griswold, Erwin N., "Preface to A Conference on the Work of Harold J. Berman," *Emory Law Journal* 42 (1993): 424–426.

Grotius, Hugo, "The Poem Het Beroep van Advocaat [The Calling of the Advocate] (February 18, 1602)," reprinted in Hugo Grotius, *Anthologia Grotiana* (The Hague: Martinua Nijhoff, 1955): 33.

Haines, Charles Grove, *The Revival of Natural Law Concepts* (New York: Russell & Russell, 1965).

Hall, Jerome, *Comparative Law and Social Theory* (Baton Rouge, LA: Louisiana State University Press, 1963).

Hall, Kermit L., ed., *The Oxford Companion to American Law* (Oxford University Press, 2002).

Hart, Herbert Lionel Adolphus, "Definition and Theory in Jurisprudence," *Law Quarterly Review* 70 (1954): 37–60.

Hill, Jane H., and Bruce Mannheim, "Language and World View," *Annual Review of Anthropology* 21 (1992): 381–404, at 384.

Hobbes, Thomas, *Leviathan, or, the Matter, Form, and Power of a Commonwealth Ecclesiastical and Civil* (London: Andrew Crooke, 1651).

Hobbs, Meredith, "Translating Western Law into Chinese: Emory Professor Harold J. Berman toured China, speaking to halls packed with Chinese students," *The Daily Report* 117 (Fulton County, GA) (June 1, 2006): 1.

Holmes, Jr., Oliver Wendell, "Science in Law – Law in Science," in *Collected Legal Papers* (New York: Harcourt, Brace & Co., 1920), 210–43, at 238.

The Holy Qur'an, trans. Abdullah Yusuf Ali (Brentwood, MD: Amana Corporation, 1989).

Hull, N. E. H., *Roscoe Pound & Karl Llewellyn: Search for an American Jurisprudence* (University of Chicago Press, 1997).

Hunter, Howard O., ed., *The Integrative Jurisprudence of Harold J. Berman* (Boulder, CO: Westview Press, 1996).

Huntington, Samuel P., *The Clash of Civilizations and the Remaking of World Order* (New York: Simon & Schuster, 1996).

Iakubinskii, Lev Petrovich "*O dialogicheskoi rechi*," in A. A. Leont'ev, ed., *Izbrannye raboty: Iazyk i ego funktsionirovanie* (Moscow: Nauka, 1986), 15–56.

Jakobson, Roman, "Implications of Language Universals for Linguistics," in J. H. Greenberg, ed., *Universals of Language: Report of a Conference Held at Dobbs Ferry, New York, April 13–15, 1961* (Cambridge, MA: MIT Press, 1961), 260–69.

"On Linguistic Aspects of Translation," in Reuben Arthur Brower, ed., *On Translation* (New York: Oxford University Press, 1966 [1959]), 232–39.

"Results of the Conference of Anthropologists and Linguists," in *Indiana University Publications in Anthropology and Linguistics: Memoir, Issue 8* (Baltimore, MD: Waverly Press, 1953).

"St. Constantine's Prologue to the Gospel," *St. Vladimir's Seminary Quarterly* 7(1) (1963): 14–19.

"Two Aspects of Language and Two Types of Aphasic Disturbances," in Roman Jakobson and Morris Halle, *Fundamentals of Language* (The Hague: Mouton & Co., 1956), 53–82.

Jakobson, Roman, and Morris Halle, *Fundamentals of Language* (The Hague: Mouton & Co., 1956).

Jemielniak, Joanna, "Subversion in the World of Order: Legal Deconstruction as a Rhetorical Practice," in Anne Wagner et al., eds., *Contemporary Issues of the Semiotics of Law* (Oxford: Hart Publishing, 2005), 127–40.

Jenks, Clarence Wilfred, *The Common Law of Mankind* (New York: Praeger, 1958).

Jerome, "To Pammachius on the Best Method of Translating " – Letter LVII, available at: www.newadvent.org/fathers/3001057.htm (formatted by the Christian Classics Ethereal Library, 1996).

Jespersen, Otto, *An International Language* (London: Allen & Unwin, 1928).

Language: Its Nature, Development and Origin (New York: Henry Holt & Co., 1925).

Mankind, Nation and Individual from a Linguistic Point of View (Oslo: H. Aschehoug, 1925).

Jhering, Rudolph von, *Geist des römischen Rechts auf den verschiedenen Stufen seiner Entwicklung*, 3 vols. (Leipzig: Breitkopf und Härtel, 1869).

Joseph, John E., "Indeterminacy, Translation and the Law," in Marshall Morris, ed., *Translation and the Law*, 8 vols. (Philadelphia: John Benjamins, 1995), 8:21–23.

Kant, Immanuel, *Critique of Pure Reason*, trans. Norman Kemp Smith (London: Macmillan, 1929).

Kantorowicz, Hermann, "Savigny and the Historical School of Law," *Law Quarterly Review* 53 (July 1937): 326–43.

Keller, Helen, *The Story of My Life* (New York: Doubleday, Page & Co., 1921).

Kluckhohn, Clyde, and Dorothea Leighton, *The Navaho* (Cambridge, MA: Harvard University Press 1946).

Kress, Ken, "Legal Indeterminacy," *California Law Review* 77 (1989): 283–337.

Kroeber, Alfred Louis, "Some Relations of Linguistics and Ethnology," *Language* 17 (1941): 287–91.

Laguna, Grace Mead Andrus de, *Speech: Its Function and Development* (New Haven, CT: Yale University Press, 1927).

Levi, Judith N., and Anne Graffam Walker, eds., *Language in the Judicial Process* (New York: Plenum Press, 1990).

Lewis, John Underwood, "Sir Edward Coke (1552–1633): His Theory of 'Artificial Reason' as a Context for Modern Basic Legal Theory," *Law Quarterly Review* 84 (1968): 330–42, at 330.

Long, Edward Le Roy, *A Survey of Christian Ethics* (New York: Oxford University Press, 1967).

Macleish, Archibald, "Book Reviews," *Harvard Law Review* 78 (1964): 490–91, at 490.

Maine, Henry Sumner, *Ancient Law*, 10th edn. (London: John Murray, 1906).

Dissertations on Early Law and Custom (London: John Murray, 1883).

Malinowksi, Bronisław, *Coral Gardens and Their Magic: A Study of the Methods of Tilling the Soil and of Agricultural Rites in the Trobriand Islands, vol. 2: The Language of Magic and Gardening*, (London: George Allen & Unwin, 1935).

"The Problem of Meaning in Primitive Languages," appended to C.K. Ogden and I.A. Richards, *The Meaning of Meaning: A Study of the Influence of Language Upon Thought and of the Science of Symbolism* (New York: Harcourt, Brace & World, 1946).

Nancy S. Marder, "Instructing the Jury," in Peter M. Tiersma and Lawrence M. Solan, eds., *The Oxford Handbook of Language and Law* (Oxford University Press, 2012), 439–45.

Mattila, Heikki E. S., "Legal Vocabulary," in Peter M. Tiersma and Lawrence M. Solan, eds., *The Oxford Handbook of Language and Law* (Oxford University Press, 2012), 27–38.

Mauthner, Fritz, *Beiträge zu einer Kritik der Sprache*, 3 vols., repr. edn. (Frankfurt: Ullstein, 1982 [1901]).

McAuliffe, Karen, "Language and Law in the European Union: The Multilingual Jurisprudence of the ECJ," in Peter M. Tiersma and Lawrence M. Solan, eds., *The Oxford Handbook of Language and Law*(Oxford University Press, 2012), 200–16.

McConnell, Michael W., Robert F. Cochran, Jr., and Angela C. Carmella, eds., *Christian Perspectives on Legal Thought* (Yale University Press, 2001).

McDowell, Gary L., *The Language of Law and the Foundations of American Constitutionalism* (Cambridge University Press, 2010).

McWhinney, Edward, ed., *Law, Foreign Policy and the East–West Détente* (University of Toronto Press, 1964).

Mellinkoff, David, *The Language of the Law* (Boston, MA: Little, Brown, 1963).

"Plain English: Why I Wrote *The Language of the Law*," *Michigan Bar Journal* 79 (January 2000): 28.

Melville, Herman, "Billy Budd, Foretopman," in *Shorter Novels of Herman Melville* (New York: Horace Liverwright, 1928), 227–328.

Mollnau, Karl A., "The Contributions of Savigny to the Theory of Legislation," *American Journal of Comparative Law* 37 (1989): 81–93.

Monroe, Kelly K., *Finding God at Harvard: Spiritual Journeys of Christian Thinkers* (Downers Grove, IL: IVP Books, 1996).

Morris, Marshall, ed., *Translation and the Law*, 8 vols. (Philadelphia: John Benjamins, 1995).

Murray, Jeffrey W., "Kenneth Burke: A Dialogue of Motives," *Philosophy & Rhetoric* 35(1) (2002): 31–34.

Newman, R. A., ed., *Essays in Jurisprudence in Honor of Roscoe Pound* (Indianapolis, IN: Bobbs-Merrill, 1962).

Ogden, Charles Kay, *Bentham's Theory of Fictions* (London: Kegan Paul, Trench, Trübner & Co., 1932).

Ogden, Charles Kay, and Ivor Armstrong Richards, *The Meaning of Meaning: A Study of the Influence of Language Upon Thought and of the Science of Symbolism* (New York: Harcourt, Brace & World, 1946).

Olivecrona, Karl, "Legal Language and Reality," in R. A. Newman, ed., *Essays in Jurisprudence in Honor of Roscoe Pound* (Indianapolis, IN: Bobbs-Merrill, 1962), 151–91.

Ortega y Gasset, José, "History as a System," in *Toward a Philosophy of History*, trans. William C. Atkinson (New York: W. W. Norton, 1941), 165–233.

Toward a Philosophy of History, trans. William C. Atkinson (New York: W. W. Norton, 1941).

Palgrave, Francis, *The Rise and Progress of the English Commonwealth* (London: John Murray, 1832).

Pei, Mario, *Voices of Man: The Meaning and Function of Languages* (New York: Harper & Row, 1962).

Polanyi, Michael, *Personal Knowledge* (University of Chicago Press, 1958).

Posner, Richard A., "The Decline of Law as an Autonomous Discipline: 1962–1987," *Harvard Law Review* 100 (1987): 778–79.

Law and Literature, 3rd edn. (Harvard University Press, 2009).

"The Present Situation in Legal Scholarship," *Yale Law Journal* 90 (1981): 1113–30.

"Savigny, Holmes, and the Law and Economics of Possession," *Virginia Law Review* 86 (2000): 542–43.

Pound, Roscoe, *The Revival of Natural Law* (University of Notre Dame Press, 1942).

"The Scope and Purpose of Sociological Jurisprudence," *Harvard Law Journal* 24 (1911): 591–619.

Prager, Susan Westerberg, "David Mellinkoff: An Affectionate Tribute," *UCLA Law Review* 33 (June 1985): 1247–49.

Radbruch, Gustav, *Der Geist des englischen Recht* (Heidelberg: A. Rausch, 1946).

Riesenfeld, Stefan, "The Influence of German Legal Theory on American Law: The Heritage of Savigny and His Disciples," *American Journal of Comparative Law* 37 (Winter 1989): 1–7.

Rosenstock-Huessy, Eugen, *The Christian Future, or The Modern Mind Outrun* (New York: Charles Scribner's Sons, 1946).

    Out of Revolution: Autobiography of Western Man, introduction by Harold J. Berman (Providence, RI: Berg, 1993).

    Speech and Reality (Norwich, VT: Argo Books, 1970).

Rückert, Joachim, "The Unrecognized Legacy: Savigny's Influence on German Jurisprudence after 1900," *American Journal of Comparative Law* 37 (1989): 121–37.

Rumble, Wilfred E., *American Legal Realism: Skepticism, Reform, and the Judicial Process* (Ithaca, NY: Cornell University Press, 1968).

Ryan, Michael J., "Berman: Losing Enemies by Making Friends," *Harvard Law Record* (February 25, 1965): 5–6.

Sapir, Edward, *Language: An Introduction to the Study of Speech* (New York: Harcourt, Brace & Co., 1921).

Sajo, Andras, ed., *Western Rights? Post-Communist Application* (The Hague: Kluwer Law International, 1996).

Savigny, Friedrich Charles [Carl] von, *Of the Vocation of Our Age for Legislation and Jurisprudence*, 2nd edn., trans. Abraham Hayward (London: Littlewood, 1831).

    "Über den Zweck dieser Zeitschrift," *Zeitschrift für geschichtliche Rechtswissenschaft* 1 (1815): 1–17.

Schane, Sanford, *Language and the Law* (New York: Continuum, 2006).

Schooten, Hanneke van, "Law as Fact, Law as Fiction: A Tripartite Model of Legal Communication," in Anne Wagner et al., *Interpretation, Law and the Construction of Meaning: Collected Papers on Legal Interpretation in Theory, Adjudication and Political Practice* (Dordrecht: Springer, 2007), 3–20.

Schwarz, Frederick A. O., *Nigeria: The Tribes, The Nation, or The Race – The Politics of Independence*, repr. edn. (Westport, CT: Greenwood Press, 1983 [1965]).

Shapiro, Barbara, "Law and Science in Seventeenth-Century England," *Stanford Law Review* 21 (1969): 727–66, at 728.

Sheppard, William, *Sheppard's Touchstone of Common Assurances*, 7th edn., eds. Edward Hilliard and Richard Preston (London: J. & W.T. Clarke, 1820).

Silving, Helen, "Notes on 'Understanding'; Translation of a Penal Code," *Revista Juridica de la Universidad de Puerto Rico* 29 (1960): 333–42.

Simmel, Georg, *The Sociology of Georg Simmel*, trans. and ed. Kurt H. Wolff (Glencoe, IL: Free Press, 1950).

Snow, Charles Percy, *The Two Cultures and the Scientific Revolution* (New York: Cambridge University Press, 1959).

Soboleva, Anita, "Topical Jurisprudence: Reconciliation of Law and Rhetoric," in Anne Wagner et al., *Interpretation, Law and the Construction of Meaning: Collected Papers on Legal Interpretation in Theory, Adjudication and Political Practice* (Dordrecht: Springer, 2007), 49–64.

Solan, Lawrence M., "The Interpretation of Multilingual Statutes by the European Court of Justice," *Brooklyn Journal of International Law* 34 (2009): 286–94.

The Language of Judges (University of Chicago Press, 1993).

The Language of Statutes (University of Chicago Press, 2010).

Starr, Robert, *Business Transactions with the USSR, The Legal Issues* (Chicago: ABA Press, 1975).

Stein, Peter, *Legal Evolution: The Story of an Idea* (Cambridge University Press, 1980).

Stone, Julius, *The Province and Function of Law: Law as Logic, Justice, and Social Control* (London: Stevens, 1947).

Stygall, Gail, "Discourse in the US Courtroom," in Peter M. Tiersma and Lawrence M. Solan, eds., *The Oxford Handbook of Language and Law* (Oxford University Press, 2012), 369–80.

Swift, Jonathan, *Gulliver's Travels into Several Remote Regions of the World* (London: George Routledge & Sons, 1880).

Symposium, "A Conference on the Work of Harold J. Berman," *Emory Law Journal* 42 (1993): 419–589.

Symposium, "American Legal Scholarship: Directions and Dilemmas," *Journal of Legal Education* 33 (1983): 403–11.

Symposium, "The Foundations of Law," *Emory Law Journal* 54 (2005): 1–376.

Symposium, "In Praise of a Legal Polymath: A Special Issue Dedicated to the Memory of Harold J. Berman (1918–2007)," *Emory Law Journal* 57 (2008): 1393–1469.

Symposium, "Savigny in Modern Comparative Perspective," *American Journal of Comparative Law* (Winter 1989): 1–169.

Teachout, Peter, "'Complete Achievement': Integrity of Vision and Performance in Berman's Jurisprudence," in Howard O. Hunter, ed., *The Integrative Jurisprudence of Harold J. Berman* (Boulder, CO: Westview Press, 1996), 75–98.

Thomas Aquinas, *Treatise on Law* (Chicago: Henry Regnery, 1959).

Tiersma, Peter M., "A History of the Language of Law," in Peter M. Tiersma and Lawrence Solan, eds., *The Oxford Handbook of Language and Law* (Oxford University Press, 2012), 13–26.

Legal Language (University of Chicago Press, 1999).

Tiersma, Peter M., and Lawrence M. Solan, eds., *The Oxford Handbook of Language and Law* (Oxford University Press, 2012).

Tunkin, Grigorii Ivanovich, *Contemporary International Law: Collection of Articles* (Moscow: Progress Publishers, 1969).

Law and Force in the International System (Moscow: Progress Publishers, 1985).

Theory of International Law (Harvard University Press, 1974).

The Tunkin Diary and Lectures: The Diary and Collected Lectures of G.I. Tunkin at the Hague Academy of International Law 1958–1986, ed. and trans. William E. Butler and Vladimir G. Tunkin (The Hague: Eleven International Publishing, 2012).

Usener, Hermann, *Götternamen: Versuch einer Lehre von der Religiösen Begriffsbildung* (Bonn: Verlag von Friedrich Cohen, 1896).

Várady, Tibor, "The Anchor Language – When the Original is Actually a Translation," in Andrew Wilson, ed., *Translators on Translating: Inside the Visible Art* (Vancouver: CCSP Press, 2009), 144–48.

Language and Translation in International Commercial Arbitration: From the Constitution of the Arbitral Tribunal through Recognition and Enforcement Proceedings (The Hague: T.M.C. Asser Press, 2006).

"Language-Related Strategies in Preparing Arbitration," *Across Languages and Cultures* 7 (2006): 209–23.

Viehweg, Theodor, *Topik und Jurisprudenz* (Munich: C.H. Beck, 1953).

Wagner, Anne, et al., eds., *Contemporary Issues of the Semiotics of Law* (Oxford/ Portland, OR: Hart Publishing, 2005).

et al., eds., *Interpretation, Law and the Construction of Meaning: Collected Papers on Legal Interpretation in Theory, Adjudication and Political Practice* (Dordrecht: Springer, 2007).

Waismann, Friedrich, "The Resources of Language," in Max Black, ed., *The Importance of Language* (Englewood Cliffs, NJ: Prentice Hall, 1962), 107–11.

White, James Boyd, *Justice as Translation: An Essay in Cultural and Legal Criticism* (University of Chicago Press, 1990).

The Legal Imagination (Boston, MA: Little, Brown, 1973, [rev. edn., University of Chicago Press, 1985]).

Living Speech: Resisting the Empire of Force (Princeton University Press, 2006).

When Language Meets the Mind: Three Questions (Nijmegen: Wolf Legal Publishers, 2007).

When Words Lose Their Meaning (University of Chicago Press, 1984).

Whorf, Benjamin Lee, "An American Indian Model of the Universe (*circa* 1936)," in John B. Carroll, ed., *Language, Thought and Reality: Selected Writings of Benjamin Lee Whorf* (Harvard University Press, 1964), 57–64.

Language, Thought and Reality: Selected Writings of Benjamin Lee Whorf, ed. John B. Carroll (Harvard University Press, 1964).

"Linguistics as an Exact Science," in John B. Carroll, ed., *Language, Thought and Reality: Selected Writings of Benjamin Lee Whorf* (Cambridge, MA: Harvard University Press, 1964), 220–32.

"A Linguistic Consideration of Thinking Primitive Communities," in John B. Carroll, ed., *Language, Thought and Reality: Selected Writings of Benjamin Lee Whorf* (Cambridge, MA: Harvard University Press, 1964), 65–86.

Wilson, Andrew, ed., *Translators on Translating: Inside the Visible Art* (Vancouver: CCSP Press, 2009).

Witte, Jr., John, *From Sacrament to Contract: Marriage, Religion, and Law in the Western Tradition*, 2nd edn. (Louisville, KY: Westminster John Knox Press, 2012 [1997]).

Law and Protestantism: The Legal Teachings of the Lutheran Reformation (Cambridge University Press, 2002).

"A New Concordance of Discordant Canons: Harold J. Berman on Law and Religion," *Emory Law Journal* 42 (1993): 523–60.

The Reformation of Rights: Law, Religion, and Human Rights (Cambridge University Press, 2007), chs. 1–4.

"The Study of Law and Religion in the United States: An Interim Report," *Ecclesiastical Law Journal* 14 (2012): 327–54.

ed., *Christianity and Democracy in Global Context* (Boulder, CO: Westview Press, 1993).

Witte, Jr., John, and Frank S. Alexander, eds., *The Teachings of Modern Christianity on Law, Politics, and Human Nature*, 2 vols. (New York: Columbia University Press, 2006).

The Weightier Matters of the Law: Essays on Law and Religion in Tribute to Harold J. Berman (Atlanta, GA: Scholars Press, 1988).

Witte, Jr., John, and Johan D. Van der Vyver, eds., *Religious Human Rights in Global Perspective*, 2 vols. (The Hague: Martinus Nijhoff, 1996).

Witte, Jr., John, and Michael Bourdeaux, eds., *Proselytism and Orthodoxy in Russia: The New War for Souls* (Maryknoll, NY: Orbis Books, 1999).

Wittgenstein, Ludwig, *Philosophical Investigations*, trans. G. E. M. Anscombe, (Oxford: B. Blackwell, 1953).

Tractatus Logico-Philosophicus, trans. Frank P. Ramsey and C. K. Ogden, (New York: Harcourt, Brace & Co., 1922).

INDEX

HB denotes Harold J. Berman

metonymy, 98–100
Middle Ages, 5
Milošević, Slobodan, 170
Montenegrin language, 173
Morgenthau, Hans, 154
Mormonism, 165

national legal languages, 113–15,
    129–30
natural law
    American law, 141–42
    revival of, 14
    Savigny's opposition to, 117–19, 125
    vs. legal positivism, 5–6
Nature and Functions of Law, The
    (Berman), 3
New York Convention on Recognition
    and Enforcement of Foreign
    Arbitral Awards, 171
Nigerian Constitution, 144–45
Novial, 55n.52

obligation (term), etymology of, 88
Occidental, 55n.52
*Of the Vocation of Our Age for
    Legislation and Jurisprudence*
    (Savigny), 116–17
Ogden, C.K., 49n.33, 68
Oldendorp, Johan, 71n.22
Olivecrona, Karl, 82–83
*On the Teaching of Law in the Liberal
    Arts Curriculum* (Berman), 3
ordinary language, 50n.35
*Oxford Handbook of Law and
    Language* (Tiersma and Solan), 31

Paine, Thomas, 138–40
Papal Revolution (1075–1122), 10
peace
    and Christianity, 160–62
    and common language, 57–59
    and communification, 150–51
    international law, role of, 154–56,
        158–59
    language, role of, 150–51, 156–58
    law for mankind, 158–60
    legal language, role of, 151–52
Pei, Mario, 41–42n.18, 53

Pentecost, 8, 54–55, 164, 184–85
Permanent Court of Arbitration
    (PCA), 166–67
phonetics, 37–38
plain language movement, 32–33
poetry, 90–91
Polanyi, Michael, 9, 41–42n.18, 43,
    61–62
Polish law, 131–32
politics, 62, 70–76
Posner, Richard, 31
Pososhkov, Ivan, 82
Post, Gaines, 125
Pound, Roscoe, 14
precedent, 94–95, 131
primogeniture, 135
privacy (term), 100
privacy, right of, 89–90
Promise of American Law, The (Ball),
    30
property (term), etymology of, 88
Protestant Reformation (1517), 10
public opinion, 140

Qur'an, 165

rationalism, 41–43
relationships, 36–39
religion
    American law, 134–35
    common universal religion, 159
    HB's beliefs, 160n.15
    language of, 62
    and law, 6–12
    natural law, 117–19
    translation, 164–65
    United States Constitution, 141n.11
    unity of mankind, 158
rhetoric, 70–76
rhetorical-humanistic school of law
    and language, 27–31
Richards, I. A., 49n.33
Romans, 47n.28
Rosenberger, W., 55n.52
Rosenstock-Huessy, Eugen, 12, 19n.65,
    34, 51, 55–56, 58, 58n.58
rules, 72–75, 81
Russia, *see* Soviet Union

CPSIA information can be obtained
at www.ICGtesting.com
Printed in the USA
LVOW13s1950080217

523633LV00011B/137/P